RED AL_

Brummie Reds—Never Far Away

STEVE GRAINGER

ISBN 978-1-9163462-5-3

Enquires – grange@redallover.org

CONTENTS

Introduction

I was born in Kingstanding, Birmingham and a few months before my 8th birthday as I watched on a small black and white TV, I saw Man United beat Benfica at Wembley and lift the European Cup for the first time. I was instantly hooked – Manchester United were the team for me. At the age of ten and living in a new house near Walsall, I was United and George Best mad and as I got a few years older my half of the bedroom was covered in United posters and scarfs. In my early teens I was traveling home and away to watch The Reds and more often than not causing havoc with my mates, especially in the early - mid 70s when it wasn't unusual for 20 – sometimes 30,000 Reds to travel away and you could be forgiven for thinking you were at a United home game. The Red Barmy Army would often take over away grounds and the town centre as well. The last time I experienced anything like this was the last game of the '92 – '93 season when United played Wimbledon at Selhurst Park and 'Harry H' tried to take the Premier League trophy off Robbo as the team attempted to do a lap of honour.

Far Away – Far Away - Brummie Reds are always there - Never Far Away! This little ditty has been sung for over 40 years. Brummie Red is a generic phrase that describes United fans from Birmingham and surrounding areas including the Black Country – Although the lads from Walsall and Wolvo will probably disagree. But from memory it was Duggins from

Oldbury and his little crew who I first heard singing Brummie Reds Never Far Away - circa '77.

The roots of the official Manchester United Supporters Club in Birmingham go back to 1974. An ad appeared in the Birmingham Evening Mail asking for local Man United fans to get in touch with the intention of starting an Official Manchester United supporters club in Brum. A subsequent meeting was held in a small terraced house in Small Heath, which was attended by my good mate Paddy Flatley, Danny Tighe (both Sr. & Jr) and another twenty or so die-hard Reds. The first Brummie Red coach ran in March '75 and during the early days, two of the founders Ron C. and Danny Tighe Sr. visited New Street station and asked the many United fans that were scattered around the forecourt if they wanted to travel to the game on the Supporters Club coach instead of the expensive train! When I first used the Brummie Red coach in September '75, I was a fifteen-year-old schoolboy and most of the lads were a few years older than me, despite my age I was soon accepting as one of the boys and became close friends to many of my fellow Brummie Reds. My membership number was 226, but at the start of the '76 – '77 season there were over 500 members and we took 4 coaches to the first game of the season, a home game against Birmingham City.

We had a great craic on the coaches especially at the away games. But after a pub was smashed up on our way back from an away trip to Ipswich in the late '70s 'The Committee' announced that they wouldn't be running coaches to away games for the rest of the season. This was the start of letting the 'Train take the Strain' and we soon latched on to Jumping (Jibbing) the train. Besides having free transport when using the regular Inter City trains it also helped us to avoid the dreaded police escorts that were becoming a real pain in the arse. It really ruined the day if you were forced by the Old Bill to stay on your coach for a couple of hours or marched directly into the ground before you'd even had a pint or three.

Because a few of my Manchester mates were so well connected, especially Ged, Jonnie, Percy and Big Andy C. - from time to time I did find myself in the company of some of the United's Boys, the most memorable was being shoulder to shoulder with Grogan at the front of the massive mob that we took to West Ham in the mid 80's, but in no way shape or form would I class myself as 'A Face' or one of 'United's Boys'.

Me and most of my mates were firstly Beer Monsters and part of what the United Boys called The Barmy Army (aka The Barmies) basically the 1000's of United supporters who went to away games for a good piss up and to cause some mayhem and if that included having a scrap with the home fans, well bring it on. As detailed in the book, I did get involved in a fair bit of football violence, but for the main part it was spontaneous and very rarely anything prearranged. Looking back, it was quite strange really, especially in the 70s and early 80s, if there were only a few Brummies at an away game we would team up with 'like-minded' Reds from different parts of the country and if we were suddenly caught up in a fight with opposing fans you had to rely on strangers to get stuck in and back you up – and that of course could go either way!

Besides having the craic with the lads, I have always been interested in the club's history and general statistics, so as a bit of a twist to the usual Boys Own football memoirs, in each chapter, I have also included a bit of background information about the game; the season in general; and a match report, which hopefully will help the reader reflect on the fact that in these troubled times where we are experiencing disappointment after disappointment on the field - it isn't anything new.

Finally – A Big Thank You to Angie and Christopher for all their help with the grammar and punctuation. Hopefully not too many mistakes have slipped through the net! Many Thanks to me old mate Sag, who once again produced the artwork for the book cover. And last but certainly not least a massive Thank You to Cliff Butler United's official Club Statistician for supplying all the match reports and relevant league positions.

Chapter 1.
Wolves '71

28th August '71
Wolves 1 – 1   Best   (46,471)

United Line–Up
Stepney, O'Neil, Dunne, Gowling, James, Sadler, Morgan, Kidd, Charlton, Law, Best. **Sub -** *Aston*

Manager
Frank O'Farrell

League Position After the Game

P	W	D	L	F	A	Pts	Pos
5	3	2	0	12	9	8	3rd

Manchester born, and United through and through; Wilf McGuinness had been sacked as manager after only 18 months in the job. After the sacking of McGuinness in December 1970, Sir Matt initially returned to the role of manager. In June '71 Sir Matt's role as manager ceased and Frank O'Farrell became United's third manager in less than 12 months. O'Farrell's appointment shocked a lot of people, as both fans and press expected Celtics Jock Stein to take over from Sir Matt and become United's next manager.

Before the '71 - '72 season kicked off in earnest, United were drawn away to the lowly Halifax Town in the Watney Cup. A good early away day for the fans turned out a disastrous one for the team, as United were beaten 2 – 1.

Even though the League campaign started better, with three wins and one draw from the first four matches – there was a subplot! The infamous Stretford Enders had thrown various missiles at opposition players for a few years. But after a knife and a large pair of industrial scissors had been thrown at the Newcastle goalkeeper the previous season, the Football League felt it had to take action. A large proportion of the Stretford End terrace behind the goal was cordoned off and made into a 'No Man's Land'. Then United were ordered by the Football League to play their first two home games of the '71 – '72 season at neutral grounds.

United's first home game of the season was played at Anfield on a Friday evening and United beat Arsenal 3 – 1. The Reds second home game was just three days later. United played West Brom at Stoke City's Victoria ground and once again, won 3 – 1.

Just before the end of the summer holidays, and a few weeks after my 11th birthday, my dad told me that Mickey *"Lock up your Daughters"* Gibbs, (Mickey was a work associate of my dad) had agreed to take me to see United play Wolves at Molineux. Mickey was a right character and a proper man's – man, and he had followed United since the late 50's. And one fine day in May 1968 (the 29th to be precise) Mickey was at Wembley to see United lift the European Cup. The one and only time I had visited Old Trafford up to this point was the previous year where I saw United play for the first time. The match was played under floodlights and was the 1st leg of the League Cup semi-final. While walking down to Old Trafford and also queuing up to get into the ground, I noticed several young United fans wearing red and white woollen scarves, which had the United players' names embroidered on them. I was very impressed by seeing the players' names being displayed on scarves and immediately thought, that's a job for my Nan. My wonderful old Nan had knitted my first United scarf and I was sure she would be more than capable of adorning my scarf with the players' names.

After months and months of nagging, my Nan finally agreed to get out her embroidery needles and decorate my scarf. I cut out the United team from a match report in a Sunday newspaper and along with the scarf gave them to my Nan to do the necessary. Being the summer holidays, I had almost forgotten about my scarf, but when I found out I would be going to watch United in only four days' time, my 'Decorated' scarf became the most important thing in the world to me. To get to my Nan's house who lived in Kingstanding, meant a 30-minute bus ride and a 15-minute walk. The entire journey to my Nan's house, I continually imagined how wonderful my scarf would look with the 11 names of United players sewn onto it.

I burst through the front door of my Nan's house and ran into the back room, where she always sat and I demanded "where's my scarf?" Before my Nan could answer, I added "I was going to watch United play on Saturday and need my scarf now" My nan calmly put down her knitting, she was always knitting, and searched in the small box next to her chair. As she produced my scarf from her knitting box, she said, "I've made a start but

I haven't finished it", as my Nan passed me the scarf alarm bells were already ringing! I quickly unravelled my scarf and to my utter disappointment, my Nan had only managed to embroider one name on the scarf 'Law' (to my shame I must admit, I really didn't know the importance of Denis Law) Georgie was my one and only United hero at the time. I didn't know that Denis Law was born the son of a fisherman from Aberdeen and played for his country when only 17, and that his football magic was a sight to see as he led Man United on to victory. And that he was the King of the Stretford End and even the King of the football league, many would say.

My Nan anticipated my reaction and before I could shout out "what the bleedin' hell have you been poncing about at Nan" She said calmly "I've been very busy, trying to finish this for Paddy" (my cousin) "and besides, I ran out of red and white wool" Without a thank you or a goodbye and with tears rolling down my cheeks I left my Nan's house and headed back home. Trying to hold back the tears all the way home on the bus, I cursed my bad luck and the fact that my Nan had put 'Law' on my scarf before 'Best' The next day I was still thinking the world was against me when I had the good fortune to bump into a school friend of mine, Tim G. Tim had a few older brothers that went to the United games and Tim had smuggled one of his brother's United scarves out of his house and was proudly wearing it around his wrist.

The scarf was a very smart factory knitted one and it had a couple of United badges sewn on it. The scarf wasn't as impressive as the ones I'd spotted on my first trip to Old

Trafford, but I thought a couple of badges on my scarf would help it stand out from the crowd. So, with the couple of bob burning a hole in my pocket, I made my way to the small sports shop in Aldridge to purchase a Manchester United badge. The Sports shop must have been the smallest in England, no sooner had you had opened the shop door and walked in, there you were leaning up against the counter. The shop was not only small, but it was like something out of the Victorian era. There were no products on display, just row after row of wall mounted wooden draws, set behind an antiquated counter. No chance of shoplifting in there! It seemed the shop owner must have looked inside almost every drawer in the shop, before he finally produced what I had asked for, A piece of white and very thick cotton was unceremoniously dropped onto the counter. In the centre of the 6 x 6'' piece of cloth was a printed Manchester United crest. That will do nicely, I thought to myself. After a few hours of nagging my mom, she finally agreed to sew the badge on to my scarf. With 'Law' on one end of my scarf and the 'United Crest' on the other end, the world seemed a better place again.

On the day of the match Mickey came to pick me up from my house, he was his normal bubbly self and seemed almost as excited about the game as me. Within seconds of him coming through my front door, I was showing Mickey the new decorations to my scarf, he inspected my pride and joy for a few seconds, then said "I thought George Best was your favourite player?' I could only answer with an embarrassed smile! We made the short trip to Wolverhampton in Mickey's small two-seater works van, and the entire journey I had my scarf tied around my wrist so I could show off 'Law' & the 'United Crest' to the rest of the world, I let the scarf hang out of the slightly open window. When we arrived at the Wolves ground, we were met with a sea of Red & White; you would've thought we had been at Old Trafford. There were thousands and thousands of chanting United supporters queuing to get into the ground. After queuing up for what seemed an age to get into the South Bank, Mickey and I finally made it on to the packed terrace. The noise was deafening, and the atmosphere was electric. The United supporters filled the South Bank and it seemed that half of the 46,000 crowds, must have been United fans. To give me half a chance of seeing the pitch, Mickey and I took our position at the bottom of the South Bank. I had never experienced anything like this; it was like watching the closing scenes of Batman, being dragged into the headmaster's office and the Saturday morning matinée – all rolled into one. I was totally awe struck and as the packed terrace echoed to the sound of UNITED – UNITED – UNITED and people swayed backwards and forwards and from left to right, I remember thinking it couldn't get better than this. But it did!

While I was still standing open mouthed and at the point where I thought I might just wee myself with excitement, Mickey jokingly said to me "I hope you're not one of those Hooligans that run out on the pitch to cause trouble" Before I could reply, I spotted a teenager, coming out of The North Bank at the other end of the pitch and he casually started walking towards us. He wore a gold and black scarf around his neck and had a couple hanging off his waistband, he also held a red and white scarf in his hand. As he causally made his way across the pitch the Wolves fan, was greeted by cheers from his fellow supporters in the North Bank and a hail of boos and general abuse from the United supporters. When he got to the centre circle he stopped, then he slowly held the red and white scarf aloft and proceeded to burn it. Amazingly, while the Wolves fan nonchalantly stood in the centre circle, holding the burning United scarf, there was no intervention from the police or club stewards, there were just cheers and applause, from one half of the crowd and the deafening jeers of disgust and contempt from the other half.

As I looked on in total shock, I thought to myself 'How the fuck can he be allowed to do that and where are United's infamous Stretford Enders?' I was just starting to feel very uneasy about the whole situation, when suddenly there was a load roar, which was immediately followed by a violent serge in the middle of the South Bank as hundreds of United fans made their way to the front of the terrace. The cavalry had arrived! My spirits were soon lifted as at first tens, then hundreds of United supporters climbed out of the terracing and onto the Molineux pitch. The display of out and out aggression from the United fans, resembled an army of invading barbarians scaling the walls of a fallen citadel. My heart was beating ten to the dozen and I had a smile from ear to ear as I watched the massive mob of United fans charge across the pitch to where the Wolves fans were gathered. It was like something out of a film and I loved it!

Not surprisingly the Wolves fan who had set fire to the United scarf, ran for his life and dived back into The North Bank as soon as the United fans got on the pitch. As the United mob made its way across the pitch, the police finally took some action and formed a blue line in front of the North Bank. The sheer weight of numbers meant that some United fans would get through and fights started to break out as United fans started to jump into the North Bank.

After police reinforcements arrived the police finally ejected the United fans from the front of the North Bank. While the police were concentrating on getting United fans out of the Wolves end, the main United mob were still on the pitch, beckoning Wolves fans to come and join them. The Wolves fans didn't take up the challenge and the United fans eventually made their way back to the South Bank, where they were greeted like a conquering army by the rest of the Red & White hoards.

Soon after the police had shepherded the last few United fans off the pitch, the main entertainment started, and the two teams entered the field of battle. I waved my scarf and jumped up and down like someone possessed as George Best trotted into the penalty area and waved at the crowd as he took a few warmup shots against Alex Stepney. Even though Georgie was on the pitch, I found it difficult to concentrate on the game because of the electric atmosphere generated by the extremely vocal United supporters and the continual swaying of the crowd.

Fortunately, I was taking notice and I had a great view as my hero George Best scored United's only goal. As most of the United players surrounded George and congratulated him after he'd scored the goal, the temptation was too great to run on the pitch and join the celebrations. However, after remembering the look of disapproval on Mickey's face when hundreds of United fans had invaded the pitch before the match, I thought I'd better stay put.

As Mickey and I left the game after the final whistle, my head was spinning with all the excitement and drama of the afternoon. The wildly animated crowd were packed into the South Bank with the deafening noise from the passionate United fans seeing my hero Georgie Best putting the ball in the back of the Wolves net, and the spine chilling pitch invasion that followed by hundreds of United Boot Boys!!

Just outside the ground I bumped into Robert, a lad who lived just over the road from me. Robert was also a Red and a few years older than me and had made his own way to Wolverhampton on the bus. Robert and I chatted non-stop about the game and the excitement of being with the United supporters until we reached Mickey's van so that I could continue my conversation with Robert I asked Mickey if we could give Robert a lift home. "As long as he's happy sitting in the back of the van," Mickey replied. Robert happily agreed and jumped into the back of the van, which he had to share with Mickey's work tools and various bits of building materials.

As per the journey to Wolverhampton, I was eager to show off my scarf. So again, with my scarf still attached to my wrist, I held my arm against the side of the slightly opened window and let my scarf hang outside the van. We had only been driving for a minute or two in very slow traffic, when a gang of about 20-30 Wolves fans came walking towards us. On seeing my red and white scarf hanging from the window they quickly surrounded the van and immediately started kicking and thumping the sides and roof of the van. Soon the kicking and thumping turned into rocking the van from side to side. I was terrified; Mickey and I were thrown about like we were on a fairground ride. I was praying for it all to stop, when suddenly I felt my arm being pulled up through the gap in the open window. Panic set in and tears rolled down my face, as I shouted to Mickey for help.

Mickey quickly lent over and tried to pull my hand back inside the van. Unfortunately for me, two or three of the bastards who were terrorizing us were pulling my arm and scarf in opposite directions. I thought my arm was going to be ripped out of its socket when suddenly the pulling stopped, and I sprung back into Mickey's arms. I gave a big sigh of relief before noticing my scarf was missing, well 90% of it. The gang of Wanky Wanderers had cut the scarf from my wrist. There was virtually nothing left of my pride and joy. 'Law' and my Man United crest had gone, and my scarf was now an oversized wristband. But there was one last sting in the tail, with an almighty crash; the van was pushed over onto its side. Mickey found himself with his face on the tarmac and me on his lap. Robert probably ended up the worst off having been thrown around in the back of the van like a ragdoll as the van turned on its side Robert ended up being battered by the metal tools, bricks and slates that rained down on him. Luckily within a few seconds a group of Good Samaritans came to our rescue and the van was tipped back up onto all four wheels and Robert was once again subject to being bombarded with all manner of objects. While I cried over the loss of my scarf and Robert cried about all his cuts and bruises, Mickey just sat in a dumbfounded silence for what seemed like an age.

Mickey's silent shock soon turned into red rage when we finally got out his van to inspect the damage. The van resembled an old tin can that had been used in a weeklong game of *"Kick & Run."* Can you just imagine the scene on the drive home? I was lamenting the loss of my scarf; Robert was continually whimpering about his many injuries and Mickey was shell-shocked over the damage to his van.

AND WHAT A DRAW UNITED
Wolves 1, Manchester United 1

Old Trafford should be ready with a mass show of thanks for the new-look Manchester United when they return to headquarters next Saturday.

A number of spectators were removed from the ground by police before the match had kicked off, after a few Man U supporters had spilled onto the pitch from the Spion Kop end and attempted to get onto the North Bank section amongst the Wolves fans. The Police were heavily outnumbered as the United fans swept down the pitch, but order was eventually restored when the Man U supporters returned to the Kop end.

There was nothing less than a thunderous reception after United's unbeaten haul of eight points from five "away" games. The skills, pride and bravery which took a point from Wolves were a superb advertisement for the recovery so soon engineered by the new chief, Frank O' Farrell.

United were brilliantly in charge of a one-sided first half when George Best put them ahead, but it needed the acrobatics of Alex Stepney to restrict injury-stricken Wolves to a point in the second half.

Danny Hegan.

The crowd of 46,479 - Wolves biggest for two seasons, watched in disbelief as Bobby Charlton arrogantly stood with the ball while United's jigsaw formations slotted into space alongside him. So it was left to Best himself to thump united into a 16th-minute lead after Brian Kidd squared a David Sadler free-kick back across the edge of the penalty area. Wolves came out for the second half with obvious instructions to chase and rattle United out of their leisurely composure and United's keeper Alex Stepney was the target for a furious bombardment as James and David Sadler lost their monopoly in the air.

Four times Stepney pulled off super class saves to hold headers from Dougan and Gould and shots from Hibbitt and Gould.

United's failure to adapt the marking system to Dave Wagstatte's switch to the right wing led to Wolves 78th-minute equaliser. Wagstaff's centre rebounded from the defensive wall and fullback Bernard Shaw met the hall 30 yards out and not even Stepney could make a move for his blistering shot.

Chapter 2.
Birmingham City '73

10th March 1973

Birmingham City 3 – 1 Macari (51,278)

United Line–Up

*Rimmer, Forsyth, Buchan, James, Morgan, Charlton, Young, Kidd,
Graham, Macari, Storey-Moore.* **Sub -** *Martin*

Manager

Tommy Docherty

League Position After the Game

P	W	D	L	F	A	Pts	Pos
32	7	10	15	32	53	24	20th

*Tommy Docherty had only taken over from the meek and timid
Frank O'Farrell a few months earlier and must have realized
what a mammoth task he had on his hands to bring the glory
days back to Old Trafford. United had gone nine games from
the start of the season without a win, and only scored three
goals in those first nine games. As The Reds lined up against
Birmingham City, there was little hope of an away win, United
had only won once on the road until this point and only ended
up winning three away games all season.*

*'The Doc' managed to keep United up, however, they finished
a lowly 18th with just a mere seven points from safety. To add
'salt to the wounds' to the Old Trafford faithful; at the end of
what was a terrible season, club legends and former European*

*Footballers of the Year - Bobby Charlton and Denis **The King** Law, left the club. George Best, United's other European Footballer of the Year, would play his last game for United in less than a year. Between them United's Holy Trinity had played for The Reds over 1,200 times.*

I was only twelve years old and this was the first United game I attended without being accompanied by an adult, and without doubt, thought I knew it all. I went along to the game with my neighbor Nick, and his older cousin Martin, whom both unfortunately were Blues supporters. Nick and I met Martin near New Street and as we stood chatting hundreds of Reds came pouring out of the station.

I immediately pulled out my new United silk scarf that was hidden around my waist, while Nick and Martin were quick to hide their blue and white scarves. Much to the annoyance of Martin, I insisted that we tagged on to the United mob and walk up to the ground with them. Making a tremendous noise the United mob seemed like an unstoppable juggernaut as it marched down the middle of Digbeth, bringing all the traffic to a standstill. The dozen or so coppers who were trying to escort the United fans to the ground were powerless to control the mass of red-and-white clad hooligans. Shop and pub windows were smashed, and several United fans were jumping on and even running across the roofs of stationary cars much to the horror of the passengers sitting inside them. As the United mob approached the infamous Greenaway pub; Blues' main pub at the time, a small army of Blues fans came storming out of the boozer and blocked the way to the ground. I had only been close enough to witness one other altercation between football fans before and that was Port Vale v Villa, where no more than seventy hooligans were involved. But now there must have been more than a hundred Blues fans and hundreds, if not thousands of United!

There was no way the small number of plod could stop the inevitable from happening and a mass brawl immediately broke out as the two sets of supporters came together. The roar that went up as the two mobs charged into each other was deafening. Bricks, bottles, and beer glasses were flying through the air in both directions with the fighting going on for a good five minutes with neither mob giving any ground. It wasn't until four or five vanloads of coppers arrived on the scene that the opposing fans were separated.

When the mass ranks of police restored some kind of order, the United mob marched up to St. Andrews. As we made our way up the hill to the Blues ground, I spotted a small trolley-cart selling my favourite food, Westley's hamburgers - manna from heaven for me and my mates. There was a small queue waiting to be served with these wonderful burgers, but at the front of the queue were a gang of United fans. Everything apparently seemed orderly when suddenly a few raised voices were heard followed by a cry for help as the poor vendor was surrounded and quickly dragged to the ground. While half the gang were helping themselves to burgers and cash, the other half were stripping the vendor of his white coat. White butchers' coats were quite a fashion accessory for certain football fans in the early 70s. The white coat must have seemed like a nice trophy of war to the United fans. The final act of terror for the vendor occurred when the United fans tipped over the trolley-cart, which sent burgers, cobs, onions and sauce bottles all over the pavement. What a bleedin' waste!

The Burger-Bashing-Boys marched off triumphantly swinging the white butcher's coats above their heads as if it were their regimental mascot. My suggestion to go in the United section of The Spion Kop fell on deaf ears so I ended up taking off my scarf and followed Nick and Martin into the main section of City's Kop. By today's standards the St. Andrews Spion Kop with its worn out concrete steps and terraces, exposed steel girders and corrugated iron cladding, would be classed as positively shabby, even dilapidated and probably was! However, I always thought the Blues main end had great character and the noise generated was tremendous; basically, a proper football ground! The United and Blues fans were divided by a six foot high metal fence that ran from the back of the Kop down to the pitch, as per the Kippax.

The fence may have prevented the two sets of fans kicking two shades of shit out of each other, but it certainly didn't stop every type of missile imaginable being thrown back and forth by the warring hooligans. Literally every few seconds there would be a brick, bottle, coin, battery, bike chains, and even the odd boot was seen flying across the dividing fence. Not far from where Nick, Martin and myself were standing, a group of Blues fans were giving a few Indians a lot of grief. It was pretty clear that the Indians were very much outnumbered and didn't want any trouble. But after an initial bit of pushing and shoving, one of the Indian's turban was pulled off and thrown into the air. Understandably this immediately changed the mood of the Indians and with outrage and anger, knives were brandished. Then one of the Blues fans produced what looked like a small chair leg, or it could have been a very ornate rolling pin! Who Knows? But at this point another one of the Blues fans wielded a small, but thick chain.

Soon a 'no man's land' gap was formed as the two antagonists waited to see who would blink first. It was bad enough dodging flying missiles but this altercation with drawn weapons was just far too hot for us and Martin quickly guided us from the troubled Kop to a safer part of the ground. Martin suggested we should stand behind the goal in the Tilton End as there was never any trouble in there. After pushing our way through the crowd, we finally took up our position behind the goals in the Tilton. I was totally shell-shocked by what I had just witnessed and completely worn out after pushing and squeezing through the jam-packed terraces. But it seemed Martin was correct about the lack of trouble and the supporters who stood around us, were nowhere near as hostile as the Blues and United supporters in the Spion Kop. So much so, that after 10 minutes of standing in the Tilton, I felt confident enough to put my United scarf back on. The much older lads and the men standing around us didn't seem to be worried about a 12-year-old wearing a United scarf until just before kickoff when the United forwards trotted up into the penalty box and started taking practice shots against Jimmy Rimmer. Willie Morgan was one the United players who was taking shots at the goal and as his ball hit the back of the net you could tell he wasn't holding back. Willie Morgan had several shots that were all on target then one of his powerful half volleys whistled past the outside of the post.

Nothing wrong in that you may be thinking. But the speedy ball headed straight into the crowd and unfortunately knocked a poor young boy clean off his dad's shoulders. If Willie Morgan had been on the fairground, he would definitely have won himself a coconut! At first there was an initial panic to make sure the boy was okay then there was plenty of abuse and anger aimed at Willie Morgan who was totally unaware of what had just happened. While the St. Johns ambulance men were making sure that the boy wasn't badly hurt, the father was restrained by a copper and a couple of his mates. I dread to think what the father would have done if he had been free to take his frustration and anger out on the unsuspecting United player.

Many of the Blues fans standing around us were fuming over what was an accident. Just a few minutes after that incident a few very scary teenage Blues fans approached me and said, "if you don't take that scarf off, we will fuckin' hang you from it." The scarf was off and in my pocket quicker than then you could say, "we've got Willie – Wille Morgan on the wing." With only a few minutes to go, United were 2 -1 down and we decided to make our way out of the ground. Martin, not only being the oldest but also by far the tallest led the way as we tried to push past the vast mass of bodies. The combined linking terraces of The Spion Kop and The Tilton Road must have held nearly 40,000 spectators, and as we tried to make our way up the steps in the uncovered corner section of the ground it felt like we were trying to push past every one of them. Even though the terraces were packed we came across several blokes having a piss on the steps. Well, when you have to go, you have to go and sod the poor bleeder in front of you who gets the splash back! Our ascent to the top of the terrace was hampered by fans continually stopping on the steps to get a last look at the match before they left the ground.

The crowd was so tightly packed, that most of the time I couldn't even see the sky, it seemed like I was lost in the forest of bodies. We had managed to get halfway up the terrace steps when there was an almighty cheer from the Blues supporters - Birmingham City had been awarded a last minute penalty. Everyone making their way out of the ground seemed to turn around as one. And as they did, I was lifted off my feet and spun around, and because it was so congested on the steps, even when the crowd surged forward my feet were still dangling in the air. I struggled to get my feet back on to the concrete steps, but we were packed in so tight I had no chance. We were crammed together so tightly I couldn't even move my arms. I couldn't see the Blues penalty taker, but I could just about see the dejected and despondent United players on the edge of the box. Even though I couldn't see that the ball had hit the back of the net, I was left in no doubt that Blues had gone 3 – 1 up. The Blues fans went wild and with my feet still dangling in mid air all the fans surrounding me cascaded forward like a massive tsunami. We must have surged 20 foot towards the pitch then back again in one stomach churning movement; and still, my feet couldn't find the steps.

As the Blues fans started to jump about and celebrate the goal, the crush subsided a little and the vice-like embrace of the crowd lightened enough for me to finally get my feet back on the ground. When I eventually made it to the back of the terraces, I collapsed up against a brick wall and over dramatically thought to myself that I was lucky to be alive. As I huffed and puffed and struggled to get my breath back, I realized that my feet were wet. It was a sunny day so it couldn't be rainwater. Then as I looked down the smell hit me; I was ankle deep in a pool of piss. I hadn't noticed when I fell exhausted onto the wall that I was next to the notorious St. Andrews bogs. Whenever the Blues had a big home game you could guarantee the toilets would overflow and rivers of piss would run down terraces. Some said - it all added to the charm of the place! It seemed, it wasn't turning out to be my day, but the worst of it was yet to come. I had lost my two mates whilst trying to get out of the ground so before I made my way back to the city centre I tied my United scarf to my waistband and hid it down my trouser leg.

The walk back to the city center was uneventful, relieved I hadn't come across any trouble I sat on a small parapet wall outside the Mulberry Bush pub. While I sat and waited for my mates to turn up, I started to read the match programme. My head was buried in the programme and I was fully engrossed in the United article when all of a sudden it turned very dark. I looked up to find myself totally surrounded by a large gang of teenage Blues supporters. My heart was going ten to the dozen, as I quickly closed the match programme and jumped to my feet then nervously looked around. I thought to myself how the fuck am I going to get out of this? To add to my confusion and alarm there seemed to be several muffled conversations going on within the gang and I felt totally disorientated. Even though the Blues fans looked like a very scary lot, I somehow plucked up the courage and said to one of them, "who are WE, looking for?" He gave me a strange look and snapped, "United fans, ya thick cunt!" I was like the proverbial rabbit stuck in the headlights!

Then I heard another one of them cry out, "There they are!" Then the gang moved, en-masse taking me with them. I can only put it down to being so hemmed in and petrified that without any thought I decided to run down the subway ramp with the rest of the gang. I had only been running for a few seconds when I felt my United scarf working its way down my leg. I looked down and to my horror I could see my silk United scarf trailing out of my trouser leg. A few seconds later my scarf was on the floor. Part of the gang who were behind me had stopped and were staring at the scarf on the floor. As I carried on running, I heard the Blues fans behind me shouting at the vanguard of the gang to stop. I went into sprint mode and as the gang in front of me slowed down, I flew past them all. I had just reached the stairs in the subway when I heard a tremendous holler and to paraphrase Bradley Walsh, 'The Chase Was On!' I could hear all types of abuse and death threats from the baying mob as I dodged in and out and pushed aside bewildered and dazed shoppers. As I approached Rackhams department store I could still hear the Blues mob behind so I decided I would try and lose them by running into the giant store. An old soldier - a Corporal Jones type from Dads Army, always patrolled the front entrance of Rackhams. He was dressed in a three quarter length coat with epaulettes and proudly wore a chest-full of war medals. He was continually on the lookout for little sods like me. As I ran up the street he certainly had me in his sights.

When I reached the grand entrance of the shop, the old git grabbed me by the arm and pulled me back. I was swung around and to my horror I could see that the Blues fans were only a few yards away. So, with my free arm I pushed the old soldier in the chest and sent him stumbling backwards into the path of my pursuers. I then raced into the shop and scrambled up the stairs onto the first floor. As I reached the first floor, I could hear some commotion being caused by the Blues fans on the ground floor.

Ducking and diving in between endless rows of dresses and old fogeys' bloomers, I came to an emergency door. I pushed it open and ran down the stairs. When I got to the bottom of the stairs, I opened another door and found myself in the basements where Rackhams delivery vans were parked. I couldn't initially see an exit, so I decided to hide under one of the large vans that were parked a few feet away from me. My heart was almost pumping out of my chest as I lay on the cold concrete floor looking up at the underside of the delivery van. I had been hiding under the van for a short while and was starting to think that maybe I had managed to escape from the Blues mob and maybe, just maybe, it might be safe for me to make a move. I was just building up the courage to break cover when I heard a few voices next to the van. Then I heard the van door close and the engine start up. How I never soiled myself as the van slowly pulled away, I will never know. As the van drove out of the basement I lay on the floor in shock, unable to move, I just couldn't believe what had just happened.

However, a few seconds later I was bolt upright, one of the porters had spotted me lying on the floor and shouted out, "What the fuck are you doin' down there?' He then called out to a couple of his mates; 'There's an intruder in the basement'. I spotted the open roller shutter doors the delivery van had just driven through and I made a run for it. I looked around as I got to the door and noticed four men in brown porters' coats chasing after me. Fortunately for me, my new adversaries weren't exactly the athletic type and after only a minute or two they gave up the chase and headed back to their dark and dreary basement. No doubt puffing and panting all the way back.

DOC'S SORRY MISFITS

Birmingham City won another vital battle in their fight for First Division survival and confirmed what the football world feared for Manchester United.

Until Lou Macari offered them brief hope with an 83rd minute goal, United were exposed as expensive misfits. United's late spurt left an unrealistic impression of their ability to arrest the million pound slide towards Division Two.

Birmingham, a club with a history of soccer's harder times, called on their traditional grit to hound United into a 2—0 deficit, by the 62nd- minute.

The lead was worthy of a performance which showed them to be better equipped for this pressure- type soccer. Five minutes from time it seemed that Willie Morgan, one man who bore the United shirt with pride, might have snatched an equaliser.

A swerving shot was on target from the top corner until Dave Latchford pulled off a save, which will he remembered to the end of the season. That was the end of United and an injury time penalty goal by Alan Campbell restored a true image of the game.

Tension spilled over in scuffles between Macari and Roberts and Graham and Bob Latchford.

Alex Forsyth was booked for bringing down Trevor Francis. A Birmingham goal in the 42nd minute was the breakthrough towards better things—though not for United's uneasy halfbacks James and Buchan.

The ball should have been cleared long before Pendrey chipped it back into the penalty area. Francis flicked it on and Latchford bulldozed it over the line. Moore, Kidd and Charlton all gave brief hints of a United revival before half-time when the limping Moore was substituted by Martin.

Hynd, Roberts and Martin all had to work hard for a spell and United's turning point came when Roberts cleared off the line after Graham's shot beat Dave Latchford for power.

With Page and Campbell winning the ball in midfield more readily Birmingham eased on top with a Bob Hatton goal in 62 minutes.

For all the craft old Morgan* and the persistence of Kidd. United's revival was a surprise.

The Inspiration stemmed from Macari stabbing in a close range shot after Birmingham had failed to deal with a Charlton free kick.

Chapter 3.
Stoke City '74

29th April '74
Stoke City   1 – 0   Manchester United   (27,392)

United Line–Up
*Stepney, Forsyth, Buchan, Holton, Houston, B. Greenhoff, Martin, McCalliog, Morgan, McIlroy, Macari **Sub -** Young*

Manager
Tommy Docherty

League Position After the Game

P	W	D	L	F	A	Pts	Pos
42	10	12	20	38	48	32	21st

I'm sure that none of the tens of thousands of United supporters that were at Wembley in May '68 would have thought in their wildest dreams, or maybe 'nightmares' that just six years after winning the European Cup, United would be relegated to Division 2. But after a disastrous season that had seen Alex Stepney as joint top scorer with two goals at Christmas. Manchester United's 36-year stay in Division 1 was guaranteed to end after their penultimate game of the season, a 1–0 home defeat against archrivals Man City. The fact that other relegation candidates obtained positive results the same afternoon, meant that even if United had beaten City they would have still been doomed to the 2nd division.

My previous visit to the Victoria ground in 1971 was a joyous occasion. I'd gotten a new United rosette and a George Best poster. The United mob had taken The Boothen End and to top it all off I had ran onto the pitch before the game and got Georgie to autograph my poster. My Second visit to the Victoria ground was bittersweet.

I was delighted to be watching United for the first time that season but heartbroken about the fact that we had been relegated and as myself and Ade approached the ground, I really didn't know what to expect from my fellow United supporters. In an attempt to stop trouble in the ground, the Stoke police had blocked off the entrance to The Boothen End. So, unless you had a Stoke accent you weren't allowed through the police cordon.

Feeling a little disappointed about United fans not being allowed access into the Boothen End, me and Ade made our way to the large uncovered terrace at the opposite side of the ground. Any thoughts of the United crowd being in a sad and sombre mood were quickly dispersed. As we queued to get into ground the United supporters were acting like they were already on the terraces singing song after song and pushing and shoving each other as they fought to get through the small turnstiles. We got into the ground a good hour before kick-off and the terraces were already filling up. Full of bravado me and Ade made our way to the back of the terrace where we thought the United main mob would congregate. We had only taken up our position for a few minutes when the word went around that the United crew from 'The Special' had just arrived at the ground. 'The Special' being the chartered train that ran from Manchester Piccadilly and transported many of United's notorious hooligans to away matches.

This news caused great excitement amongst the United fans and the atmosphere instantly became incredible. It seemed like a bolt of Lightning had hit the United supporters. Everyone started chanting as loudly as they could and danced around like people possessed. As the boys from 'The Special' poured through the turnstiles, the mayhem continued on the terraces and we repeatedly sang - *'We'll be back – We'll be back – We'll be back – We'll be back We'll be back – We'll be back – back –back!* Ten minutes or so before kick-off the large open terrace was packed to bursting.

Ade and I were being slowly crushed to death at the back of the stand. We decided to move down the terrace, and as we did, we noticed first one, then two, then three large gaps appear in the crowd towards the front of the terrace. Wondering what was going on we made our way towards the nearest of the three gaps, there was a loud roar from the United fans on the periphery of the gap, that's when I noticed smoke had started to drift up from the terraces. This made us even more eager to find out what was going on, so we pushed and ducked and dived until we were at the edge of the mysterious gap. To my utter astonishment and delight several United fans had started a fire and this had been repeated in the other two gaps along the terrace. The dozen or so coppers who were standing on the edge of the pitch looked totally lost for words as were Ade and myself but definitely for different reasons! To date, it was the most outrageous and exciting thing I had ever witnessed. While the United fans were in raptures for a few minutes the coppers looked on helplessly. Then suddenly from out of nowhere half a dozen police dogs appeared at the front of the terrace. The dog handlers didn't hesitate at letting the dogs into the packed United fans, barking and snapping. The dogs were on twenty to thirty foot leashes and had boundless amounts of energy forcing hundreds of Reds away from the fires. When the fleeing United fans couldn't move any further into the packed crowd a few brave souls turned and faced the four-legged foe and started kicking out at the snarling beasts. One of the lads trying to put the boot in was Decca, a lad we knew from Walsall. He was backing into the crowd and simultaneously swinging his Dockers to keep the fang-baring dogs away from him. As man and beast were testing each other's metal, a few coppers had jumped into the crowd and were doing their utmost to put out the flames on the terraces. They may have literally put out the literal flames, but the presence of police in the crowd (pardon the pun) only added fuel to the metaphorical fire. In no time the few brave boys in blue were surrounded and vastly outnumbered by the United mob that were jostling and pushing them. It was only a matter of time when some coppers found themselves on the floor. After a few minutes the coppers escaped from the baying mob without any serious injuries and with only their pride taking a battering, because several of them had lost their helmets. The United fans went into party mode and there were massive cheers as several coppers' helmets were tossed around the terrace. What a trophy of war a coppers helmet would have been. While the coppers helmets were still flying around the crowd, a line of police came marching round the side of the pitch and stood in front of the baying United supporters. The much-needed reinforcements were marched into position with the help of the massed ranks on the terraces, whistling the Laurel and Hardy tune, aka *"Dance of The Cuckoos."* It was almost mandatory in the late 60's and 70's for a group of young football hooligans to whistle the Laurel and Hardy tune whenever two or more coppers walked past. After the fun and joviality of Dance of the Cuckoos had died down, many of the older and well travelled boys started to sing, *Harry Roberts is our friend, is our friend, is our friend. Harry Roberts is our friend, he kills coppers,* which went right over my head. The small army of coppers faced the unruly United mob and stood shoulder to shoulder, forming a human barrier across the entire width of the pitch, Ade and I counted over seventy of them. The younger coppers looked petrified and the older ones looked disgusted by the mayhem that was in front of them. After the game had started, Decca miraculously found us in the crowd, and he was quick to tell us about the carnage that United fans had caused after they left the railway station in Stoke and made their way to the ground. Hundreds of windows had been smashed, cars tipped over, pubs ransacked and Stoke fans had been run all over the place. Decca was a couple of years older than me and he had quite a reputation of being a hard nut. Decca also had a reputation of supporting any team in red and white. Man United was definitely his first team, but he would also go and watch Walsall and rumour had it, he even went and watched Liverpool. I had heard a few people say that if Leeds or Man City ever played in red and white he would also go and watch them. However, there weren't many people in Walsall who would actually say that to Decca's face. Because of Decca's reputation and age, Ade and I really looked up to him and we felt privileged to be in his company. That said, Decca was a certainly a strange kettle of fish. Throughout the game all manner of missiles would be thrown at the small army of coppers who were bravely keeping their positions along the side of the pitch. At the time it was great entertainment to watch the police dodging coins, bits of concrete and the odd bottle or two. When Stoke City were just about to take a corner kick, a copper's helmet was thrown in the penalty area and for virtually the entire match we all sang, *We'll be back - We'll be back - We'll be back - We'll be back - We'll be back - We'll be back - back - back!* As the three of us left the ground at the end of the game, I was astounded to see a mob of chanting Stoke City fans coming towards us. Especially after Decca had earlier informed us that United had ran Stoke Fans ragged before the game. I was a thirteen year old cocky wanabee and not surprisingly my bouncing stride instantly turned into a snail's pace as I gingerly made my way towards the oncoming Stoke fans. I could physically feel the bravado and thin veneer of invincibility that I had experienced over the last few hours on the terraces drain out of me. I was just about to shout 'Mom!!' when I heard the battle cry from behind me and was brushed aside by the charging United storm troopers. My fickle bravado and fantasy of being a football hooligan quickly returned when the rampaging United fans smashed into the Stoke fans and quickly dispersed them into the dark side streets of Stoke.

Thanks for the memory...

Of Carey, Rowley and Pearson...
Of Edwards, Byrne and Taylor;..
Of Charlton, Law and Best...
Of precious moments of spectacle and high drama

Stoke City 1, Manchester United 0

FEW sporting idols have fallen harder than Manchester United, who last night left the First Division after 36 crowded years

But even this night was blackened by the stupidity of young hooligans who have clung to the coat tails of fame.

Their bonfires on the terraces and clashes with police were just another ugly reminder of the disciplinary fate awaiting Old Trafford next season.

This season ended the way it began, with a defeat away from home.

Stoke, who must surely emerge as serious championship contenders next season with Alan Hudson adding his dimension to the talent we always knew was there, wait to see if this result will be good enough to take them into Europe.

A goal by John Ritchie from close in after a line run and cross by Sean Haslegrave in the 19th minute was enough to secure them a fairly comfortable win.

Having seen their last 1< matches the only conclusion of any constructive value that though their future is uncertain there is no lack of determination.

And young player', have aged years through bitter experience.

Last night, with discovery of the season Brian Greenhoff captain for the night in opposition to his brother. Jimmy, of stoke. United might have snatched a draw but Stoke were the far more confident side.

They might have had a second goal five minutes after the first when a shot from Jimmy Robertson was deflected for a corner by United goalkeeper Alec Stepney and Denis Smith headed against the crossbar.

There was a shock for United in the second minute when left back Stewart Houston was carried off on a stretcher after being injured in a tackle by Robertson.

But he was able to step back into the action seven minutes later.

United's best chances came when a Sammy McIlroy shot hit Smith. He had another one saved by John Farmer, and Mick Martin shot Wide, all in the first half, and Greenhoff shot wide in the second half.

—John Roberts

Chapter 4.

Leyton Orient '74

17th August '74
Leyton Orient   0 – 2   Morgan - Houston   (17,772)

United Line–Up
Stepney, Forsyth, B. Greenhoff, Holton, Buchan, Houston, Morgan,
*Macari, Pearson, McCalliog, Daly **Sub -** McIlroy*

Manager
Tommy Docherty

League Position After the Game

P	W	D	L	F	A	Pts	Pos
1	1	0	0	2	0	2	3rd

It was real! United were in Division 2 for the first time since 1938 and playing Leyton Orient on the opening game of the season. The Doc had decided to stick with the young side that had been so disappointing the season before.

The manager seemed happy that United had a strong rear guard that would be the backbone of the team - Brian Greenhoff, Alex Forsyth, Stewart Houston, Jim Holton and class act Martin Buchan were all very reliable defenders. Alex Stepney was the sole survivor of the 1968 European Cup winners and was one of the few senior players in the team which included captain Willie Morgan. United's only major signing in the summer was Stuart (Pancho) Pearson.

The Reds paid Hull City £200,000 for the striker and he made his debut at Leyton Orient. With his do or die attitude Pancho soon became a firm favourite at Old Trafford and in his first season he scored 17 league goals – the previous season Sammy McIlroy was The Reds top scorer with just 6 goals. Even in Division 2 United had the highest crowds in the football league with an average home gate of 47,781, they also recorded the biggest crowd of the season when almost 61,000 saw United beat Sunderland 3 – 2 at Old Trafford.

United's first game of the 1974 – '75 season was just seven days after my fourteenth birthday, and we had played Leyton Orient away. I had no idea who Leyton Orient was, or where their ground, Brisbane Road was. Soon after I had read in the Sunday papers where United's first game in division two was going to be played, Decca informed me that he would be going to London to see the match. My eyes lit up with the thought of seeing United in London and running wild with Decca and Ade and the rest of the United mob.

Problem was that I only had 50p or so in my pocket. Knowing that I needed a few more bob, I topped up my away day money with a trip to the scrap yard. My dad kept all his scrap metal that he removed from various jobs in a car pit in our garage. He weighed in the scrap each Christmas and split the money between his men. This particular year however, they were going to be light. The day before the game with the help of Ade and Decca I helped myself to almost half of the valuable metal and took a couple of large bags full of lead and copper to a nearby scrap yard. Knowing that my dad was also a tealeaf like me helped me justify taking the scrap metal. To quote the Gospel of Matthew, *"He who lives by the sword."* and all that.

The two sacks of scrap metal were ridiculously heavy, so we had to stop every few hundred yards for a rest, but when we eventually got to the scrapyard it was all worthwhile. With no questions asked of where this scrap came from or whom it belonged to, I simply dropped the two bags on the old rusty scales. A fella with the dirtiest hands and face that I'd ever seen checked the weight of the lead and copper and handed me a 'Bluey' (£5). Christ was I over the moon! This was more than enough for my train fare to London and admission into the ground!

When I told my parents that I was planning a trip to watch United in London the next day, they hit the roof and made it abundantly clear that there was no way they'd let me go. After endless rounds of me saying, "I'm going," and my parents replying, "you are not," I stormed out of the house in frustration. To be fair to my parents it had only been a few weeks since I'd had my first appearance in juvenile courts for smashing the windows in the school swimming pool.

They probably thought, and rightly so, that I would be running riot in London with thousands of other young tearaways, which would undoubtedly lead to another court appearance. It probably didn't help my cause that leading up to the new season, Man United's notorious fans were regularly making headlines in the Sunday papers, and always for the wrong reasons. The press had dubbed the United hoards, *'The Red*

Army' and stated they were the most infamous and feared supporters in the land, causing one riot after another as they followed their team up and down the country. Teams in the second division needed to brace themselves when United were due in their town. I'll have a bit of that, I thought.

To avoid any further confrontation with my parents, on the morning of the game I sneaked out of the house nice and early with my red-and-white scarf stuffed up my jumper and my £5 safely in my pocket. I called at Decca's home, which was only a few minutes' walk from my house. Decca lived with his dad who never seemed to be around, leaving Decca to fend for himself. It was just before 7am when I approached Decca's house and headed for the front door where I heard what seemed like loud music coming from inside. I had to bang on the door for quite a while before he finally answered. Once inside, I was pretty shocked as to how spartan the house was.

The only furniture in the living room was a tatty old table in the centre of the room with a few rickety chairs around it and a sideboard that had a record player sitting on the top of it. The noise I'd heard from outside was coming from the record player and would you Adam and Eve it, Decca was only playing an LP that had been recorded on the Liverpool Kop! I was sitting in one of his rickety old chairs and almost bursting inside with excitement at the prospect of going to London to see my beloved Man United but having to listen to scousers singing 'Walk On'. This surely can't be right I thought, but Decca was indeed a strange one. Just before we left his house, Decca handed me a heavy carrier bag and said, "I've fuckin' paid for it, so you can fuckin' carry it". After feeling the weight of the bag, I took a quick peek inside and saw it was full of beer. Not wanting to lug it around London, I suggested we buy beer on the train. Decca immediately snapped back, "D'ya wanna pay thirty fuckin' P for a can of shit Tartan?" I didn't really know what he meant so I simply shook my head and picked up the weighty carrier bag. When we met up with Ade, he was doing his best to look mean and moody with his United scarf wrapped around his head. The packed lunch tucked under his arm kind of spoilt his image though.

With supplies in hand the three of us jumped on the bus to Birmingham and then boarded the train at New Street Station to London. I was delighted to see a large group of United fans already on the train and they had certainly made their presence noticed by smashing most of the light bulbs and throwing toilet paper all over the carriages they were sitting in and of course they were singing United songs at the top of their voices. We arrived at Euston Station at the same time as another train that was packed full of rowdy United fans. A handful of police tried to keep the United fans on the platform, but the rampaging Reds simply swept the coppers aside and charged out of the side entrance of the station, followed of course by me and my two mates. When we got to the front of Euston station, we were thrilled to see hundreds of United fans all over the concourse. With all these United fans around us and Decca at our side, Ade and I felt six feet tall. However, the feeling of invincibility was short lived after we followed the United mob down to the tube station, me and Ade got separated from Decca and had to wait for the third train to arrive before we could start our journey to Leytonstone. There were another twenty or so United fans on the train but like Ade and me, they were only in their early teens and didn't seem to have any idea of getting to their destination either.

Our train stopped at two or three stations without incident but as we pulled into the next station, I noticed there was a large group of much older lads wearing blue and white scarves. When the tube train doors opened, we soon discovered that they were Chelsea fans. The blue and white cladded mob cried out *"Chelsea Agro - Chelsea Agro,"* as they ran into a carriage and attacked the United supporters who were unlucky enough to be standing near the exit doors. In a flash Ade and I were out of our seats and running for cover in the next carriage, followed quickly by the other United fans that had managed to avoid the Chelsea supporters.

Ade and I were naïvely under the impression, that if we wore a Man United scarf all other football fans would be frightened of us. Well, as we found out that day, it certainly wasn't the case. Our United scarves were on and off like a whore's knickers when a bunch of drunken sailors were in town. At the next station a few of us decided to leave the train and try and find someone that could give us directions to Leyton Orient's ground. Ade and I were making our way up the escalators in the tube station when a mob of Spurs fans appeared on the opposite escalator. As soon as they saw us, they immediately became extremely hostile and a barrage of abuse came our way. The aggressive insults from the Spurs fans soon turned to jeers of contempt, disdain and belittlement when they noticed me and Ade gingerly taking off our scarves.

After getting directions from a copper and getting off the train at the wrong station a couple of times, we finally made it to Liverpool Street, where to my relief we discovered we could get the Central Line direct to Leytonstone. Thank fuck for that, I thought. No more jumping on and off bleedin' tube trains. It had taken us almost as long to get from Euston to Liverpool Street, as it had from Birmingham to Euston.

Both Ade and I were relieved to see loads of United fans waiting on the platform to get the train to Leytonstone and our red-white and black scarves were soon on show again. We were packed like sardines on the tube and with all the singing and swaying backwards and forwards we could have been on the terraces. It was a great atmosphere on the train and being surrounded by much older United supporters, my fickle boldness soon returned.

After three or four stops we were once again greeted by a welcoming party – this time West Ham fans! It was a very frightening sight and even before the train had stopped, they were punching and kicking at the windows and doors. These Happy Hammers obviously hadn't fancied the trip up to Maine Road to support their own team but seemed content to stay on their own manor and fight with the Man United fans instead. My Moodometer immediately swung round from WE'RE THE BOYS to OH FUCK! However, this encounter with marauding hostile fans wasn't like the encounter with the Chelsea fans. As soon as the tube doors opened the vast majority of the United fans poured onto the platform and piled into the cockney gang. Ade and I decided to keep the seats warm and watched the action through the large train window.

We had a great view as the two sets of fans got stuck into each other. It was just like watching a wild-west saloon brawl on a giant screen. As the fighting continued, I thought the train driver must be a United supporter, or like me and Ade an excited onlooker because the train didn't leave the station until all the West Ham mob had been chased off the platform and the triumphant Reds were back inside the carriages. When we finally made it to Leytonstone, we were relieved to find Decca waiting for us.

Decca was outside the tube station talking to a fellow Red and like me he was wearing white skinners, however with a major difference; his white skinners were covered in dried bloodstains. Decca introduced us and quickly explained that his new mates had travelled down from Manchester the night before and while he and a group of other United supporters were trying to find a way into the ground on the previous evening, they had been attacked by a large mob of West Ham fans and he had been stabbed. He must have been quite a tough cookie because he didn't receive any medical attention. He simply shrugged his shoulders and said he would get it sorted when he got home to Manchester. A group of about forty of us left the tube station and started to walk to the ground. Our journey was soon interrupted when all of the lads in front of us stopped off at the first pub that we came to.

The pub was divided into two rooms and a walk-thru at the back of each bar allowed you to see into the opposite bar. The one room in the pub was fairly packed so Decca, Ade and I chose to go into the quieter bar and found seats in the corner while Decca went up to the bar to get the drinks. As soon as we sat down Ade got out the remainder of his food supplies and said to me, "Grange do you want this last ham cob?" Before I could answer, an old dear sitting nearby piped up, "Ham cob! – Ham fuckin' cob! You're in London now boy, you thick northern cunts, it's a fucking ham roll!" The old dear initially reminded me of my old Nan, she was 70 if she was a day and she looked like butter wouldn't melt, until she opened her gob. I was flabbergasted - I'd never heard an old woman or old man for that matter using such lovely language before.

Both Ade and I sat open mouthed as the old dear puffed on a fag and continually mumbled to herself, "Ham fuckin' cobs – Northern monkeys" I thought the West Ham fans were a frightening sight until this old woman frightened me to death. I tried my hardest not to look at the old dear sitting next to me, but I couldn't help noticing that she was chain-smoking and almost nodding off as she knocked back the port and lemons. As I sat drinking with Decca and Ade, I continued to take the occasional sly look at the foulmouthed pensioner and I was surprised to see her without a fag in her mouth but there was a reason for that, I noticed her head ratcheting backwards and forwards indicating that she had fallen asleep. I was just about to point this out to Decca and Ade when Ade said there was smoke coming from that old lady's handbag. The silly old cow

45

had put her open handbag on her lap and dozed off and the fag must have dropped out of her mouth and into her handbag.

Our fits of laughter alerted the barmaid as to what was happening. The barmaid casually walked over, picked up the old dear's drink and poured what was left of it into the smoking handbag then she closed the handbag and left the drunken hag to enjoy her forty-winks. The quiet bar that we had chosen to sit in had soon become packed with fellow Reds including our new friend with the blood-stained white Skinners. His Skinners were now also grass-stained after he had just taken part in a 100 a side kick-about in a local park. I think he said it was 27 – 34 when he left with a further 47 goals disallowed for offside and 63 sending offs! He also told us of his adventures from the previous night and went on to delight us with his tales of the infamous pitch invasion against City and how United battered every City fan who had been brave enough to turn up at Old Trafford that day. I was in my element listening to tales of United Agro, but sadly the tales of United's Red Army were interrupted when one of 'Stained Skinners' mates came over to him and said there were a few Cockney's in the other bar. 'Stained Skinners' was immediately on his feet and pushed his way to the bar counter, so he could see into the opposite bar. He stared menacingly into the other room for a few seconds then picked a beer glass and hurled it into the crowded bar opposite us. There was the familiar sound of breaking glass that I knew so well followed by a short silence, then uproar and several glasses and bottles came flying at us.

The whole pub went crazy and anything that could be thrown was thrown. Besides glasses and bottles flying through the air, ashtrays, stools, and chairs were also used as flying missiles. When the ammunition ran out, the bar emptied out into the street, so Ade and I left the pub and the only person left inside was the pissed-up sleeping beauty. Out in the street was a strange Mexican stand off with a couple of United fans jumping into no-man's land and taking up their best martial arts poses. They were doing their very best impression of Bruce Lee with their arms flying all over the place and legs kicking out, ready for an opponent to challenge. Finally, a few lads from the opposing gang jumped into the ring and squared up to the martial arts warriors.

They very gingerly checked each other out but no one getting near enough to an opponent to land a meaningful blow. It was like a cross between shadow boxing and ballet. No doubt being frustrated by the lack of action, one United fan suddenly ran out from the crowd and with a single punch, knocked one of the Cockney spark out. This was the spark that lit the blue touch paper for the rest of the United fans to steam into the Cockneys who were saved by the appearance of the coppers. Very quickly the size of the United mob doubled, maybe even tripled in size and all the coppers could really do was to form a human barrier around the Cockneys.

A few of the Cockneys had been knocked about a fair bit so a couple of coppers were either side of the injured parties, assisting them to the safety of the pub. One United nutcase blocked the path of two of the coppers assisting an injured

Cockney and as they stopped, he started examining the damage to the Cockneys battered face. "Wow, that's great," the United fan said to the shell-shocked Cockney. "I wish I had done that to you," he continued.

Then while the two coppers were still holding the Cockney, the United fan head-butted him. The United nutter then wandered off like he was taking a Sunday stroll. I don't think even the two coppers could believe what they had just witnessed. When we arrived at the ground there were United fans everywhere. The Doc and a couple of the players had been quoted in recent times as stating, 'they weren't sure if there would be 500 or 5,000 United fans at Orient for the first game of the season.' They needn't have concerned themselves, there were probably somewhere in the region of 15,000 United fans in and around the ground. At a guess, 12,000 inside and 3,000 outside the ground.

Turnstiles were being closed well before kick-off, and as me Ade and Decca queued at the junior turnstiles, a United fan walked past us carrying what seemed like a sledgehammer. The hammer carrying Red approached a locked turnstile that was about 20 yards away from us and proceeded to smash the small wooden door into small pieces. Then still holding his large hammer, he disappeared over the turnstile followed by scores of other United fans. Even though there were no roofs over the terraced areas situated behind each of the goals, the noise from the United fans was deafening. United practically took the ground over with The Red Army packed into the terraces behind both goals and alongside the pitch. I can only remember hearing the Orient fans singing from the seats situated over to our left. Just like at Stoke City, a long line of coppers stood shoulder to shoulder in front of the packed terraces. However, because of the number of United fans at the ground, it wasn't just one terrace, but three that the coppers had to try to protect.

The coppers didn't do a great job; before kick-off several teenagers ran onto the pitch and gave the police the runaround. I will never forget one lad in particular around my age, he was wearing a United scarf wrapped around each wrist and once he got on the pitch, he zigzagged from touchline to touchline, constantly avoiding the three coppers who were pursuing him. As he ran around the pitch, he swirled his scarves around his head gaining rapturous applause from the United fans. At one stage the cheeky sod even stood still for a few moments and let an out-of-breath copper get within a few inches of him. The copper was just about to put his hand on the young tearaway's shoulder when he produced a neat bit of foot work that Georgie Best would've been proud of and left the flat-footed plod looking like a right clown. Determined to get the little sod, half a dozen police came on the pitch to try to apprehend him. One quite athletic plod chased after him and made the rugby dive towards the youth, but he missed, and it resulted in the copper crashing into the advertising hoardings. Immediately after this the pursued youth dived back into the crowd and wasn't seen again.

Throughout the game there were a steady flow of coppers escorting United fans around the pitch and out of the ground.

Each time this happened the United mob directed a shower of abuse at the heavy-handed coppers. I really couldn't understand why so many United fans were being thrown out. It seemed like a party atmosphere amongst the thousands of United fans on the terraces, especially after United's captain Willie Morgan had scored a great goal and put United into a 1-0 lead. Then when Stewart Houston made it 2-0, it was job done. The only lighthearted aggression from the United fans was while they were chanting, *"STRETFORD – SCOREBOARD - STRETFORD – SCOREBOARD"* or *"Celtic"* and *"Rangers"* at each other.

After the game we made our way back to the tube station and after queuing for what seemed an eternity, we finally got onto one of the packed platforms where a gang of United fans were trying their best to pull the cigarette and chocolate machines off the tube station walls. Flying kicks and rubbish bins were thrown at the wall-mounted machines, but it wasn't until someone appeared with a wooden plank that had been ripped from one of the platform seats that any success was achieved. To great cheers from the crowd one after another machine was pulled off the wall. As the various machines hit the concrete floor, they smashed open and their contents including the money went flying everywhere. While the older lads were on all fours fighting for the cigarettes and the cash, Ade and I were content to fill our pockets with the chocolate bars. Well, I was starving; I had not had anything to eat since the infamous Ham Cob incident in the pub earlier.

FULL-BACKS SEE UNITED THROUGH

By RADFORD BARRETT

Orient 0, Manchester United 2

Two policemen were hustling a pale, thin- faced, red-scarved boy of about 15 out of Orient's ground as I entered it on Saturday.

The constables looked a little lost—and no wonder, since hooliganism must be for them an excruciating blend of boredom. danger and disgust.

Yet the boy's features were calm, set as if in a trance, almost exalted. Now, he imagined, he truly belonged to the casualty destructive brutal bands who have nothing and everything to do with football, and. like hyenas, hunt in packs and laugh a lot for no good reason.

Kept in Awe

Until someone discovers how to break the pattern, the game will still need their admission money and their applause while suffering from the other ways in which they indicate devotion.

United's fans now command more acres of print than their team and will certainly dominate my recollections of this match.

One and a half sides of the pitch were filled by visiting fans. Jackson, Orient's goalkeeper, said after the game that his match concentration blots apprehension about such unpleasant spectators, yet it was surely not United themselves who kept Orient in such awe in the first half. They were possibly distracted despite themselves.

United pressed busily, but none too sharply, until Roffey failed to pick up Morgan as the Scot came away with Greenhoff's long pass. Morgan went on to beat Jackson with a rising shot in the 28th minute.

Persistent Bullock

Orient came to life alter the break mainly thanks to Bullock's persistence in the air and the youthful impudence at No. 2 of Fisher, a coloured boy, 18 this month.

Fairbrother missed the best chance, and Orient did not punish the known hesitancy of the United full backs as they should have done.

Forsyth and Houston had the last word, Houston heading in a free- kick after Forsyth had been fouled with 16 minutes to go. To this pair gain confidence. United's prospects are good, for Pearson looks Docherty's best buy so far, and Holton and Buchan locked the middle up completely.

Chapter 5.
West Ham '75

25th October '75
West Ham United   2 – 1   Macari   (38,528)

United Line–Up
Stepney, Houston, Buchan, B. Greenhoff, Nicholl, Daley, Coppell, Jackson, McIlroy, Pearson, Macari. **Sub** *- McCreery*

Manager
Tommy Docherty

League Position After the Game

P	*W*	*D*	*L*	*F*	*A*	*Pts*	*Pos*
14	*8*	*3*	*3*	*24*	*13*	*19*	*2nd*

United's immediate return to the First Division got off to a flyer, winning 5 and drawing 1 from their first 6 games – and United were sitting top of the table as they travelled to Upton Park.

Both on and off the field, all football fans wanted to put one over on the great Man United. One of the teams that wanted the United scalp more than most was West Ham. There had been bad blood between the supporters since May 1967, when United clinched the Division One Title on the penultimate game of the season by crushing The Hammers 6 -1 at Upton Park. The humiliation on the pitch was matched by humiliation on the terraces as United took over the ground. It's gone down in United folklore that over 25,000 Man United fans were packed in the ground, and even though the turnstiles were closed by 1:30pm, literally thousands of United fans gained free admission to Upton Park after scaling the perimeter walls with the help of wooden ladders. The fun and games had started on the Friday evening, when hundreds of Reds got inside the ground, and on the Saturday morning they even had a kick about on the pitch.

Once the game had got underway Upton Park was bedlam, all hell broke loose as the United team were roared on by near hysterical supporters. Several times the referee had ordered the ball boys to try and clear the goalmouth which was littered with toilet rolls and streamers. The St. John ambulance men were running along the sides of the pitch, their stretchers laden with fans who had succumbed to the violence on the terraces.

At full-time, thousands of United supporters invaded the pitch and were digging up lumps of turf. Matt Busby eventually arrived in the stands to address and applaud the fans for their support. Outside the ground, United ran the shell-shocked Happy Hammers all over the place. With everything that had happened on that day the police records show that amazingly only one Mancunian was arrested, a sixteen-year-old, whose father was ordered by the authorities to travel to London to collect his delinquent offspring.

I had recently joined the Birmingham branch of Manchester United Supporters Club. The supporters club had been running for a few seasons and regularly took two coaches to all home and most away games. I was still at school and most of the Brummie Reds on the coach were three, four, even five years older than me. I was over the moon to be travelling to see United with older, wiser, and harder lads than me. They came to be my Big Red Brothers. It was a great atmosphere travelling down to London on the coach, learning all the famous United songs and listening to the exploits of all the older lads and of course swigging back cans of beer. All went well on the M1 but as soon as we left the motorway our coaches were flagged down by waiting Police and we were told that all United coaches were to be escorted to West Ham's ground, and to add insult to injury, our coaches weren't allowed to arrive at Upton Park until after 2pm.

What a load of bollocks! This meant a very boring and frustrating two hours waiting on the side of the North Circular Road. It was all well and good the police and local authorities planning for a few coaches to arrive at Upton Park an hour before kick-off, but by 1pm almost 200 coaches full of crazed United fans were parked up on the side of the North Circular Road. When we eventually started to make our way towards Upton Park, the line of 200 coaches stretched for over a mile and not surprisingly we were in bumper-to-bumper traffic and our progress through the East End was painstakingly slow.

We were going stir-crazy on the coaches and it was almost 2:30pm when we finally caught sight of the Upton Park floodlights. With the traffic still going at a snail's pace a lot of the older lads decided it was time for us to make our way to the ground on foot. We were all in great spirits, and I felt privileged to be included in a mob of fifty to sixty Reds. We were all wearing our red and white scarves and quite a few of us had denim jackets covered with United badges. So, it was understandable that we got several strange looks from other United supporters when they heard us chanting, *"Birmingham lal – lal - la, Birmingham lal – lal – la"* and the old Stretford End favourite *"We all agree Crossroads is better than Corri."*

As we got to within a hundred yards or so from the ground, our high spirits were dampened when we saw the number of United fans in front of us and the massive queues at the turnstiles. Then when the turnstile doors started to close my heart really sank. A dozen or so of us rushed to the side of the ground and tried to get into the seats but again we were met with closed turnstiles and it was the same story at the North Bank. In desperation we circled the ground one more time in a last-ditch attempt to find a way into the ground. But when we heard the crowd applauding the players onto the pitch, we knew it would be a lockout! There must have been thousands of United fans locked out and for a few minutes it was a great atmosphere as we all stood outside the South Bank chanting United songs just as if we were on the terraces. Understandably the Old Bill weren't very happy with so many Reds outside the ground and with the help of mounted police and coppers on motorbikes, they soon set about dispersing the massive mob of United fans. As the police pushed us away from the ground, I noticed a few blocks of high-rise flats, which were only a few hundred yards away and I immediately thought we would be able to see the pitch from the roof. After pointing out the flats to several other United fans, a small mob made our way to the flats. When we made it to the top floor, our progress onto the roof was halted by a locked door. There was a large sign on the door that read, Emergency Use Only. Well this was an emergency! After a few minutes of us taking it turns kicking at the door it finally flew open and we ran onto the roof of the flats just like excited school kids. We jumped up and down chanting United songs as if we had just gained entrance to the terraces. But once again our excitement was short lived. We soon discovered the roof on the Upton Park stands blocked out most of our view and we were limited to only seeing a very small section of pitch. But it was better than nothing. We had been standing on tiptoes and stretching our necks to get the best view for about ten minutes when an irate and out of breath caretaker turned up on the roof. He called us all the names under the sun and demanded we got off the roof immediately. We in turn politely told him to 'Fuck Off'! We continued to trade insults with the caretaker until half a dozen coppers turned up. The relationship between football hooligans and the police was not very cordial at the best of times so the fact that the old bill had to march up almost twenty flights of stairs to remove a bunch of yobs from the rooftop didn't go down too well at all. The first few United fans that the boys in blue grabbed hold of were unceremoniously thrown down the first set of stairs. When the remaining lads on the roof protested about the heavy-handed treatment, truncheons were drawn and United fans in the front line were subjected to a few cracked heads. With this type of police aggression, I'm sure they would have happily thrown us off the roof. I'm certain they only refrained because of the 'concern' that we would land on the police vans parked outside the block of flats. When police reinforcements arrived, the coppers started to escort the United fans down the stairs. JH and I were one of the last ones to leave the roof and soon noticed no coppers following us down. So just for the craic I knocked on one of the front doors and to my surprise an old dear answered and gave me a big smile as if she almost thought she knew me. Being ever the opportunist, I said to her, "Can we come in and watch the football?" "Of Course," she replied, and moved to one side and beckoned us in. The charming old lady immediately got out the biscuits and offered us a cup of tea, which was all very nice, but I had more pressing matters to deal with, like finding a window with the best view of the match. After quickly scouting around the flat, I discovered that our genial host lived at the back of the flats and Upton Park wasn't at all visible from her windows. We really should have given the old lady a bleedin' good kicking for wasting our time, but instead, we left her with biscuit crumbs on her carpet and tea stains on her table. *Ya Doe Fuck with The Infamous Brummie Reds!!!*

After we left the block of flats, we continued with our mission to get into the ground. As we approached the back of the South Bank there were a mob of United fans kicking and banging on one of the exit gates. It didn't seem that they were causing any major damage to the gate but amazingly and unexpectedly the gate opened, and three very menacing looking blokes dressed in white stewards' coats appeared and looked like they were ready for action. Now I don't know if the three amigos fancied themselves as being a bit tasty and had opened the gates to sort out the northern hordes, but when they noticed how many United fans were outside, their faces soon turned white.

Before they had any chance to turn around and close the gates, the stewards were swept away as hundreds of United fans, tried to rush through the open gates. I can only imagine that my fellow Reds who gained access to the terraces had hit a bottleneck because the flow of United fans getting into the ground suddenly stopped and this immediately caused a large crush outside the ground as the United fans pushed in vain to get inside. Unfortunately, the bottleneck gave the heavy-handed coppers time to get the United fans away from the gates and get them closed again. Little did we know about the mayhem going on inside the ground, but I was glad I didn't get inside when I later found out what had happened on the terraces of the South Bank.

Because the coaches that were carrying thousands of United fans turned up so late at the ground only a small minority actually got through the turnstiles. The South Bank soon resembled the Alamo, with the West Ham fans playing the part of the Mexicans. A United mob of two or three hundred were being totally overwhelmed and had been forced into the top corner of the stand. The Reds somehow managing to give as good as they got but I'm sure many of them must have given a big sigh of relief when the Old Bill turned up in numbers and started to separate the warring fans by forming a very large no man's land. Forming such a large gap in the crowd caused its own problems as hundreds of United fans were getting crushed at the front of the South Bank. Not only crushed, but they were also being attacked by the West Ham mob, with many of them using weapons against the outnumbered Reds. John Mc., one of the older Brummie Reds, who had helped run the coaches, was struck on the back of the head with a hammer. With blood gushing out of a deep wound in his skull, John just about managed to scramble onto the side of the pitch before collapsing. John immediately received treatment by St. Johns ambulance and a photograph of him being stretchered away from all the turmoil was splashed all over the Sunday papers. John Mc. wasn't the only Brummie Red to end up in the limelight. Sharky, Tartan, Les, Daz and few others made it onto the back pages of the Monday tabloids as well.

Being totally naïve and full of youthful arrogance, I was gutted that I didn't get into the ground when we rushed the gates, but I did manage to watch a bit of the match. Initially, I stood on the steps of one of the large TV vehicles that was filming the game. Neither the police nor any of the technicians inside the van told me to move, so I slowly but steadily made my way inside the van and watched the game on a six-inch square black and white screen. Maybe the technicians were too busy to notice me or maybe because they just weren't bothered by my presence. No one asked me to leave so I stayed put and managed to watch most of the second half. I didn't get to see the end of the second-half because with less than 10 minutes to go I heard a roar from the United fans outside the ground, and as curiosity, of course got the better of me I went to the door of the TV van to see what was happening. I was told by a couple of animated United fans that the gates to the North Bank had been opened and the United mob that had been outside the South Bank for the entire game were making their way there. I jumped down the steps of the van and immediately followed the United mob to the opposite side of the ground. I was far from the vanguard of the mob and by the time I got around to the North Bank the police were guarding the exit gates so that no more United fans could enter the ground. When the final whistle blew there was pandemonium outside Upton Park with large gangs of United and West Ham getting stuck into each other. The police were run ragged as they tried in vain to stem the violence. Police horses, dogs and motorbikes were all used but to no avail. I was beginning to think that I was out of my depth with all that was going on around me, then something happened that shocked me even more. I had no idea where the coaches were parked and with only a few bob in my pocket, I had no other way of getting home. After asking every copper I saw where the coaches were parked, I finally found the awe-inspiring line of United coaches that just seemed to go on and on into the distance and was extremely relieved when I eventually found the Brummie Red coach. I was just about to drop into my seat when one of the lads came up the coach steps and shouted, 'West Ham are here.' The lads who were on the coach immediately got off, quickly followed by myself. Full of bravado and adrenaline I followed a mob of about fifty United fans but when the mob got to a 'T' Junction in the road, they suddenly stopped and quite a few of the Reds turned and ran back towards me. I was a bit taken aback as to why the United fans had turned and ran without even engaging with the enemy. My curiosity got the better of me and I trotted over to the "T' Junction. I froze on the spot and my eyes nearly popped out of my head when I saw what was coming - an enormously packed street of West Ham hooligans. This mob wasn't made up of school kids like myself, or even older teenagers, they were men! Fully grown men wielding weapons wearing steel toe-cap boots and singing, *"Where's ya famous Cockney Reds?"* I turned on my heels and ran so fast I ending up beating most of the lads back to the coach. As I got back on the coach, I was relieved to see a couple of police vans going full speed towards the West Ham mob. I'm pretty sure that if the Old Bill hadn't turned up when they did there would have been a very long line of smashed coaches and broken heads. When all the fun and games had eventually died down and we had started making our way out of the east end, the coach pulled up at a set of traffic lights and right outside the coach window stood an old geezer wearing a claret and blue scarf and carrying his groceries. Ade and I immediately started to bang our fists on the coach window and launched a very over the top verbal attack on the poor old fellow. We were on our feet screaming all sorts of obscenities and doing our best to look rock hard, but probably looking more like a couple of animals in a zoo. During this barrage of abuse, the old geezer just stared up at us and remained poker-faced. Just as the coach started to pull off, he really slowly lifted his one arm and with a final little thrust, gave us the 'V' sign and mouthed, 'Little Wankers.' His comedy timing was immaculate. Our schoolboy aggression immediately turned into fits of laughter. The old geezer was right of course, Ade and I fancied ourselves as a pair of hardcases, but he saw us for what we were, a pair of school kid wannabes on a day out with the big boys.

A little Foot Note: – every single one of the West Ham players in the 1975 team who played that day were English. How times have changed!

ATTILA RIDES AGAIN

West Ham United 2, Manchester United 1
By Brian Granville

THE visits of Manchester United and their hooligan fans to London are about as welcome as those of Attila the Hun to the declining Roman Empire. Yesterday, at Upton Park, play in the second half was held up, both teams left the field, for 19 minutes, while spectators spilled off the brawling South Bank terracing on to the pitch.

Desperate situations demand desperate remedies. Perhaps we should make admission to all Manchester United's away games by ticket only, giving no allocation to Manchester. One of the sadder aspects of this sorry affair is that the team itself it is playing so well, as indeed it did yesterday, despite a dire beginning.

Six mere minutes had been played when Day, the West Ham goalkeeper, took a mighty kick from hand. High and long into the Manchester half it soared, pursued by little Alan Taylor, for whom no cause was ever lost. Round Greenhoff he ran, over Buchan the ball bounced, and as Stepney came despairingly off his line and Taylor nodded it past him and snuggly into the net. Manchester recovered from this traumatizing start astonishingly well and must still be wondering how on earth they lost. Only in the final quarter hour or so after they had surprisingly scored their second goal did West Ham, deprived of Bonds and Lock get hold of the game, though Brooking had an imposing second half.

Having given away that ludicrous goal, Manchester showed their spirit by quickly shrugging it off and attacking West Ham with a will, taking tight control of midfield and putting together any number of fast, dangerous, intelligent attacks. Coppell, with his speed, quick turns and tricks, clearly had the mastery of Lampard, Macari was busy and energetic, Pearson ready to swoop on the smallest chance.

It was extraordinary that West Ham should reach the interval with their lead intact. A 30-yard left-foot shot by 'the young right back Nicholl was turned around the far post by Day, who also look a left-foot shot by Coppell. McIlroy was just wide of that same post when Pearson flicked on a fast cross from Nicholl. Twice in the space of a minute Pearson struck, first when T. Taylor and Holland were slow in shepherding a ball to Day, bounced off the keeper to safety then Pearson got a foot in, and the shot bounced off the 'keeper to safety, then Pearson homed in from the right and Day took his shot low at the near post.

Pearson should 'have scored just after half time, following what appeared a handling offence by Daly. He had only Day to beat but shot straight at the goalkeeper. Perhaps it was sheer lack of-activity, which soon afterwards caused a strange mistake by Stepney, who allowed A Taylor's cross from the goal line to bounce off his legs. Gould lunged in for the ball and was then violently embroiled on the ground with Buchan. Belli might have been sent off; neither was.

Vicious fighting on the South terraces then led to the game being held up. Both teams eventually walked off the field while loudspeakers optimistically and ana-chromatically appealed: "Will you please be British sportsmen and get back into the crowd?" The roar of derision was predictable.

Finally, the walking wounded, and a few arrested youths disappeared down the tunnel, the rest climbed back over the fence and the game at last resumed. "Well done police, thank you very much," said the loudspeakers. The moral is that, just as the British sportsman is no more than a memory, so is the time when clubs could afford to be without a safety fence.

Scarcely had play resumed when United equalised. A foul by Lampard on the left, a free kick by Coppell, energetically headed on by Houston, a clinching header by Macari. At this point Manchester's defenders, most unwisely, decided to play keep-ball and West Ham gratefully got off the ropes, hit back, then scored again; a goal which heavily underlined the difference in quality between Manchester's defence and their attack. Paddon, brought down by Greenhoff out on the left, accepted a short free kick and crossed to the far post where Gould hit his shot low into the opposite corner Altogether an unusual afternoon.

Chapter 6.
Newcastle Utd. '76

11th September '76
Newcastle United   2 – 2   Pearson B. Greenhoff   (39,037)

United Line–Up
*Stepney, Houston, Buchan, B. Greenhoff, Nicholl, Daley, Coppell, McIlroy, Pearson, Macari, Hill **Sub** - Foggon*

Manager
Tommy Docherty

League Position After the Game

P	W	D	L	F	A	Pts	Pos
5	1	3	1	8	7	5	3rd

Once again, we had a disappointing start to the season, only winning one of our first four opening games. The week before the trip to Geordieland a crowd of over 60,000 at Old Trafford saw a 3 - 2 defeat at the hands of Spurs. United may not have been the best team in the league, but they were still the best supported team and the young Stretford Enders were proudly wearing badges proclaiming, 'I am one of the Loyal 55,000! After finishing a very respectable 3rd place in the league the previous season, United were back in Europe after a seven year absence and had been drawn against Ajax in the UEFA Cup. Well it was seven years absence if you didn't include the Mickey Mouse Anglo - Italian cup, which United took part, in '73. Ever since Jim Holton had left Super Mac unconscious on the Old Trafford turf a few seasons previously, there had been some bad blood between the teams. The previous seasons game at St. James's Park was a bruising affair both on and off the pitch, but thanks to 2 goals from Pancho, and 2 o.g's from Newcastle, The Reds won the game 4 – 3 and helped keep United 2nd in the league.

The Brummie Reds who had travelled up to Newcastle the previous season, had all said that it was the roughest ground they had visited that season, closely followed by White Hart Lane. So when it was announced that United had been drawn to play Ajax away in the UEFA CUP, just a few days after playing Newcastle away, it was hardly surprising that a vast majority of the lads chose to go and sample the erotic delights of Amsterdam rather than face the ferocious lunatics up in Geordie-land. I had tried desperately to get on the Brummie Red coach after undertaking a two-hour journey, which included catching three buses to take my £5 deposit to Ron C, who ran the Birmingham supporters club. When I finally got to his high-rise flat, Ron told me that the last seat on the coach had been taken half an hour ago! I was extremely disappointed to put it mildly and was gutted that I would be missing out on the chance of watching United abroad. It would have been my first trip overseas and I knew that I would be green with envy when I met up with the lads after they had returned from Amsterdam, no doubt bursting to tell me of all the wonderfully exciting adventures they'd experienced. No way was I going to sit in silence and listen to all my mates rabbiting on about their tales of glory, so I decided I'd get a few sagas of daring deeds myself. Even though I had heard all the horror stories regarding how wild it was visiting Newcastle, I booked on the Brummie Red coach for the trip up to the wild north and St. James's Park to see United. Because of United's pending game against Ajax, it wasn't surprising that there was only one coach travelling up to Newcastle. But I was surprised and a little alarmed that the coach was only just over half full. "Oh Fuck!" I mumbled through gritted teeth. What if only a few hundred of us turned up in Newcastle? We'll get slaughtered! My thoughts of impending doom weren't helped by the fact that from the moment we left Brum the rain was pelting down by the bucket load and the further north we went the clouds got lower and darker and the rain seemed like typhoon levels. Probably because most of the lads were suffering from hangovers and had to get up earlier than they normally did for work to catch the coach, the first hour or so of our journey was pretty mundane and monotonous. It certainly livened up a little when we made our first stop on the service stations just south of Sheffield. The service stations back in the 70's could be very moody places and you never knew who you might cross paths with. If there were two or three coach loads of us it was usually ok, but with only about forty of us on our coach, I was a little apprehensive when we pulled into the services and spotted a couple of coaches with Northamptonshire written on the side. They could have been anyone; so, erring on the side of caution we thought it best to leave our scarves on the coach. Martin S., Black Country Pat, and I made our way across the car park and were just about to walk into the services when a large group of lads wearing United scarves and clutching loads of booty to their chests came flying out of the doors. The three of us quickly made our way inside the services to see what was going on. The scene that greeted us was a cross between a Carry On film and Oliver Twist. The shop looked like it had been raided by Fagin and his merry bunch of helpers. There were a bunch of lads behind the counter robbing the till and helping themselves to the cigarettes. Another gang of lads were emptying the shelves of sandwiches and pies. There were also four lads carrying out a metal display unit, which was full of drinks. And while all this chaos and disorder was happening a couple of misguided and deluded shop staff were running from one bunch of lads to another and trying to take the stolen goods off them. The have-a-go-hero shop-staff were simply brushed aside by the rampaging mob. We observed from a safe distance for a few seconds then Martin suddenly shouted out, "Porn Mags!" He then rushed directly into the shop and gathered as many off the top shelf magazines as he could carry. After helping ourselves to what food was left on the shelves, we headed back outside. As we made our way over to our coach, we saw the two Northampton coaches drive off with what looked like a real party atmosphere going on. It did appear that the drivers and passengers were celebrating as if United had just won the cup. With the aid of a dozen or so porno mags the next two hours on the coach was far more enjoyable because we had copious amounts of tits and fanny material to gawp at. For a little act of caring and sharing, we ripped out most of the full-frontal shots and stuck them to the back and side windows, which certainly cheered up many of the passing lorry drivers. It seemed like we were being beeped every couple of minutes and even when a police patrol car passed by the coppers were giving us the thumbs up. As we approached Gateshead the driver agreed to stop at the pub. It wasn't even 12 o'clock and we were hoping for a hassle-free pint but unfortunately as we turned onto pub car park, we were followed by a van full of coppers who boarded our coach and started searching for weapons and contraband. Their search was fruitless, and being the 1970s, nothing was said about the porno pictures we had stuck to coach windows. We were politely informed by the old Bill that no Man United coaches would be allowed to stop anywhere near Newcastle and all coaches would be escorted to a marshalling yard near St. James' Park. We were all initially pissed off but when we approached the city centre there was a certain sense of relief having the police escort.

It was still pouring with rain when we passed the first pub and about thirty mad Geordies came running out, none of them wearing coats, and they started throwing glasses and beer cans at our coach. While they were throwing these missiles at our coach, the old Bill in the van in front of us just let them get on with it. We had only travelled a few hundred yards when we came across a mob of about a hundred United fans being escorted to the ground by almost as many coppers. I later found out this small number of Reds were the total amount of lads who had travelled on United's *Special* from Manchester. On the opposite side of the road to the United mob must have been twice as many Geordies being held back by a stable load of police horses. As our coach passed between the two mobs another hail of missiles were thrown at our coach by the Newcastle fans.

We gradually made our way through the city centre towards the marshalling area, only to be given a nice reception by the Geordie welcome committee at virtually every pub we passed. Our police escort didn't even bother to stop the crazed locals throwing glasses, bottles, and beer cans at the coach and it was a minor miracle that none of the windows were smashed. We were in sight of St James Park when we pulled up at a set of traffic lights. Unfortunately for us there was a pub on the corner when the coach pulled up to stop and yet another mob of Geordies piled out onto the street. But this time it wasn't just glasses, bottles and cans that were thrown at us. They also dragged out chairs and barstools from the pub and started throwing them at the windows, totally ignoring the police van in front of us. The Geordies surrounded our coach and violently banged on the windows and kicked the side panels. It was a very scary situation and the lad sitting opposite me refused to look out of the window even though three or four Geordies were doing their best to get his attention by banging Newcastle Brown Ale bottles on the window. He seemed to be frozen with fear and sat bolt upright looking straight ahead and slowly he took off his red and white scarf from around his neck. I don't know what good removing his scarf on the coach was going to do him - they had got his number and that was that. There were so many Geordies around the coach that even when the lights changed to green there was no way the coach could go forward. Fortunately, the coppers eventually got out of the van and headed towards our coach just as the Geordies had managed to open the coach door. When the coppers cleared a way for us through the Geordie mob, Pat, Martin and I tried to put on a brave face and traded insults with them while waving goodbye. But as soon as the Geordies were out of sight the reality of what lay ahead sank in and we all just stared at each other without saying a word.

The marshalling area in the coach park turned out to be a grey and dull cattle market located about half a mile from the ground with the surroundings none the better, especially as it was still raining cats and dogs. Even more worrying was that there were only three United coaches parked in the coach park. As I looked out of the window at our wind swept, bleak location in the pouring rain, my heart sank and I thought, what the fuck have I come here for? If the Geordies didn't kill me then I would probably end up with pneumonia! It was lashing down and all I had was my denim jacket to protect me from the elements. Martin, the daft sod had gone native and was only wearing a T-shirt.

The coppers informed Ron C that they would be escorting us to the ground at twenty coach loads a time. But looking at the car park, I thought it would probably be around 3:30pm before they actually got twenty coaches together. My enthusiasm to leave the safety and warmth of our coach slowly but surely picked up over the next hour as coach after coach arrived to bolster our numbers. Just before 2pm the police decided it was time to start marching us down to the ground. Alarmingly the Brummie Reds were in the first wave. There were about 1,000 of us huddled together walking down the hill towards the ground with about a hundred coppers walking alongside us. It was a relief and heartening to see most of the coppers with dogs by their side, and even more evident was the sight of a dozen mounted police with their 3-foot long riot sticks. The riot sticks were soon put to good use almost as soon as we left the cattle market where the Geordies were lying in wait. The mounted police happily whacked the hostile Geordies and backed their horses into them to keep them on the opposite side of the road from us. This method of Geordie control worked well until we went past the infamous Strawberry pub where all hell broke loose.

The entire pub emptied onto the street to challenge us, throwing glasses and bottles as they left the bar. The mounted police charged straight into the enraged mob, but the Geordies didn't budge, and we witnessed Newcastle fans punching and kicking the police horses. Ferocious looking police dogs were thrown into the melee and after a few minutes the police managed to bring things under control and get most of the Geordies back into the Strawberry. To ensure the mad Geordie bastards didn't come charging back out at us, several coppers with dogs went into the pub and even a mounted copper parked itself in the front entrance to the pub.

When we arrived at the back of the Gallowgate end, we immediately came under attack from bricks and bottles. Unfortunately for us the area outside the ground resembled a small wasteland, with an endless supply of bricks for the locals, which included girls and young boys. Even though the missiles were coming down almost as heavily as the rain, most of our police escort marched back up to the cattle market to collect the next bunch of Reds to run the gauntlet. To my utter dismay there were only a handful of coppers to separate us from the Newcastle fans, which were queuing up to get into their side of the Gallowgate end. While we stood in the pouring rain waiting to get through the turnstiles, the Geordies regularly attacked us with suicide charges, by bursting out of nearby ranks. However, the old Bill stopped most but some did get through and fought like men possessed. For all their bravado, they ended up with a jolly good kicking before the old Bill removed them.

The Gallowgate End was a large open terrace that was divided in two by a high metal Fence. The fact that the Gallowgate End didn't have a roof meant there was no escape from the rain and by the end of the game we would all end up looking like drowned rats. And the fact that we had to share the Gallowgate with the Geordies meant there was no escape from the flying missiles. That said, missiles weren't only being sent over from the Geordies who were inside the ground. I had noticed several objects flying over our heads that were very clearly thrown from outside the ground by some very athletic bar-coded barbarians. The coppers that were inside the ground didn't seem interested in stopping us or the Geordies throwing bricks and bottles at each other. Their main objective was to remove the twenty plus Reds that had scaled the giant floodlights. A task in which the coppers failed miserably as the hardy group of United fans defiantly stayed perched on the flood lights for the entire game. By the time the teams came onto the pitch, the rain was coming down so hard we could barely see the other end of the ground. The large puddles that had already formed on the pitch made me think, there is no way this match will go to ninety minutes. Even when the game was in full swing, the Geordies would send over a few missiles consisting of bricks, coins and bottles, which we returned in kind. There was a skinny old fellow in his seventies standing near to us who was a game old sod and was throwing anything he could get his hands on back at the Geordies. Every time a missile fell anywhere near him, he would dive on the floor and try to retrieve it. The old soldier may well have been game but sadly he couldn't throw a half-ender more than ten yards. So instead of splitting a few Geordie heads, he inadvertently hit one of his own. It was noticed by a few of the lads that the brick didn't even make the fence that was dividing the two sets of fans, so we made damn sure he only threw coins after that! With so many missiles flying in different directions, there was bound to be a fair few casualties and unfortunately just before half-time we had the first casualty in our ranks. I was talking to Pat when he suddenly dropped to the floor as if a sniper's bullet had just hit him. The offending object that had poleaxed Pat and given him a two-inch gash on his forehead was a large battery. Pat was out cold for a few minutes but soon came around after a few of the lads helped get him into the St John's ambulance.

During halftime, While Pat was receiving medical attention, I went to the back of the stand to see if I could shelter from the rain for a few minutes. I couldn't believe the sight that greeted me when I got to the bottom of the concrete steps. On the opposite side of the dividing fence was a gang of men, in their early twenties, who stood staring at us in a menacing and very intimidating silence. They were all wearing kilts and shin high hobnail boots and had long straggly hair that had been soaked by the rain. A few of them wore shirts, but even though it was pissing down, most of them were bare-chested.

Half of them were pressed hard up against the fence – others stood immediately behind them, looking like a real life terracotta army. But I must say, I had never seen any terracotta warriors who looked as frightening as this bunch of lunatics.

Even though I was scared to death, I couldn't help but stare wide-eyed at them, until one of them made eye contact with me that nearly made me shit my pants. I immediately turned around and ran back up the concrete steps to the relative safety of the packed terraces. We didn't see Pat again until halfway through the second half and when he did return his head was heavily bandaged. This of course was a source of great amusement to everyone, except for Pat of course. Boys being boys, we took the piss out of Pat for the rest of the match and we all cracked up when a coin bounced off Pat's bandaged head just before the game finished. Through tears of laughter Martin suggested that Pat should paint a couple of black stripes on his bandage to stop them taking aim at him. At the end of the game we tried to go down the steps to the back of the stand but because the Geordie mob outside the ground was so big, the police just couldn't disperse them. Once again, we were showered with bricks and bottles from our genial hosts. After standing on the rain soaked terraces for a further fifteen minutes, the coppers decided they would lead us along the side of the pitch and take us out through the Leazes end. As we got out of the ground, there were a small army of police to escort us back up to our coaches at the cattle market. For a few minutes it seemed we would get back to our coaches un-challenged. No such luck. Hundreds of Geordies came rushing down the side streets and piled straight into the police escort. Once again, the Geordies that did manage to get through the thin blue line were given a good kicking by the Reds. With the help of mounted coppers and scores of fearsome Alsatians, we finally got back to our coaches.

As we piled onto our coaches, en-masse everybody stripped off and the coach soon resembled Mr. Wu's Chinese laundry with soaking wet clothes hanging all over the place. When we got a safe distance from Newcastle we stopped at the services. The coach that we parked next to had certainly been in the wars with a couple of smashed windows and 'NUFC' and 'MUNICH SCUM' sprayed all down the side and back of the coach.

If we thought our trip to Newcastle was fun and games, nothing compared to the sight that greeted us at the service station. There was no theft, nor vandalism or fighting with rival fans, just complete pandemonium, with hundreds of barely dressed Reds pushing and shoving each other so they could get their wet clothes under the hand dryers in the toilets. United fans had taken over both the gents and ladies' toilets in a vain attempt to dry their sodden clothes. It was certainly a very strange sight to see so many lads huddled together and only wearing their Skidders and Dockers! To onlookers it must have looked like some sort of dodgy nudist convention.

SWINGING IN THE RAIN

John Dougray
Newcastle 2, Man Utd 2

Considering the thoroughly wretched conditions – gale force winds and icy rain this match at St James Park was more entertaining than one could have reasonably expected. But still only 29,642 spectators of 39,037 who bought tickets braved the elements.

Manchester complained about Newcastle's first goal, but it was a good example of a referee using his discretion and of a side being punished for not playing to the whistle.

It came after 13 minutes when Manchester moved out quickly following a corner to try and play Newcastle offside. The ball came to Kennedy who sensibly decided to go past the defence on his own. Although a lines man flagged for offside against Barrowclough who was behind the defence, the referee indicated he was not interfering with play and Kennedy was allowed to continue his run before crossing to Cannell who scored with a diving header.

4 minutes later Manchester equalised when Pearson ceased on a mistake by McCaffery who tried to casually to pay the ball out of the goal area and near the interval they went ahead when Greenhoff scored with a well struck drive from 30 yards.

Newcastle looking more effective with Cannell playing alongside Gowling and Burns operating slightly behind them, deservedly drew level early in the second half when Burns profited from a rare error from Greenhoff to side foot past Stepney as the keep came out.

Chapter 7.
Southampton '77

26th February '77
Southampton   2 – 2   Macari – Hill   (29,137)

United Line–Up
Stepney, Houston, B. Greenhoff, Buchan, Nicholl, Coppell, McIlroy, J. Greenhoff, Macari, Pearson, Hill. **Sub -** *McCreery*

Manager
Tommy Docherty

FA Cup 5th Round

United had made it into the 5th round draw of the FA Cup thanks to a Lou Macari goal in the 4th round, against QPR at Old Trafford. When United were drawn away to Southampton, only one thing was on the minds of both United fans and players – Revenge! In a disappointing performance from The Reds the previous May, Southampton had beaten United 1 – 0 in the FA Cup final. The '75 – '76 season had been full of hope and expectation; United could have gone into the '76 cup final as Division I Champions, IF they hadn't lost three out of their last six games. Sadly, United ended '75 – '76 season without a trophy; the only morsel of comfort was that they qualified for the UEFA Cup. The Reds went into the 5th round FA cup tie against Southampton full of confidence after comfortably beating Newcastle the previous week at Old Trafford, courtesy of a hat-trick from Jimmy Greenhoff.

Because the FA Cup held a great excitement, it was a ritual for my work mates and I to have our ears glued to the radio for the

5th round draw. With great anticipation there would always be the customary shout of cheers ringing around when the respective teams were drawn out of the hat and equally loud boos and curses hollered when rival teams were announced. When the radio announcer said, "Southampton," I instantly shouted, "Wankers," in recognition of them beating United in the previous years' cup final. Then with clenched fists and a loud cheer of joy, the announcer said, "play Manchester United." Wow, Southampton away - I was over the moon because it would be payback time! I was super-confident that United would not only take over the Dell but the whole of Southampton. And surely the boys would do the business on the pitch this time. Not being able to get tickets for the cup-tie at Southampton's pokey little ground, Banker, Eddie R, Pat, Dave S and I all decided to travel down the day before the game in search of tickets. None of us had a car, and with a train journey being far too expensive, we decided to make the five-hour journey to Southampton on a National Coach from Digbeth. Later that Friday morning we all met up in a pub near to the coach station for a few bevvies before we boarded the coach for the long journey South. We wore our scarves with pride and boarded the coach carrying cans of beer. We did however sense that our aggressive looking coach driver wasn't too pleased to see us when we filed past - and if looks could kill, he gave each one of us a long and hostile stare. Unperturbed, we marched to the back of the coach to claim our seats. We had only sat down for a minute when the driver came stomping to the back of the coach and with a strong south coast accent, proceeded to read us the riot act. "Right you lot, there'll be no messin' about on my coach. For a start, off you can take those bloody scarfs off, also, no drinkin' and no fuckin' swearin' either, you hear?" "No" and "Bollocks" shouted Banker. Before the driver could continue with his little speech, Banker opened a can of beer and much to the annoyance of the driver the froth sprayed all over the window. More often than not, once Banker had downed a few pints it was inevitable he was going to be trouble. He wasn't exactly a hardcase, but he would never back down. "If you think I'm going five fuckin' hours without a drink, then you're off your fuckin' rocker," Banker continued. The driver looked like he was going to burst a blood vessel. The situation wasn't helped when Banker glared at the driver and added, 'We've only been on the coach for a couple of minutes and you're already having a go at us. We haven't upset anyone, have we? - Have we? - No! - So, fuck off and drive us to Southampton, you carrot cruncher'. You could just tell that the driver was using all of his powers of restraint to stop himself striking out at Banker. After a staring match that lasted for a couple of seconds, the driver turned around and stormed to the front of the coach. Banker shouted after him, "You'd better have a fuckin' bucket on board so we can take a piss!" On hearing this, the driver stopped for a split second, then regaining his composure he got off the coach and soon returned with a couple of his colleagues and an inspector. As soon as the driver started to approach us Banker yelled out, 'We've done fuck-all wrong. You don't own this fuckin' coach. You just drive it!' 'That's it, I want that cheeky bastard off my coach,' snapped the driver to the inspector. After a couple of further verbal exchanges between the driver and Banker the inspector managed to calm things down. We agreed not to drink beer on the coach and promised to keep Banker in order. Very reluctantly the driver said we could stay on board. The coach had only travelled a couple of hundred yards, when would you Adam and Eve it; Banker pressed his well-worn self-destruct button again. He jumped up onto the seat, dropped his trousers and did a moony against the coach window. Then the mad bastard shouted at the top of his voice 'I've got the best fuckin' arse on the coach!' The coach came to an abrupt halt and Banker, still with his trousers round his ankles, was catapulted into the next seat where an unsuspecting and totally shocked passenger was sitting.

Banker was still trying to get his trousers on, when the coach driver came running up the aisle. 'That's it! you're off, you're off this coach and it doesn't move until you're off.' Not surprisingly the driver took us straight back to the coach station and this time he wasn't going to back down, but unfortunately neither would Banker. The inspector came back on the coach for a good 15 minutes and tried his best to persuade Banker to leave the coach. Banker wasn't having any of it and was still claiming that he hadn't done anything wrong and flatly refused to get off the coach. Digbeth cop-shop was right opposite the coach station and it wasn't long before the plod turned up and boarded the coach. A young copper and a policewoman, at first, tried their best to reason diplomatically, patiently and politely with Banker. Even being reasonable had little effect, Banker simply continued making lewd and suggestive remarks at the policewoman and the young copper who by now had lost all patience, grabbed Banker by the arm and tried to pull him out of his seat and in turn, Banker gave the copper a right-hander. Both coppers pulled out their truncheons and within seconds there were four more coppers on the scene. Well, Banker being game to the very end, held onto every headrest as he was dragged kicking and screaming down the aisle. It must have taken the old Bill about ten minutes to eventually get him to the front end of the aisle and off the coach.

Apparently when Banker appeared in court the next day, the courtroom erupted with laughter when a stern and pompous Sergeant read out, "The defendant stood on his seat, dropped his trousers, pressed his bare buttocks against the window of the coach and shouted, I've got the best fucking arse on the coach." Banker's reward for having 'the best fuckin' arse on the coach was a £110 fine, plus costs.

After all the earlier commotion, the four of us kept a very low profile on the journey down to Southampton and were all very glad to get off of the coach when it finally arrived at our destination. After a few swift pints it was time to go and sort out some digs. The barman pointed us in the right direction and told us where we would find most of the towns B&B's, and fortunately, it was only a ten-minute walk from the pub. I'm not sure if it had anything to do with Man United being in town, but almost all the B&B's were closed or had 'No Vacancy' signs in the windows. After walking the streets for what seemed an age, we finally came across a B&B with a vacancy sign. We rang the bell, knocked on the door and rang the bell again. Eventually a weird looking bloke answered the door, whom I guess would be in his mid 40s and dressed like someone from the 1940s. He wore a couple of cardigans over his pullover, a shirt and tie, Oxford bags that were obviously two sizes too big for him and old ladies' boot-slippers. Instead of switching on a hallway light when he opened the door, he used a torch to slightly illuminate the doorway. The Strange fella smiled at each one of us, then after a long silence, said, 'Hello boys, what can I do for you?' Well, isn't that pretty bleedin' obvious! I thought. 'We're after a couple of rooms for the night,' Pat replied. "Rooms – Rooms," said the man quizzically. "Yes Rooms! You are a bed-and-breakfast, aren't you?" Pat snapped back at him. After another uneasy silence where the daft old sod stood grinning at us and nodding his head like he was a toy dog on the parcel shelf of the car, he replied. "Oh yes, we're a boarding house, do you want a room?" "For fuck sake," spurted Dave. "Yes, we want a couple of rooms." Once again there were a few seconds silence before he said, "Oh right, you want rooms, I'll just go and ask the wife." The man then turned around and shut the door in our faces, but to our amazement we could hear him locking and bolting the front door. We were losing valuable drinking time and were getting pissed off with the antics of our would-be landlord. "That twat is fuckin' mad," exclaimed Eddie. "Any more fucking about from the old bastard and he'll get a kick in the bollocks and a brick through his window," added Dave. We had been waiting on the doorstep for about five minutes and Dave was just about to go and find a brick to put through the window, when we heard the door being unlocked and the bolts sliding back. When the man eventually opened the door, he stood there with the same stupid grin and once again began to nod his head. It was all too much for the four of us now and we just burst out laughing. In-turn the man started to chuckle to himself. After a minute or so we gained our composure and asked him again if he had any rooms. "What type of rooms?" came a frustrated response? "Two double rooms!" I sighed in frustration. "Yes, I think we can let you have two double rooms – I'll just get the keys off the wife." Then once again he closed, locked and bolted the door. After yet another wait, he returned with the bedroom keys and eventually let us into his B&B. We all followed him upstairs and after he had shown us our rooms, he sat down on one of the beds and said, "my name is Cyril." Before we could respond, he continued, "I suppose you will be off to the pub now or chasing girls in night clubs and getting into all sorts of scrapes." Our mad, but friendly landlord then started chuntering on, down memory lane. Dave and I weren't the least bit interested to what Cyril had to say, so off I trundled in search of the bog. I soon returned and told Cyril, who was still talking to himself, that there was no bog paper. "I'll go and ask the wife for some," which by now was becoming a predictable reply. When Cyril returned with the bog roll Eddie suggested to Cyril that he should come out on the piss with us. Cyril gave a coy little smile and said that would be nice, but he would need to ask his wife. Dave, being Dave piped up and said, "Bring your wife along Cyril so we can all give her a good seeing to." Poor old Cyril was lost for words. Once we had crossed Cyril's hand with silver, he handed over the bedroom keys, but no front door key. When I pointed out we needed a front door key because it would be the early hours of the morning before we returned. Cyril replied, (and you've guessed it) "I'll just go and ask the wife," and off he went. With the front door key safely in my pocket, we were ready to make a move. But before we left Dave stressed to Cyril, "Make sure you don't put the bolts on the front door, because if you do, you won't have a front door when you get up in the morning." When Pat made the mistake of enquiring about the time for breakfast. Cyril's usual response only got to, "I'll go and ask," when Dave interrupted him with, "Don't fuckin' bother, tell your Missus we'll be down at nine."

After wandering in and out of several pubs, we were disappointed to discover that there weren't that many United fans about. We were expecting to come across hundreds of United fans on a mad night out and to hopefully pick up a few match tickets. No such luck! There were only a handful of United fans about, and one of them, a cockney Red who soon latched on to us. He had hitchhiked down from London and we soon discovered he was more than a little crazy. After talking to him for only a few minutes, he produced a leather cosh and announced he would "either do a couple of Southampton fans or a copper at the game". Just before closing time we met a more sane and agreeable Red called Steve. He was a Red from Yorkshire and he'd been in the Navy for almost 15 years and had endless tales of his adventures on the seven seas. Steve was in Southampton for some 'specialist' Naval training and was very generous with his Naval expenses, buying us not only beer but shots as well. We were having a great craic with sailor

Steve, and after god knows how many pints, the mad Cockney had even grown on me. When we were thrown out of the pub and the door slammed shut behind us, Steve offered to take us back to his hotel. Dave moaned about how expensive the drinks would be in a hotel, but Steve certainly put a smile on all of our faces when he told us it would all be at the courtesy of the Royal Navy. What a night! The Senior Service could have refurbished a small battleship with the bar bill that we must have ran up.

The next morning, I wandered into Eddie and Pats room and to my astonishment, wasn't sure what shocked me the most, the broken windows and glass on the floor, or the sight of a naked Eddie (not a pretty sight) drying himself on the curtains. Eddie had taken a shower but because he couldn't find any towels, dragged his bed over to the broken window and was using the curtains as a towel. When Eddie noticed me staring at him opened mouthed, he just grinned and said, "Fuck 'em." Still flabbergasted, I asked him what the fuck happened to the window? To which Eddie looked surprised and replied, "Don't you remember all that aggro with the mad Cockney last night?" I certainly didn't. I had been pissed out of my head when we got back to the B&B and couldn't remember the cockney coming back with us because as soon as my head had hit the pillow, I was out for the count. Eddie & Pat filled in the gaps for me. When we left Navy Steve's hotel we had apparently agreed to try and sneak the Cockney back into our B&B. Pat told the Cockney that our landlord would be waiting up for us and suggested that it would probably be best for him to wait down the street for a bit while we opened a window for him to get into one of our rooms, but only when the coast was clear. Once all the lights were turned off at the B&B, the Cockney started throwing small stones at the windows. Pat said he did hear what seemed like stones hitting the window but was too pissed and tired to get up and do anything about it. After a few minutes of throwing stones at the windows the Cockney must have ran out of patience and he picked up a large rock and threw it straight through the window of Pat and Eddies room. This got the attention of both Pat and Eddie who then approached the broken window in a drunken stupor. The Cockney threw another stone through the window which saw Eddie and Pat stumble for cover inside the B&B. He then started calling them all the cunts under the sun after running out of ammunition and energy before disappearing into the night. The combination of an extremely heavy night and all of us wondering if Cyril would notice the broken window before we left, meant there wasn't much talking going on around the breakfast table or none of us noticing the woman who was serving us. I just assumed she was probably Cyril's wife but when I caught a glimpse of the woman's face I nearly died of shock! Had Cyril married his twin sister, or has he become Cynthia in drag? Cynthia reminded me of Dick Emery's character Mandy, and I was expecting her to shout out, *"Ooh you are awful – but I like you,"* then pushing one of us over, like he did in his famous comedy sketch. The problem of the broken window instantly became insignificant.

The previous night Pat had said he wasn't sure that Cyril actually had a wife and every time Cyril told us he was going to talk to his wife, the mad bastard was probably talking to a life size cardboard cut-out or a freaky blow up doll. "If Cyril has a blow-up doll, then I want to see him fuckin' the thing" quipped Dave. It seemed Cyril had more dark and bizarre secrets than I wanted to know about. I thought it best not to say anything to the other lads until we had left Cyril's B&B. Pat and Eddie were shocked and disgusted by the revelation as expected but Dave wanted to go back and try on Cynthia's knickers.

We continued the thankless search for tickets, and I for one, hoped we didn't come across our mad Cockney friend. We soon discovered that there were loads of United fans in Southampton but unfortunately most of them were in the same position as us - looking for tickets. The situation wasn't helped that most pubs were closed or displaying large signs stating, 'Locals Only'. We made our way to the ground, but it was the same story there, all of the pubs were closed, and thousands of United fans were without tickets. I did my very best to get inside the ground just like scores of other Reds. I even tried to jump the turnstiles a couple of times but was pulled back by the stewards on each occasion. I also tried to pay the turnstile operators in the seating section, but they were having none of it. I would have climbed a tree to get a glimpse of the match but the trees at the back of the United end were full of Reds an hour before the game had kicked off. While thousands of frustrated Reds were milling about in the streets surrounding the ground, the few United fans that had managed to infiltrate the Southampton end were having a hard time of it.

A small mob led by Southampton's answer to Black Sam were roaming the terraces looking for United fans. The United fans had no one that measured up to Southampton's Black Goliath and were getting battered all through the game. The status quo certainly changed when the gates were opened five minutes before the final whistle and hundreds of United fans charged into the Southampton end. Because many of the coppers were outside the ground, some who were even shuttled in from London only saw the odd skirmish. As soon as the United fans started to get a little excited, the coppers would send in the ubiquitous police dogs, and of course to protect the boys in blue, all the Alsatians were on twenty foot leashes. As was often the case there were always a few barmy Reds who were happy to challenge their four-legged foe, and a few of the dogs had to be carried away from the hostilities by their handlers. Just before the end of the game Dave and I were lucky enough to be walking past the main stand as the gates were being opened. We rushed past the stewards and pushed our way up the stairs and into the seats and was amazed by the abuse and resistance we got as we tried to get up to them. The stairs were packed with have-a-go OAP Southampton fans. They certainly weren't happy about a couple of United hooligans invading their territory. One of them punched me in the face as I passed him and another one grabbed Dave around the neck and tried to pull him back down the stairs. The old fuckers were behaving worse than us. We got into the seats and cheered

United on for the last few minutes of the match. Our vocal support for United was met by more hostility from the elderly home fans when we were pushed and jostled by both elderly men and women! 'Cheeky bastards' I thought. At the final whistle hundreds of Reds poured out of the United end and started celebrating on the pitch. At the other end of the ground Southampton fans were getting on the pitch to escape the United fans that had invaded their end. On seeing the Southampton fans on the pitch, the United fans charged straight at them and for a few minutes there was chaos in front of the Southampton end. When the United fans had finished with the Southampton supporters behind the goal the conquering Red Army made its way to the main stand where Dave and I were cheering them on. Much to our delight the massed ranks of United fans started digging up the pitch and throwing lumps of turf at the sneering, pompous Southampton fans in the seats. The Southampton Silver surfer ultras were furious at the sight of their precious pitch being destroyed and they went crazy when Dave and I stood on the seats and started shouting at the top of our voice *"Hello – Hello United Agro, United Agro, Hello – Hello, United Agro!"* A small gang wearing blazers and ties tried to pull us off the seats that we were standing on and a few of the daft old gits were turning a bit nasty, hitting us with walking sticks and brollies. Embarrassingly if the old Bill hadn't turned up and thrown me and Dave out of the ground, the Darby and Joan club may well have battered us.

A RED RIOT

By Mike Langley
Southampton 2, Manchester United 2

The Docs Red Army hurled two divisions of Manchester United's unruliest storm troops over the terrace wall at the finish of this enthralling repeat of the 1976 Cup Final. They beat up a steward, fought with police and chased into a humiliating retreat a battalion of Southampton supporters daft enough to challenge them. Then the Mob trooped away to flex their muscles for the reply on Tuesday week – Southampton are in Belgium this week in a quarter-final of the European Cup Winners Cup

This was the match we should have had last May, not one opportunist goal, but four smashers, even though one was a penalty. And capping it all a display by Channon that should silence anyone who believes he's lost his way into the second division.

United were twice ahead, twice lost the lead and from the start of the second half showed their willingness to settle for a draw.

Southampton defenders Blyth and Waldren were in continual early trouble especially in the air, and it was no surprise that Macari only 5ft and bit should out jump everyone

and side head the first goal.

A piercing pass by ball set Channon running free behind United's defence to be fouled as he entered the box by Houston and then Stepney. A penalty of course, and Peach smashed it past Stepneys left hand.

Ambush

The defence isn't born that could've prevented the second goal. It was like a shot from ambush by Hill on the right.

It came off his left foot and flashed the essential inches wide of a fine dive by Wells.

The Stretford End jubilation was strangled almost in mid verse by a perfectly executed goal.

Channon won the ball off McIlroy and slid through a pass that caught United square and Holmes refrigerated calm, pushed it past Stepney with his left foot. After that it was nearly all Southampton. United must be relieved to get a second chance!

Chapter 8.
Norwich City '77

2nd April '77
Norwich City   2 – 1   O.G. Powell   (24,161)

United Line–Up
Stepney, Houston, Buchan, B. Greenhoff, Nicholl,
*Coppell, McCreery, McIlroy, J. Greenhoff, Macari, Hill **Sub -** McGrath*

Manager
Tommy Docherty

League Position After the Game

P	W	D	L	F	A	Pts	Pos
30	14	8	8	54	40	36	6th

After an outstanding league performance in the previous season United didn't have a great first half of the '76 – '77 season. However, things started to look up in the New Year, when Gordon Hill 'King of all Cockneys' hit some great form. It wasn't just his stunning wing play; he also scored many vital goals and ended the season as The Reds top scorer with 22 goals in all competitions. United had won 9 of their 12 games before travelling to Carrow Road, which included back to back victories over City and Leeds. The only defeat in the previous 12 games was away to United's bogey team, Ipswich town. The Reds would only win 4 of their last 12 games and finished the season in 6th place.

British rail had started advertising reduced price weekend tickets called 'Shoppers Specials' with the price of tickets reduced by at least 50%, the tickets were aimed at couples and families to help them travel around the country for a nice day out. I couldn't believe our luck when one of the lads told us that British Rail were running a special train to Norwich the day United were due to play Norwich City at Carrow Road. A return ticket was £4 that's a quid cheaper than the Brummie Red coach, and a quid meant four pints back in '77. The 'Shoppers Special' was scheduled to leave New Street at 07:30am - returning at 6:30pm. The timings and price would do nicely.

When I arrived at New Street on the morning of the game there were already about 30 lads there that usually travelled on the Brummie Reds coaches.

A few of them were talking to four or five lads that I initially didn't recognize. But as I got nearer, I recognized one of them as being the horrible little bastard that I had had a run-in with a few months previous after we had returned to Brum from the United game. A few of the lads and I had gone for a drink in the Horsefair pub and while I was at the bar waiting to get served, standing next to me was an oversized dwarf. I just happened to make a very innocent comment about liking one of his tattoos and to my astonishment he gave me a look as if I had just called his mother a whore, then stormed off. When I returned and stood with the rest of the lads, I could see this mad little sod at the bar with a large gang of Blues fans being very animated and pointing in my direction. I asked the lads if they knew who he was and one of them recognized him from a notorious family in Small Heath. He had several older brothers, all mad Blues fans and also had cousins all over the South Birmingham area. By all accounts my feeling was that my little tattooed friend lived off his family's reputation. After a few minutes a couple of the Blues fans came over to us and told me that I'd upset their mate and he wasn't going to take any shit from someone like me. Because we were vastly outnumbered by the Blues fans, I told them that I really didn't want any trouble and all that I had said to their mate was that I liked his tattoo, but this didn't seem to cut any ice with them. So, it seemed it was either going to be fight or flight. I made my way over to the Blues fans and said to the deranged twat, "let's go downstairs and sort this out." Without saying a word, he pushed me aside and very aggressively made his way through the crowded pub to the door that lead down to the basement toilets.

Thinking this geezer was completely off his head, I cautiously followed him down the stairs. As I got halfway down the stairs, I could see that he was waiting for me, but after taking a few more steps further I could see that he had armed himself with a bottle. "Come on ya cunt," he yelled at me as I stood hesitantly on the bottom steps. I was looking around the basement to see if there was anything I could use to even the odds, when I heard footsteps behind me. My heart rate went through the roof and I feared the worst. I thought it must be his Blues mates who had come to join him but was extremely relieved to see two of the bouncers come running past me. The first bouncer immediately tried to calm down my crazed adversary. The second bouncer said to me, "If you know what's good for you, you'll get out of here now, this guy's always a nightmare in here." As I turned around and started walking back up the stairs, the mad little bastard threw his bottle at me and was screaming his head off while the bouncers tried restraining him.

And now, here he was laughing and joking and being as nice as pie. I really should have gone over and kicked him straight in the bollocks. But it was a bit early for me to get involved in that type of thing, and besides, I hadn't had my Weetabix that morning.

After we had been travelling for a short while myself and a couple of the lads decided to go and have a mooch around. We were strolling along one of the carriages that had a very narrow gangway and six-seater individual compartments, when I did a double take. Sitting in one of the compartments were four very attractive young ladies, and one of them was so gorgeous that my eyes nearly popped out of my head and my tongue hung out of my mouth. I wasn't sure if the butterflies in my stomach were caused by a few of cupid's arrows or by my one-eyed trouser snake getting so big and hard that I could've beaten a rhino to death with it. It may have been a tad too early for a bit of aggro, but it was never too early to chat up these lovely lasses.

Leaving the other lads in the corridor, I stepped into the compartment and sat myself down between two of the girls and introduced myself and asked their names. You could have knocked me down with a feather when they replied in a foreign accent. They were only Brazilian students who were studying at Birmingham University and they were off to see friends in Peterborough. There seemed to be an instant attraction between myself and the gorgeous dusky Brazilian and she whispered to me, "onde voce asteve toda a minha vida, voce homem novo viril consideravel," which loosely translated to "Is that a small canoe in your pocket, or are you just pleased to see me?" All of the girls were very friendly and chatty, and it wasn't long before the rest of the lads found out that there were four beautiful Brazilian girls on the train and were soon fighting each other to get into the compartment with me and the girls. Most of the lads were understandably excited and acting a bit immature but were very polite. Dave of course was the exception; he couldn't resist asking the girls if they took it up the shitter? I stayed chatting to my Brazilian beauty until the train pulled into Peterborough station. As we approached the station platform, she asked me to get off the train with her so we could spend the day together. Even though she was definitely Miss World material; I couldn't miss out on my first trip to see United at Carrow Road and a wild day with all the lads - You've got to get your priorities right – right?

I told her unfortunately Pancho was out injured and there was a chance I'd get a game. So as much as I would have loved to have spent the day with her, sadly it had to be, 'not today Josephine'. She gave me a kiss and passed on her phone number and we arranged to meet the following Saturday back in Brum. With my heart all in a flutter and my trouser snake desperate for some action, I gave her a soppy wave goodbye only to later remember that we had Stoke City at home the following Saturday.

As was the norm, as soon as we arrived in Norwich, we went in search of the local pubs. After being thrown out of a couple of pubs for singing we came across a picture postcard pub that had a small restaurant in the lounge and was frequented by stuffy locals wearing tweed suits and old school ties. While the locals were enjoying their Saturday afternoon drink and meal, in we strolled on this very civilized English pub scene and were made to feel as welcome as a dose of crabs.

Much to our delight and the utter frustration of the locals, Banker had his clowns head on, and he was about to put on a show. While we were at the bar waiting to get served, Banker produced a long thin plastic tube and dropped it into the beer glass of the bloke who was standing next to us. We looked on in amazement as Banker took a massive sip from the bloke's beer. We then went into hysterics as Banker blew back down the tube. which of course created loads of bubbles and made the beer spill over the top of the glass. The blokes face was a picture when he turned around and noticed that his beer had come alive and was escaping from his glass. After Banker had been served his first pint the barman turned away to serve another customer. At this point Banker quickly drank half of his pint and then took a small plastic lion out of his pocket, dropped it into his beer, and in a very commanding and confident voice, shouted, "excuse me barman." The barman immediately walked back over to Banker who lifted his glass and said, "This isn't on pal – there's a lion in my beer." The barman was lost for words as he stared at the small toy lion floating in Bankers beer. Even though Banker had drunk almost half his beer he insisted the barman gave him a new pint. As soon as the barman had given Banker his new pint and moved on to serve another customer, Banker took a big swig and dropped an elephant into his glass. He then beckoned the barman over and shouted out at the top of his voice, "What sort of pub are you running here? This one's got an elephant in it." By now it was pretty obvious the barman wasn't amused, while we, on the other hand were all in fits of laughter. Banker then decided it would be fun to rope a few more people into his fun and games. He quickly chose a middle-aged couple sitting having a meal. They looked very well-to-do and were well turned out, they wouldn't have looked out of place at a Buckingham Palace garden party. Banker brazenly walked over to the couple's table and dropped several of his toy animals onto each of their plates. He then stormed back over to the bar and banged his fists on the counter, "That couple over there have got safaris in their meals – I demand to see the manager," Banker said to the pissed-off barman. Bankers request was answered in just a few seconds as the manager made an appearance. When the manager introduced himself to Banker, he immediately took the manager by the arm and walked him over to where the infuriated couple were sitting. Banker then pointed out the various animals that had been dropped in the couple's meal and said to the bemused manager, "What's going on in your kitchen? This just isn't good enough ya know, these people are vegetarians." When the manager asked the diners if there was a problem, the man snapped back, "Of course there's a problem, this bloody young hooligan has just ruined our lunches." Banker sarcastically tutted in response, "Temper, Temper," then added, "What about the poor animals? One minute they're minding their own business, the next they're up to their neck in salad cream and dandruff." With that the man sprang up from his seat and squared up to Banker and gave him a piece of his mind. When he had finished giving Banker a bollocking, Banker said, "I hope you're finished now, because the animals need a drink." He then picked up the man's plate and dropped it into the large ornamental fish tank, which was the centrepiece of the pub. Both the customer and the manager were stunned into silence, but the man's wife sprang into action and picked up her handbag and smacked Banker straight around the head. With the manger and the husband looking on, Banker pulled the handbag from the woman and it too followed the man's meal into the fish tank. There was a deathly silence for a few seconds, then the pub was in uproar. The locals were shouting for the birch to be brought back and our little crew were either rolling around the floor in fits of laughter or jumping onto the tables singing United songs. When the manager ordered his staff to get us off the tables, they were greeted with the contents of the brown & tomato sauce bottles. After only a minute or two the place looked like St Trinian's dining room on a bad day. All of the staff were covered in sauce and most of the locals had become collateral damage. Even the landlord's dog that had been released to see us off the premises got a nice splattering of sauce. We left the pub in a right state with beer glasses all over the place, tables tipped over and chairs thrown around the room. As I took one last look at the carnage in the pub, I knew then it was going to be one of those special days.

We had only gotten a few hundred yards away from the pub when we saw two younger lads come running towards us. From their demeanour it looked like they were being chased. As they passed, they handed us a bottle of vodka and a bottle of Bacardi, which was quite bizarre. "What about the fuckin' bottles of coke?" Banker shouted out as the pair of them disappeared around the corner. The next pub that we came to had United fans packed inside like sardines. A few of the lads and I went in to get the beer leaving the other boys milling around on the car park drinking vodka. While they were passing the bottle around, they were approached by three young but very game girls who had travelled across from Great Yarmouth especially to meet some United hooligans; and in fact, needed to look no further. The girls immediately asked for a drink of vodka and started asking corny questions like 'how many fights we'd had that day', 'had we ever been in prison', and 'had we ever put someone in hospital'? Banker and Mad Dog soon realized the inexperienced girls were hooligan groupies and it took little persuasion for the girls to disappear round the back of the pub with them, and of course the vodka went with them too. I was stuck in the pub for ages but when I finally got outside with the beers, the lads, girls and vodka were all gone.

When we approached Carrow Road many of the United fans we came across seemed to be in extremely high spirits. Maybe they had been given free bottles of vodka as well. Whatever the reason, it was obvious everyone was up for some fun and games. A vast majority of the United fans had decided to go into the Barclay End, which was usually reserved for the home fans. While we were queuing to get into the ground; we were filmed by the BBC's Nationwide News team. The TV crew walked up and down the ranks of United fans, so we did our best impersonations of a bunch of out of control lunatics, which I suppose we were. We happily played to the cameras – singing, swearing and giving the 'V' signs every time we knew we were being filmed. We soon found out that the film crew had travelled up from London on the train with the Cockney Reds and the Nationwide TV programme intended to do a special feature on the infamous football hooligans.

The Barclay End was divided into four sections by metal railings and by the time we got onto the terraces, United had packed out two sections. The Old Bill had moved the Norwich supporters into the fourth section with the third section left empty and used as a buffer to separate the rival fans.

Just before kick off the atmosphere in the United section was fantastic. Most of my mates, including myself were up against the dividing fences giving the Norwich fans as much abuse as we could. Then out of nowhere a large group of Cockney Reds appeared and took over our position at the fences. Even though I was well pissed and full of bravado, I was also a little shocked at how wild and mental they were. Because so many

United fans were continuing to swarm onto the terraces, the police were forced to open the gates into the empty section. As they did, the Cockneys were the first through and ran straight across the open terrace and jumped over the dividing fence into the home fans. Thirty or forty of them must have gotten over into the Norwich section before the coppers made an appearance and started pulling United fans off the dividing fence. Most of the coppers didn't stay around for long and were drafted into the Norwich section to form a cordon around the Reds that had gotten in there and were terrorizing the home fans. The empty section was soon as packed as the other two sections and United had three quarters of the Barclay stand. Throughout the first half the coppers were helpless to stop the steady flow of United fans jumping over the fence and joining the Cockneys. By half time a good size United crew had formed in the Norwich section. The quiet backwater of Norwich had never experienced anything like it before. The worst violence recorded at Carrow Road up to date occurred with a serious outbreak of cushion throwing between the Canaries and their deadly rivals, the much-feared Tractor Boys.

By half time we needed some relief from the crush on the terraces, so we made our way to the back of the stand and down to the open ground at the bottom of the steps. There were so many Reds about that it was almost as packed as the terraces. The few Norwich fans that foolishly came down for a pie and a piss were immediately attacked and needed rescuing by the few coppers on hand. At the back of the stand, there were two small catering huts selling the normal rubbish you could find at football grounds – cold pies, watery hotdogs, stale crisps etc, etc. Because there were so many Red & White nutters packed around the flimsy wooden huts, you could barely see the structures, let alone get anywhere near them. It wasn't long before many of the United fans became impatient with the doddering old carrot crunchers who were serving from inside the huts. While I was still standing on the bottom of the concrete steps, I saw one of the huts move from side to side, then backwards and forwards. It didn't take long before one of the huts was completely turned over with the serving staff still inside! This of course was greeted by a massive cheer from the massed United fans. The second hut came off much worse, as it was being rocked back and forth the whole thing suddenly burst into flames. The burning hut caused even louder cheers and the excited United fans wrestled with each other for the pies and burgers that had been tossed onto the ground from the destroyed huts. When the coppers eventually turned up, they were pelted with everything from saucepans and cans of pop to flaming pieces of wood.

During the second half the coppers did their best to control the United mob in the home section and to avoid further clashes outside the ground at the end of the game the coppers escorted the Norwich fans around the side of the pitch and into the seats to relative safety. But even as the Norwich fans were being led onto the side of the pitch, United fans in their section were breaking free of the police cordon and charging into the bewildered home fans. All our pushing and shoving enabled us to leave the packed terraces to finally reach the exit at top of the concrete steps where I could hardly believe what I was seeing; a large mob of United were ripping the corrugated iron sheets off the back of the Barclay Stand. Many other Reds were using whatever missiles they could lay their hands on and throwing them at the police who were standing behind temporary barriers positioned just outside the ground. It was pretty obvious that none of the coppers fancied being a hero and stood rooted outside the ground while the Barclay Stand was being demolished by the United mob. Always being up for a bit of vandalism, the lads and I soon joined in and helped with the destruction of the stand. A few over enthusiastic Reds even clambered up onto the roof and started kicking in the corrugated roof panels. We thought this was great stuff until one of the lads on the roof went straight through a corrugated panel and fell onto the concrete terraces below; miraculously he didn't receive life threatening injuries but he did spend several weeks in the local hospital, where I bet the porters spat in his food.

The Nationwide TV producer must have thought he'd hit gold! All the time we were ripping out the stand, their TV crews were filming it from outside ground. Over the years I had experienced far worse violence than I saw at Norwich, but to this day I have never witnessed vandalism on the scale that had occurred at Carrow Road. Even part of the ground's perimeter fence was set on fire and still the coppers were no more than bystanders while the cameras kept on rolling. When we were making our way out of Carrow Road, a cameraman was spotted filming from the window of a first floor bedroom in one of the terraced houses. Loads of bricks were thrown at the window and one hit the bullseye, sending the camera and its operator flying back into the bedroom. Just because the camera had been put out of action, it didn't stop the United mob from continuing to smash the house windows and neighbouring windows. I'm sure the money the owner of the house received from the Nationwide TV film crew wouldn't have covered the cost of all his broken windows, let alone the broken windows of his neighbour's properties. While on the subject of payments, because of the violence and the amount of vandalism that day, I still wonder if the Nationwide TV team handed over any cash to some of the Cockneys and encouraged them to cause as much chaos as possible. Who knows?

The papers had a field day and pictures of United mobs on the rampage covered many of the tabloids front and back pages. Then on the following Monday evening after the Nationwide News programme had aired their footage of the day's violence and vandalism, the government promised to act!

NEW BOY ENDS UNITED'S RUN

Norwich 2, Manchester United 1

KEVIN REEVES, an 18-year-old who was playing for Bournemouth in the Fourth Division three months ago, is the main reason Manchester United no longer look invincible (writes MICHAEL EATON)

Reeves scored once with impressive coolness and was denied a second goal by Alex Stepney's one handed save, and generally showed great maturity as United lost for the first time in 15 games.

Since losing to Norwich's East Anglian rivals Ipswich in January, United had been climbing the table to a position from which they were attracting money as championship contenders. That ambition no longer looks credible, especially as 8 of their remaining 12 matches are away from Old Trafford.

HELP

Norwich sailed into United during the first half and were 2-0 up after only 32 minutes having a displayed a confidence that bordered on arrogance. But their sheer effrontery brought a reaction in the second half when United who couldn't be faulted for their work rate briefly hauled themselves back into the match. United were given considerable help by United them- selves because Tony Powell got into an almighty mix up with his keeper Kevin Keelan and conceded a 53rd minute own goal with a deliberate header.

United defence was at fault for the first goal after only 7 minutes, Colin Sullivans free kick alluded them, Martin Peter's had a header half cleared and Colin Suggett was allowed a free shot from the rebound. A long ball from Peter's and a run down the wing from Robin Gibbins gave Reeves the chance for the second goal, his fifth in 12 matches.

Chapter 9.
Bristol City '77

May 7th 1977
Bristol City 1 – 1 J. Greenhoff (28,864)

United Line–Up
*Stepney, Houston, Buchan, B. Greenhoff, Nicholl, Albiston, Coppell,
Jackson, McCreery, J. Greenhoff, Macari.* **Sub -** *McIlroy*

Manager
Tommy Docherty

League Position After the Game

P	W	D	L	F	A	Pts	Pos
39	17	10	12	63	53	44	6th

*Going into the Bristol City game, United had lost their last
four away games in the league, which included a 4 – 0
battering at the of hands of QPR.*

*Fortunately, United's form in the FA Cup was much better,
and after recently beating Leeds 2 – 1 in the semi-final at
Hillsborough, The Reds had secured a second successive trip
to the FA Cup final at Wembley.*

*Off the pitch, United fans had their wings well and truly
clipped. After the disturbances at Norwich the previous month,
the government was forced into action, and the minister of
sport, Dennis Howe, announced that United supporters were
to be banned from all away games for the rest of the season.*

The government naïvely thought they would be able to enforce the ban by making United's remaining away fixtures 'All Ticket' and only home supporters would be allowed to purchase tickets for the games.

For a few years the 'I HATE' badges had become very popular amongst United fans 'M.U.F.C. I HATE CITY' - 'M.U.F.C. I HATE LEEDS' - 'M.U.F.C. I HATE COCKNEYS' Now there was a new 'I HATE' badge at Old Trafford 'M.U.F.C. I HATE DENNIS HOWE'

When the Labour Minister for Sport announced United's away ban Dave, Sharky and myself immediately made plans to take a day off work and travel down to Bristol and buy as many tickets for the game as possible.

Sharky picked up me and Dave and we drove down to Bristol thinking it would be an easy task to just go to Ashton Gate ticket office and purchase half a dozen tickets each. No such luck; the jobsworth in the ticket office would only sell one ticket to each person. Frustratingly this meant we had to wait 30 minutes or so before we could return to buy another ticket. On my third visit to the ticket office, the jobsworth recognized me and refused to sell me another ticket. It was the same story when Sharky and Dave tried to buy their third ticket. Luckily there was a small gang of young kids hanging around the ground and after negotiating a small fee, we persuaded them to go and buy tickets for us. We planned to sell the 80p match tickets to fellow Brummie Reds for £2.00. Much to my surprise and frustration a lot of the lads were very critical about us selling the tickets for over twice the face value. We certainly, weren't Super Touts, and the £1.20 profit on each ticket just about covered my lost wages for the day and the petrol money down to Bristol.

When Dennis Howe announced that United's remaining away games would be 'all ticket affairs', he also stated that none of the official Manchester United supporters' clubs could run coaches to any of United's away games. So, for the twenty of us who had decided to go to the game it was a case of spending a few more quid and letting the train take the strain. With everything that had been said in the daily papers, we all knew that there would be a massive police presence at Bristol, so wearing our colours was a definite no-no and for once, most of us turned up dressed as if we were going out on a Friday night. Sure, enough when we got to Bristol Temple Meads station it was swarming with coppers and to avoid being an immediate target for the Old Bill, we left the train in ones and twos and planned to meet up a few hundred yards from the station. I was stopped a couple of times before I got out of the station, but I just put on a stupid West Country accent and said that I was a Bristol City fan, producing my match tickets convincing the coppers that I was local and I was allowed to go on my way. A few of the lads obviously weren't so convincing and they were frog-marched back to the platforms and put on the first train back to Brum. I was flabbergasted when I later found out that the thick bleeders had headed straight back to New Street. If I had been forced onto that train, I would have simply gotten off at the first station stop and returned to Bristol and tried my luck again.

Fortunately, the majority of us got through the police interrogation at the station and rendezvoused as planned, then we went in search of a watering hole. I was expecting it to be a little challenging to find a pub in the city centre but having walked around for well over half an hour all the pubs we had passed had locked doors. After chatting to a few locals, we found out which buses headed toward Ashton Gate. We jumped on the first bus that was heading towards Bristol City's ground and asked the driver to drop us off at any pub that was open. The bus driver was a great bloke and very sympathetic to our quest for a few pints. The driver pointed out that all the pubs near to the ground would be closed or at least only open to home supporters. Noticing our frustration, the driver told us not to worry and would drop us off at a nice little pub that he regularly frequented. Sure enough after a five-minute drive he made an unscheduled stop and directed us down a small street that looked like a dead-end. At the bottom of the street, hidden away on the right-hand side, the driver pointed the pub out to us and stated that we'd have a great time in there and to make sure to tell them 'Billy the Bus sent you'. We thanked the driver and made the short walk down the road towards the concealed pub. From the outside the pub looked a little shabby to put it mildly and it looked like it hadn't had a lick of paint since the war, while the interior was almost as bad.

Not surprisingly when we first strolled into the boozer, we were greeted with suspicion from both the regulars and the bar staff and when the scary looking landlord appeared, he said in a very curt manner, "regulars only." As soon as we mentioned *'Billy the Bus'* his attitude suddenly changed toward us. But he still felt the need to read us a mini riot act and told us that, 'any trouble, and there would be broken heads'! Although it wasn't even 12 o'clock, I soon noticed that several of the scruffy looking locals were already worse for wear and a couple of them were even nodding off. When we ordered our normal drinks of bitter or lager, we were given looks of disapproval from the bar staff. After we had drank two or three pints, the landlord suggested we should try the local brew, Cloudy Scrumpy. So, to be sociable most of us agreed to sample pints of the house specialty, which seemed to be an icebreaker as both the customers and the bar staff found it amusing to see our contorted faces which confirmed our dislike for the super strength cider. It was bleedin' horrible! And one pint was enough for everyone, except Banker, who of course had another and another and another. The locals loved his enthusiasm and his ability to down the local scrumpy and very soon we had struck up a conversation with several of the locals and somehow Banker got himself into a drinking race with one of our newfound drinking buddies. The barmaid pulled six pints of scrumpy and placed them on the bar. The rules were simple, you had to drink three pints as fast as possible and the loser had to pay for all six pints.

With the whole pub cheering, Banker was the first to down all three pints. Both the Scrumpy and the congratulations from the locals went straight to Banker's head and he went around the pub trying to find his next opponent who came in the unlikely form of a skinny old lady. The lady said she couldn't manage three pints but would bet him a quid that she could drink a pint faster than him. As well as the £1 bet, the loser also had to pay for the drinks. After the way Banker had downed his previous three pints, I thought the old woman must either be made of money or mad. The pints were placed on the bar and the landlord counted them down...... "3 – 2 – 1". The beer went down the old dear's throat like water going down a plug hole, while Banker was struggling with his last few gulps, she triumphantly slammed her glass down onto the bar. With that the pub went wild while Banker went bright red. He was visibly embarrassed as he handed his quid over to the old women and paid the barmaid for the drinks. To repair his damaged ego, Banker soon went in search of a new challenge, and all the locals, including the landlord were clapping and shouting out, "Bring out the Rough, bring out the Rough," and encouraging the barmaid to take him on. After a little bit of cajoling and flattery the barmaid agreed, and the landlord produced two ceramic containers, each holding four pints of Rough Cider, which was not only the cheapest that the pub served but also the strongest. Before proceedings got underway the landlord placed a large metal bucket at the feet of Banker and the barmaid. Then pointing at the ceramic container, he said to Banker if he could empty the ceramic container, it would be on the house, if not, it would cost him 30 Bob! Once again, the landlord did the countdown.... "3 – 2 – 1", and to great fanfare the two adversaries commenced battle. Banker lasted less than thirty seconds before he had to remove the large container from his mouth and throw up into the bucket. With the fantastic atmosphere in the pub, you would have thought they had been participating in an Olympic Sport.

After a minute or so the barmaid took a breather but didn't throw up. Just as she was about to continue, Banker stopped, and for a second time, threw up into the bucket. The barmaid had to stop a couple more times before she finished the four pints of Rough Cider, but she managed to finish without throwing up. Banker on the other hand was struggling. After every two or three gulps he had to stop and be sick. Mindful that it would cost him £1.50 if he didn't finish his four pints, Banker soldiered on.

Even though there must have been two pints of vomit in Bankers bucket, he finally emptied the ceramic container, and the landlord congratulated him and shook his hand, and most of the pub regulars followed the landlord's lead. Led by Banker, we must have made quite an impression on the landlord, because when it was time to head off to the ground, he gave us half a dozen bottles of Scrumpy to take with us. What a great afternoon we had in there with such a generous landlord and full of such wonderful characters. We hadn't walked very far from the pub when we were stopped by a van-load of coppers who politely informed us we couldn't take the bottles of Scrumpy any further. Reluctantly we put down the bottles and carried on walking, all except Banker, who informed plod that there's no way he's giving up his drink. "I'd rather go back to the pub than give it to you wankers." With that, Banker picked up a few of the bottles we'd abandoned on the pavement. The coppers were already getting out of their van when Banker staggered away. He was soon apprehended just outside a grocery shop. Giving all kinds of verbal abuse as he struggled to break loose from the coppers, Banker more importantly held firmly on to his three bottles of cider. In the struggle however, he stumbled into a long trellis table that displayed all kinds of fruit, and went 'arse over tit', taking a couple of the coppers with him. At least one bottle of cider got smashed as Banker, the coppers, and all the fruits crashed to the pavement below. Within seconds another four coppers dashed over to assist their fellow officers, and once again Banker was nicked. We were all a bit wobbly after the session in The Cider House and we were pretty lucky to get into the ground without incident, especially taking into account that we were searched by coppers outside the ground and the club stewards inside. Once inside the ground we recognized a few faces and soon had a little mob of about thirty strong. We made our way onto the large open terrace and pushed and shoved our way to the back of the stand. I was comforted by the amount of red and white scarves on view but being half pissed, I didn't notice the red and white scarves belonged to Bristol City supporters.

Thinking we were surrounded by fellow United supporters, we started to chant *"Manchester la- la- la, Manchester la – la – la,"* and immediately we were overrun by hundreds of Bristol City fans. I was kicked from pillar to post, and while on the floor, one of the bastards tried to slash me. Fortunately, he only nicked the back of my neck, but he did manage to inflict a

12-inch long cut into the back of my jacket. When the melee was over, Kevin R. was the only one of The Brummie Reds that I could find. He pointed out the large rip to the back of my jacket and the small cuts to the back of my neck and said, "And you've only got one shoe". Fuckin' great! They were my best shoes as well.

As soon as I noticed that I only had one shoe, it seemed as if everyone on the packed terrace was trying to tread on my foot. I lasted until half-time then told Kevin I'd had enough and was off to find some new shoes. Kevin wasn't keen to be left in the hostile terracing on his own, so he agreed to join me in my quest to find a new pair of *'rhythm and blues'*. I only had a quid or so on me so getting a new pair of shoes was going to be challenging. Walking barefooted, I finally spotted a shoe shop and was about to go inside when Kevin pointed out it would look very suspicious if I were to walk into the shop without any shoes on my feet. So, he offered me his shoes and the plan was to get the shop assistant to go back and forth to the stockroom and get me loads of different shoes to try on. When I found a suitable pair and the assistant was in the stockroom, I would pick up Kevin's shoes and do a runner. It all went very smoothly in the shop and I ran out wearing a brand-new pair of shoes. I had a massive smile on my face by the time I met up with Kevin, but he quickly took the smile off my face when he said, "And where the fuck are my shoes?" I'd only gone and left them in the shoe shop. I wanted to burst out laughing but could see that Kevin didn't see the funny side and wasn't in a laughing mood. I offered Kevin my new shoes, but he snapped, "They look fuckin' shit," and stubbornly refused my kind offer. There was an off-licence nearby, so I offered to go and get us a couple of cheap bottles of cider. Opposite the off-licence was the entrance to a small park with a few benches. So, we decided to wander over and figure out what our next move would be. We hadn't been sitting down too long when a lad about our age came and sat on a bench a few feet away from us. Kevin's eyes were immediately drawn to the lads Dockers. Without saying anything to me, Kevin got up and walked over to the lad and said, "Nice Dockers, what's the size?" The lad nervously replied that he was a size-9 and then Kevin went into Scouse mode and said. "Take the fuckin' things off or I'll smash this bottle over ya fuckin' head." The poor lad went white with fright and initially refused to give up his Dockers. Kevin had to take a swing at him with his bottle before the lad decided that his Dockers weren't worth a headful of stitches.

When we got back to Temple Meads we met up with the rest of the lads, all but Banker of course. He'd had the pleasure of spending the weekend in Bristol, before yet another court appearance on Monday morning. On the train journey home, we were having good craic and chatting about the wild time in The Cider House and whether Banker would go down this time. It wouldn't have surprised anyone if he did get a custodial sentence as he had certainly been riding his luck for a while. Things had gone a little quiet for a while, when Big Vern suddenly jumped off his seat and announced, "It's too fuckin' hot in here," and then took off his jacket and to the amazement of us all, threw the jacket straight out of the train window. Big Vern's crazy antics were a source of great amusement to everyone in the carriage - well everyone but his younger brother, who looked visibly upset and was holding back the tears.

After a few minutes Big Vern's young brother couldn't contain himself any longer. "Ya bastard." he yelled out, "that was my jacket you threw out the window." I don't think I stopped laughing until we got back to Brum.

UNITED SADNESS

By Bruce Perry

Bristol City 1, Manchester United 1

Sammy McIlroy, substituted for Manchester United full-back Stewart Houston after he broke an ankle, was sent off along with Bristol City's Gerry Gow.

It was a sad end to a game that wrecked Houston's Cup final dream and saw three other desperate City players booked in the fight against relegation—Norman Hunter, Gary Collier and Gerry Sweeney.

Hunter and Gow now face suspension, though Hunter said he would be appealing. The all-ticket 32,166 crowd didn't take kindly to referee Ray Toseland's decisions and he came close to losing control in the second half.

A fortnight from their big day, United were desperately trying to avoid any threat to their Wembley chances.

It didn't seem to bother them too much when City went a goal up after only 6 minutes. Chances galore were being missed by the Bristol side.

Tom Ritchie, top scorer in last season's promotion run, was the chief culprit. He hit the upright from only two yards, and missed a second chance after a superb centre from Whitehead had split United defence

But they paid for those missed at the start of the second half when Collier conceded a penalty by bringing down McCreery in the 49th minute.

Man of the Match Jimmy Greenhoff scored from the spot kick, and that goal will almost certainly take City down to the Second Division.

With Whitehead tormenting the United defence, it was no surprise when City took their early lead.

United were slow to clear his left wing centre and Chris Garland stabbed the ball home from close range.

Chapter 10.
St. Etienne '77

14th September '77
St. Etienne   1 – 1   Hill   (33,678)

United Line–Up
Stepney, Nicholl, Buchan, B. Greenhoff, Albiston, Coppell, McIlroy,
McCreery, McGrath, Pearson, Hill. **Subs** *Grimes, Houston*

Manager
Dave Sexton

Cup Winners Cup 1st round – 1st leg.

Much to the dismay of many United supporters, just after
United had won their first major trophy in almost 10 years, the
board sacked 'The Doc'. The reason Docherty was dismissed
was due to 'revelations about his personal life' – Namely he
was shagging the club physio's wife! The experienced but
slightly dull Dave Sexton was soon appointed as United's new
manager. As Chelsea manager, Sexton had won both the FA
Cup and the Cup Winners Cup. Sexton's previous club QPR,
had a reputation for playing stylish attacking football. So
initially it seemed like a good fit for The Reds. While managing
United, Sexton also took charge of the England under 21 side.

After beating Liverpool in the FA Cup Final, 2 -1 (in doing so,
stopping a scouse treble) United were now in the Cup Winners
Cup competition for the first time since 1963 and United were
drawn against French side St. Etienne in the first round.
Before the trip to central France, United had gotten off to a

reasonably good start to the season - drawing one & winning
three out of their first four games. Unfortunately, immediately
prior to the St. Etienne game, United experienced their first
defeat of the season – losing 3 -1 away to bitter rivals Man
City.

After missing out on the trip to see United play Ajax in
Amsterdam the previous season, there was no way I was going
to miss the trip to St Etienne. I had never been abroad before
so my trip to France to see United was a double first. After
paying my deposit to the Brummie Red committee, my next
step was to get a passport. Back in the 70's it was an easy
exercise to obtain a passport. You simply filled out a form
from the post office, supplied a couple of black and white
photographs, handed over a quid or two, and Bobs your uncle -
you had a one year passport.

The day before the game fifty Brummie Reds waited
expectantly for the top of the range coach, that we had been
promised, to arrive at Digbeth coach station and take us on the
expected 16-hour road trip to France. With the majority of us
intent on drinking ourselves into a stupor, a toilet on the coach
was a must. When the coach eventually arrived my heart sank,
it was no better than the coach that took us to the United games
in England.

Frustratingly there was no time to swap my beer for vodka, so
it would have to be a piss in the bottle trip. By the time we got
onto the Ferry at Dover I was so out of it that I'd slept all the
way across the channel and missed all the fun and games. As

per usual when English football fans were on cross-channel ferries they caused havoc, breaking into the slot machines, raiding the duty-free, robbing and smashing up the bars and generally giving the crew a load of grief. I didn't really come around until our first pit stop in France where we picked up a couple of extra passengers, Clive and Bowie from Gorton. While the two of them were having a jimmy in the French service station, their mates thought it would be a laugh if they drove off without them and they would then have to hitch hike down to St Etienne. Luckily for Clive and Bowie our driver spotted them running out of the service station just as the coach was pulling out of the car park. Less than twelve months later, while watching United during a pre-season tour, I would find myself in a certain bar in Düsseldorf with Clive!

I woke up again just as we arrived on the outskirts of Paris, and just in time to witness their ridiculous morning rush hour. It was bumper to bumper for well over an hour and the restless lads wanted to stop in Paris for a few hours, but the driver wasn't having any of it. He insisted we would only be stopping at designated service stations in France. Most of the journey from Paris to St Etienne was uneventful, except for the odd individual throwing-up or pissing on the seats as they tried to relieve themselves into beer bottles. I really didn't know what to expect in France, but I certainly hadn't imagined France to have such spectacular countryside and to be so hot. By 1pm it was red hot and we were nearly passing out on the coach because of the heat, and of course, there was no AC on-board. When we got to the outskirts of Lyon, which is only forty miles from St Etienne, we started to see gangs of teenagers waving green and white St Etienne flags. Besides flags and scarves being waved at us, there was also the occasional brick thrown at our coaches. I must say it made me feel quite at home. Having a few bricks thrown at the coach is one thing, but when we were south of Lyon, several cars mostly draped in green and white flags drove past us with the passengers brandished various weapons. When all the United coaches met outside St. Etienne later that afternoon, we discovered that the mini convoy of cars had attacked one of the United coaches that was in front of us. Apparently one of the cars positioned itself in front of the coach so it could control the speed. Then with the skill that a synchronised swimming team would have been proud of, the rest of the cars positioned themselves both sides the coach. After one of the drivers sounded his horn for about 10 seconds, the passengers inside the car lent out of the windows and started pulverising the coach with hammers, chains and timber clubs. The attack lasted for less than 30 seconds, but in that short time the French nutters made a right mess of the coach. The lads on the battered coach said the cars were so well organised that they were sure this must have been a regular welcoming committee. We were all pretty shocked to hear this because I really thought we would simply stroll into St. Etienne and take over the place.

When we reached the outskirts of St Etienne all of the United coaches were parked on a large piece of wasteland and the two Manchester lads were finally reunited with their so called mates. A few of the coaches looked like they had suffered the same fate as the coach in front of us and the general feeling was that St Etienne fans would have a high price to pay for the attacks on our coaches. When we eventually drove into St. Etienne and parked near the ground it was a real culture shock. I had seen quite a few shabby properties whilst working in the building game but nothing to compare with the hovels that surrounded the Stade Geoffroy-Guichard. Almost all of the properties were small, rundown single-story buildings with paint peeling off the walls and broken roof tiles. The shops were dreary and the windows so dirty you could hardly see through them. The small drab bars initially seemed ok and the French lager was cheap and very acceptable. However, acceptable wasn't a word you could use to describe the toilets! The first French toilets I saw really were a massive culture shock. The toilets were set in a glorified 3ft x 3ft alcove, and for privacy there was a very short saloon type door that was almost falling off its hinges. In the centre of the floor was a 4-inch diameter hole that was surrounded by shit and no bog paper to be seen anywhere. 'Dirty Bastards'! As we approached the ground, I was amazed to see the local coppers not only walking around with 2-foot-long riot batons, but also carrying guns. The guns fascinated me and Banker so much so that Banker with his little bit of Pigeon-French asked the Gendarmes if we could hold their side arms. When the stern looking officer refused, Banker made a grab for his holster. The Gendarme immediately struck Banker in the chest with his baton, he then swung Banker around and held him up against the wall with his baton pressed tightly against his throat. Amazingly they didn't arrest Banker; the other Gendarmes just gave him a few whacks round the legs and a good kick up the arse.

With the ground in sight we bumped into, dare I say, the main little crew of the Brummie Reds. Tartan, George, Chris, John, Les, Daz and co. They had all travelled to St Etienne by train along with a few of the crazy Telford Reds and a small mob of Manchester lads who had been causing havoc in St Etienne the previous evening. Windows were broken, a few bars were smashed up, and even a hotel reception was robbed and the interior trashed. On the day of the game a mob of United fans raided the newly opened St. Etienne club shop. After they had smashed the large front windows, they destroyed the internal display units and stole or burnt much of the green and white merchandise in the shop. As kick-off approached you could have cut the atmosphere with a knife, and the situation wasn't helped when along with the Telford Crazies, Tartan and the main Brummie Reds crew attacked a tram full of St Etienne fans. The French fans on the tram out numbered our Boys three to one but it was the St Etienne fans that were running for their lives and begging for mercy. When we got to the ground we tried to find out where the United section was situated. We soon realized it didn't exist. There was no segregation at all, and it was going to be a 'free for all' once inside the ground. Once we got through the turnstiles, we found ourselves in the massive terrace behind the goal and soon discovered we were in the wrong part of the ground. We were spat on and jostled and had plastic bags full of piss thrown at us. Then, one of the strangest things I've experienced at a football ground was being pelted with stale French bread sticks. At the time there was a bread strike back in the UK so our French hosts thought they would let us know what we were missing. Having bread thrown at you perhaps doesn't seem that serious, but after a few days those long French sticks become as hard as stone and when they are thrown at force, I can tell you it bleedin' hurts. Fist fights started to break out on the terraces after we started to sing *"Ve Te Les Vert"* (Fuck the Greens). The riot police rushed to the scene wearing crash helmets and with batons drawn ready for action, hitting out at anyone wearing United colours. At one stage Banker had three overzealous French riot troops whacking him with the riot sticks and kicking him. Many of the St Etienne fans around us got very brave once the Robo Cops arrived. When a United fan got knocked to the ground by riot batons, the home supporters would happily stick the boot in. United fans were scattered around the ground and throughout the match sporadic fighting broke out and several times this led to minor pitch invasions.

The home fans had never experienced anything like it, and gripped by fear, many of them sought refuge by climbing the fences that surrounded the pitch. It was reported later that almost fifty St Etienne fans were injured inside the ground, five of them seriously. The St Etienne chairman called us *'A Red Storm of Gangsters Pirates,'* which I quite liked. However, the Froggy Chairman failed to make any mention of the hundreds of United fans that were beaten by crazed CRS riot troops.

After the game the trouble continued outside the ground. I was in a mob of well over a hundred Reds and as we made our way back to our coaches, St. Etienne fans followed us. They weren't interested in a toe-to-toe confrontation. Instead they were content with throwing bricks and bottles at us while playing a dangerous game of chicken by riding their mopeds and scooters at us. One cheeky local on a moped pushed his luck to the limit and when his moped sped towards us for the umpteenth time, Eddie stood his ground and with the bike just a few feet away, did a little side step and caught the moped rider with a cracking right-hand which knocked him clean off his two wheeled steed. As a few of the lads started laying into the fallen St Etienne fan, Eddie was picking up the moped and taking it back to our coach. Without the knowledge of the driver or the United stewards, Eddie and a couple of the boys stored the moped in the unused luggage compartment of the coach. The disturbances around the coaches went on for some time and most of us picked up the odd trophy of war. When I finally got back on the coach, I noticed virtually everyone was either wearing St Etienne scarves or hats. The drive to Calais was pretty none eventful but once we got on to the ferry things immediately changed. It was standing room only in a large bar - restaurant, and *Allez Les Rouge* rang out around the ferry. Another song was introduced to the United ranks that day. Banker had been working on a certain little ditty and after we finally managed to get our fellow Reds quiet enough, Banker and I got on the table and gave them the world premiere of Bankers new song *"HOW WOULD YOU LIKE TO BE GOING TO FRANCE WITH ME, SINGING AND*

SHOUTING UNITED FOOTBALL, WE'LL BE SO PISSED, WE'LL REMEMBER FUCK ALL. ARRIVING PISSED IN CALAIS, WATCHING THE REDS AWAY WE'RE BRINGING 8,000 OR POSSIBLY 10! SO FUCK OFF St. ETIENNE." We brought the house down and did encore after encore until the rest of the bar knew the words and could join in.

Just to piss off the French bar staff even more, many of the lads were doing moonies by putting their arses on display, with perverts like Dave suggesting we should have a competition to see who had the dirtiest arse on the boat. The self-appointed panel of pissed-up judges staggered around the bar inspecting our arses. Even though completely bladdered, I just wanted to die with embarrassment when they came over and held up my arm stating I was the winner. The whole bar started cheering and singing, *"You dirty bastard – You dirty bastard."* Thankfully, my embarrassments were very short lived because the judges realised there was a slight error in their choice of the dirtiest arse and immediately made amends by pointing in the direction of another bloke. "You've got the wrong one - it's not him - it's HIM," they shouted simultaneously pointing at Eddie. You would have thought from Eddie's reaction he'd just won the pools and not the dirtiest arse on the boat award. Eddie had a smile from ear to ear and was punching the air with delight and excitement. He didn't even wait for the judges to lift his arm, instead he threw his arms up in recognition of his victory and took the chants of *"You dirty bastard"* as recognition of indeed having the dirtiest arse on the boat. After all the applause had died down, I asked Eddie why he was so proud of his new title? With a massive grin on his face he proudly responded, "I've never won anything before in my life, Grange!" There was no answer to that!

While we were busy drinking the bar dry and holding the world's first dirtiest arse competition – the Grafters were once again busy turning over the fruit machines and emptying the shelves in the duty-free shops.

After driving off the ferry and back onto English soil we were met by the old Bill who informed us that we had to disembark and go through passport control, which basically resembled an oversized garden shed with a dozen or so border control officers. While many hundreds of United fans rampaged unchallenged straight through passport control, Banker and I took a leisurely ride on the baggage carousel, usually meant for the passengers claiming their luggage. Usually that sort of behaviour would have resulted in me and Banker spending a few days in the cells, but with the amounts of drunken Reds running riot in the arrival sheds, the border control just wanted rid of us. After making our way through passport control, we were greeted by a couple of dozen or so of our wonderful gutter press and several film crews. The film crew and cameramen must have been delighted with the scenes of United fans running unchallenged through passport control. Of course, without knowing any of the facts, the great British press had already told the whole nation what a disgrace we were, and should all be birched, or even better; hung, drawn, and quartered!

With a history of hooliganism in Europe, our reputation without doubt preceded us. Therefore, the British press certainly wouldn't mention in the morning papers of the heavy-handed Gendarmes and St Etienne militia who beat us senseless for no reason or the fact that we were drenched in French piss. Their agenda was to print a juicy story of rampaging United fans at the expense of facts and provocation. So, when approached by the tabloid hacks, the United fans sprayed them with beer and cheap red wine, while some got the occasional smack in the mouth for good measure.

When we finally got to Brum we headed straight to the boozer for a couple of pints. At the end of the bar was an old fella reading the Birmingham Mail and splattered all over the front page was a large photo of Banker and a some of the other lads being attacked by the French riot police. We were all delighted to see we'd made the front page of our local paper, so sprits were obviously high and the beer flowing nicely. Then Eddie suddenly yelled, "Oh fuck! I've left me moped in the coach!"

I feel I can't leave this chapter without having mentioning United's game, four days after our own fun and games in St Etienne. Throughout the summer, The Sun newspaper was obsessed with two things, the first being Teddy Boys and Punks having running battles up and down the Kings Road in Chelsea. (Never in a month of Sundays could I understand that fabricated Punk Rock look. Vivienne Westwood and Malcolm McLaren must have been laughing all the way to the bank. Talk about the king's new clothes!)

The Sun's other obsession was Man United and Chelsea's hooligans. While United had been running riot at away games in Division one, Chelsea had been doing exactly the same thing in Division two. So, when Chelsea was promoted, The Sun made a big deal about the bitter rivalry between the two sets of supporters. The Sun published photographs of so-called Chelsea and United hooligans with scarves around their faces to hide their identity. The Sun sensationally wrote that both sets of fans were planning their battle strategies and stockpiling all manner of weapons including petrol bombs, ready for when the countries most feared hooligans came face to face at Old Trafford in September. They promised that the public would witness the worst outbreak of violence ever seen at a football ground. Just like Malcolm's and Vivienne's Punk Rock fashion, it was a load of bollocks! Without doubt there would be trouble when the two teams met, but it wasn't going to turn into World War 3 as predicted by The Sun. When photos were circulated of United fans running riot, not only in St Etienne but also on the cross-channel ferry and at the Port of Dover, it played right into the hands of the tabloids and helped to fuel the red-hot flames of the imminent clash of Britain's most feared hooligans. On the day of the Chelsea game, I made my way to The Rotunda in Brum ready to get the coach up to Manchester. Just before I got to the Rotunda, I walked straight into a large mob of Villa fans that were also waiting for coaches at the same spot. I was wearing my Green and White St Etienne scarf and got several strange looks as I nervously made my way through the Villa mob. I was hoping and praying that no one would challenge me, then someone actually grabbed my scarf. That's me done for, I thought. However, a familiar voice said, "Your lot caused some trouble in the week." It was Big Abdul from Walsall Wood; one of only a very few Villa from my neighbourhood that didn't give me serious grief for being a Brummie Red. Abdul still carried the physical and probably emotional scars from his trip to Millwall when Villa was in the old Division three and he was now with Villa's top firm, 'The Steamers' the first Villa mob to be made up of lads from different parts of Birmingham and the surrounding towns. Before 'The Steamers' came on the scene, as in all other cities, football gangs tended to come from the same area such as Salford & Collyhurst or Kingstanding & Quinton, who were Villa's top boys in the early 70s. Still holding onto my scarf, Big Abdul started to quiz me about what had happened in France and on the ferries. To my amazement, I was soon surrounded by a load of Villa fans who were also keen to find out how we got on with the St Etienne supporters and riot police. Big Abdul and the rest of 'The Steamers' were much older than me and seemed very impressed that a young kid like me would travel overseas to follow his team, even though it was Man United.

We got into Manchester late morning and made our way straight to the ground. There must have been well over a thousand United fans on the forecourt waiting for the arrival of the Chelsea firm, and the excitement and anticipation made for an electric atmosphere.

When the Chelsea fans eventually turned up, they had such a big police escort it was impossible to get anywhere near them.

Mounted police and dogs were charging all over the forecourt to keep United at bay. As the Chelsea fans queued to get into the Scoreboard, United made several attempts to get at them but there were so many coppers, horses and dogs surrounding the Cockneys, it was impossible to break through and get stuck into them. To be fair to the Chelsea twats, I'd never seen Man City or Liverpool turn up at Old Trafford in such numbers, the Cockneys almost filled the Scoreboard. As usual I stood in the middle of the Scoreboard Paddock along with the usual crowd of Brummies and I can honestly say I'd never experienced The Paddock so packed before and I'm sure everyone packed in the corner terrace were singing continually throughout the match. In my humble opinion the atmosphere that day was only bettered against Barcelona in '84. It was well known that both the Stretford and Scoreboard Paddocks always had their fair share of nutters, but the Chelsea game had bought all of the old United *'head-the-balls'* out of the woodwork. Chelsea had an infamous hooligan known as *'One-Arm-Babs,'* who was a tall well-built black geezer, and as the name suggests, only had one arm but nevertheless had a fearsome reputation. United also had a giant amongst their mob who bravely stood bare-chested on top of the barriers in the middle of The Scoreboard Paddock and mockingly put one arm behind his back and with his free arm, beckoned the Chelsea fans to bring One-Arm-Babs to him. The United fans in The Paddock and K Stand went wild at the act of bravado from the giant Red. I don't think the scenes outside Old Trafford after the game has ever been repeated. Thousands upon thousands of United fans waited for Chelsea outside Old Trafford and some even tried to storm the gates of the Scoreboard to get at the Cockneys but they were pushed back by the old Bill. At one stage the United mob stretched from the bridge next to the forecourt across the Chester Road and right back to the Trafford pub. There were running battles with the police for almost an hour and once again it took police dogs, horses and coppers on motorbikes to finally disperse the massive United mob. It was almost 6 o'clock before the old Bill finally gave the all clear to open the Scoreboard gates and escort the Chelsea fans the short walk back to Warwick Road Station.

After the crowd violence in St Etienne and the subsequent trouble afterwards on the ferries, and all the mayhem outside Old Trafford days later, several United players openly criticized the United fans in the press and TV. Alex Stepney, Willie Morgan and even Sir Matt were interviewed on the TV and they stated 'they didn't want the United hooligan element to come to the games any longer'. I was genuinely shocked at the players' response and as an innocent and very naïve 17-year-old, thought the players would be as proud of their fans off-the-field prowess as we were of the players' endeavours on the pitch. Well, not so apparently!

WORTH MUCH BETTER

David Lacey

St. Etienne 1, Manchester United 1

The opening leg of Manchester United's first round European Cup Winners' Cup tie against St Etienne ought to be better remembered for the quality of its entertainment rather than the trouble on the terraces which at one stage threatened to prevent the game from being started.

United, resilient in defence, well organized in midfield and sharp in attack in spite of the absence of Macari and Jimmy Greenhoff, drew 1-1 and will be expected to win the return at Old Trafford in a fortnight's time.

Inevitably the night will be as closely identified with the police baton charges which swept several hundred fighting Manchester supporters from the ground as with the greater success which the team had in withstanding a series of intense French attack.

The familiar official repercussions are bound to follow disturbances which resulted in 37 people going to hospital and will surely lead to further calls for a restriction of English clubs competing in Europe. This would be a gross over reaction, and it should be that last season United supporters caused virtually no trouble on the visits to Amsterdam

and Turin. No one would condone last night's violence, but UEFA are entitled to ask why, in spite of the pleas from Denis Howell, the Minister for sport, a sizeable crowd of United fans were wedged in among the St Etienne supporters behind on goal with nothing to separate them

Try as they might, Barthenay, Synaeghel and Santini could not bring sufficient accuracy to the movements to disrupt the zealous covering of Buchan and Brian Greenhoff. This meant that while Sarramagna and Patrick Revelli headway on the wings many a promising French came to nothing although Stepney was given plenty to do. The replacement of Barthelemy by Rocheteau just before the hour did not have a significant effect.

The Ugliness before the match had intensified the atmosphere and for a few minutes it seemed that United might be a bit effected by it as they nervously gave away corners, but McCreery, McIlroy and Coppell steadily broke up French movements before they had time to develop fully and the play remained evenly and intriguingly balanced throughout.

Chapter 11.
FC Koln '78

29th July 1978
F.C. KOLN 1 – 1 J. Greenhoff (11,000)

United Squad
*Roche, Albiston, B. Greenhoff, McQueen, Buchan, Coppell, J. Greenhoff,
Jordan, Macari, McIlroy, Hill, McCreery, McGrath, Grimes*

Manager
Dave Sexton

Part of United's Pre-Season Tour of Germany

*Nowadays, The Reds regularly travel to USA, Australia and
the Far East for their pre-season friendlies but back in the 70's
Germany, Scandinavia and of course Ireland was usually as
exotic as it got. The previous season had been Dave Sextons
first as United's manger and we finished a disappointing 10th
place in the league. To add insult to injury United's top scorer
and fans favourite, super winger Gordon Hill was transferred
to Derby County where Tommy Docherty was the manger.*

After my little adventure in St. Etienne I was keen to broaden
my horizons. When we heard United were touring in Germany,
all of the lads made a lot of noise about going there to see
them, but by the time it came to travel the only ones from our
crowd who decided to go was Banker, Mad Dog Bradbury and
myself. The Flahertys (Tom, Coleman and Shay) and their
merry band of Non-Red mates were also travelling over to The
Fatherland but probably in the back of a lorry or jibbing a
freight train.

The three of us made our way to Victoria Station in London and caught the boat train to Harwich. After all the excitement of the St Etienne trip, I was disappointed to discover we were the only Reds on the ferry. Most of the other passengers were back-packers and students and the atmosphere on the boat was very subdued. We certainly weren't going to spend our beer money on a cabin, so we spent the night drinking until we finally fell asleep in the chairs. We arrived in Ostend bleary-eyed at about 7am and after a lovely cuppa outside an extremely posh Belgian café, we did a runner without paying! Well, being served outside and then leaving us to our own devices, what else did they expect us to do? Soon we made our way to the local train station where we boarded a train direct to Cologne. Walking through the train we found an empty six-seat compartment and were amazed to find the seats could be fully reclined, so we took the 'RESERVED' card signs from the seats and threw them out of the window, and in doing so, had turned the six seats into one very large bed for us to catch up on our beauty sleep. We pulled down the blinds and jammed the door shut to stop any unwanted guests from joining us. Anyone who did try the door got an earful of good old Anglo-Saxon abuse and quickly moved on to find seats elsewhere, well most of them did. After being asleep for an hour or so someone continually tapping on the glass woke me up. I gave Mad Dog a nudge and mumbled, "Tell 'em to fuck off," which he did so immediately.

Despite the abrupt abuse, the tapping continued. Mad Dog who was lying nearest the door eventually lost his patience and jumped up and released the blinds covering the door. Just as he was about to give the 'gate-crashers' another mouthful, he realised they were nuns. Mad Dog was a good Catholic boy and the sight of the nuns tapping on the glass sent him bright red with embarrassment. He quickly turned around and shook us to wake us up. I thought I was dreaming when I looked up and saw a couple of nuns in the doorway. "I won't keep you a minute," Mad Dog told the nuns as he pushed Banker and me to one side, put the seats back into the upright positions and tried to make himself look presentable. The two nuns nodded with gratitude as Mad Dog finally beckoned them into the carriage and offered them a seat. The rest of the journey was quite surreal; Mad Dog sat bolt upright with a nervous smile as if he was waiting for one of the nuns to ask him when was the last time he'd been to confession? Banker continually tried out his rusty schoolboy French on the nuns and from the look on their faces, they couldn't understand a bleedin' word he was saying. It could have been worse for us though; fortunately, Dave missed this trip and spared us any further embarrassment because no doubt he would have mentioned 12-inch dildos, anal love eggs, and asking them if they were wearing stockings, suspenders and peekaboo bras!

On arriving in Cologne, the three of us headed straight for the rail bar, which started my wonderful love affair for German beers that continues to this day. We could have easily stayed in the bar all day because the local beer was like nectar. But after a couple of hours we were already a bit unsteady and thought it might be a good idea to find somewhere to stay before we were totally wasted. Luckily the tourist information was only a hundred yards from the railway station, however, we soon found out the hotel rooms were way off our budget. So, just in case our plans would go tits-up, plan B was put into action with a tent that Mad Dog had previously nicked from his brother. A beautiful blonde babe in the tourist office pointed us in the direction of a tram that would take us to a campsite that was on the Rhine, and just a few miles out of the city centre. Apart from how absolutely gorgeous the blonde girl looked, I was flabbergasted that she spoke perfect English and without a trace of an accent. I thought for a moment, should I ask her out for a drink? But it also occurred to me that she spoke better English than I did. Anyway, Mad Dog put the dampers on any notion of me asking her out when he piped up with, "What the fuckin' hell is a Rhine?" Banker looked at him in astonishment and snapped, "It's one of the longest fuckin' rivers in Western Europe, ya thick cunt." Banker then looked at the girl for confirmation, to which she nodded in agreement and added, "But I wouldn't have put it QUITE like that." Even though Banker was a pisshead of the highest order, he was also grammar school educated until he was expelled at fourteen for continually bringing alcohol into school. Besides speaking a little French, he could also get by in German, which really impressed me. Before we jumped on the tram, we decided to make full use of the liberal licensing laws and have a few more drinks. What a country, four in the afternoon and sitting outside a bar enjoying the weather and watching the girls go by. Back in 'ol Blighty our boozers were closed from 2:30pm until 5:30pm.

After copious amounts of German beer, we finally made it to the campsite and were in no fit state to open a hotel bedroom door, let alone pitch a tent. We handed over our Deutsche Marks to the manager of the site and there was no mistaking he was as bent as a nine-bob note. He literally skipped in front of us as he took us to where we had to pitch our tent. He pointed out our pitch and with a little giggle said, "I'm a very friendly man. I MEAN VERY FRIENDLY. If you boys need anything just whistle," then he minced off back to his little site office.

Meeting our first bent Kraut along with the heat and the drink was starting to have an effect on us and eventually one by one we dropped like flies to the floor, and using our bags as pillows, were in the land of nod before we knew it. It was just starting to get dark when we woke up and like it or not, we had to put up our tent. It was the first time any of us had attempted to erect a tent and it didn't take long for us to prove that we were completely useless at it and were making complete fools of ourselves. The gathered crowd of amused onlookers seemed to take great delight in our drunken efforts; however, after we finally managed to get the ground sheet and internal section in place, our efforts received a sarcastic applause by some of the other campers. Cheeky bastards!

We struggled for a short while with the outer section of the tent but soon gave up and simply threw the top sheet over the internal skin. "Bollocks to this. Let's go and have a beer in the site office," Banker announced. "No fuckin' way," shouted Mad Dog. "That dirty fuckin' German poof has probably already had a wank over us." So, to keep Mad Dog happy

Banker agreed to go to the site off-licence and bring some bottles back to the tent. Mad Dog and I sat on the grass and looking at the state of the tent for a few seconds, and burst out laughing at our pathetic construction, which looked as if it had been spat out of a washing machine. While we sat on the ground waiting for our beer to arrive, two Asian kids approached us wearing T-shirts with the Swedish flag splashed across the front. When they got nearer Mad Dog's expression changed. "Fuck me, you just can't get away from the bastards can ya?" Snarled Mad Dog. The two Asians stopped a few feet away from us, and with their bright eyes and broad friendly smiles, spoke in perfect English and said, "Excuse me, but we saw you were having problems with your tent, can we assist?" Before I could say, Thanks, that would be great, and get up on to my feet to help them, Mad Dog replied, "Fuck off ya Paki cunts." I shook my head with embarrassment and said to Mad Dog, "Oh, For fuck's sake!" Although the two Asian guys looked totally bemused, they still felt the need to explain. "No, I don't think you understand, we would like to help," one of them said. "I don't want any Pakis touching my tent," snapped Mad Dog. I felt so sorry for them as they stood rooted to the spot, completely lost for words. I guess they had never encountered such abuse before, "thanks a lot," I said, "but I think we'll be ok." The two Asians who were obviously perplexed by Mad Dog's response, just turned around and slowly walked away understandably quite upset by the whole incident. Mad Dog was very good company and an extremely generous bloke once you got to know him. But over the years he saw Sparkhill, the neighbourhood where he grew up, rapidly been taken over by non-English speaking foreign hordes. This obviously pissed him off greatly because he no longer felt he belonged in the place where he was born. Mad Dog was simply a 'Product of his Environment'.

When Banker returned with the beer, we decided to leave the tent exactly as we had erected it with the outer section just thrown over any old how. I had to admit, it looked a right bleedin' eyesore. After having a great night out in the City, we found it hard to pull ourselves away at 1am to catch the last tram back to our campsite. The tram stop was about mile away from the campsite, so we had to walk the rest of the way, but not before we noticed a small bar with a beer garden attached to it. The garden was illuminated with small lamps suspended from a Pergola. A couple of people were seated outside so I thought we'd chance it by trying for a cheeky one before bedtime.

Thinking that foreign bars had the same opening hours as Blighty, Banker asked the waiter in German if he was still open. To our surprise the waiter replied in English. "Of course." This was my first taste of real foreign culture and being served by a waiter outside in the early hours of the morning, drinking ice-cold beer and not even paying until we were ready to go, as was the German way, the waiter simply put a pen mark on our beer mats every time he served us. To me it could have been a moment from one of those poncy arthouse movies that I had never watched!

The friendly German waiter was keen to show off his English skills and sat down to talk to us every chance he got. The other Germans in the bar also spoke very good English and we had a night I'll never forget, talking of cabbages and kings until the sun came up. I kept thinking how relaxed everyone was and what a great atmosphere it was. At the time I felt slightly embarrassed but also in awe that these fine folk spoke my language as well as I did, but I couldn't even order a beer in their native tongue.

We didn't see much of the next day, waking late in the afternoon. After a shower and a good nosebag, we were ready to hit the beer again. We made our way to the Altstatd (old town) where we discovered bar after bar in the long narrow streets. It was here where I first met my very good friends, Ged, Clive and Wilky from Gorton, Manchester. I was also introduced to Dutch Pete a very likeable and very loud Red from Amsterdam. Pete was United mad and travelled to England several times a season to watch the Reds and knew more about English football than the rest of us put together. Ged and the other lads from Manchester had met Dutch Pete at QPR the previous season. Ged had kept in touch and had arranged to meet him in Cologne for United's first match on their German tour. We all hit it off straight away and another great night was had by all. It was nicely topped off when we walked into a bar to find Joe Jordan, Gordon McQueen and Paddy (I've got that covered) Roche, having a few beers. The players were generously quick to get the beers in and we were soon having a good craic with them and teaching them plenty of the old terrace chants. Even though the game was the next day, Joe was all for stopping out the rest of the night with us but the other two were a bit more sensible and wanted their bed. We knew it was time for them to go because Paddy kept dropping his pint! Once again it was getting light when we finally left the bars in the Altstatd. The three of us must have made for a sorry sight as we got the early morning tram back to our campsite.

On match day the meeting point for lots of the United fans before the game was the Rose and Crown in the Altstadt. As the name suggests the bar followed an English style pub with mock beams and rough plaster walls to the interior. We had only been in the mock English pub for half-hour when the Flaherty's and their little crew piled in. They were all in a very buoyant mood after just selling their blood to the local hospital. I pity the poor sods who got their blood from a transfusion. They'd surely feel pissed soon after. I can't remember exactly what they got paid for their pint of blood, but it was enough to keep them in drink for the rest of the day. With that in mind, Banker, Mad Dog and I soon made our way to the local hospital. The blood bank had all kinds of undesirable street urchins waiting to give an arm full of blood so I thought I would have no problem getting a pocket full of Deustche Marks for my services. For once I thought I would be honest and give the correct details to the receptionist at the hospital, but when she discovered that I was only 17, she told me, "Kein Kleiner Junge," which roughly translates to, "Sod off ya little shit, you're not old enough" In Germany you needed be 18 years old before you could sell your blood. Luckily, my two mates split their blood money with me, and we soon returned to the Rose & Crown two pints lighter. To our amazement the bar staff handed out large felt tip pens and encouraged us to graffiti the walls and ceiling. I was in my element writing several 'MUFC RULE OK' on the walls and on the ceiling. I also added 'GRANGE and BRUMMIE REDS' until the pen was snatched from my hand by another Red wanting to leave his mark. I later found out the kid who snatched the pen from my hand was another Brummie called Paul Evans. Paul would go on to be the Top Man on the Brummie Red coaches for quite a few years.

I revisited the Rose and Crown about twelve years later and to my astonishment and delight, my graffiti was still very much visible on the ceiling. Nice!

In keeping with the rest of the trip, we all had a skinful beforehand and were worse for wear yet again as we made our way the ground. We had only gone a couple of stops on the tram when we were joined by a mob of army boys who were based near Cologne. Talking to them on the way to the ground we discovered that only one of the army boys was a United fan. All the others had turned up just so they could kick fuck out of the Cologne fans, and maybe a few local coppers to boot. As soon as the tram stopped outside the ground, the army boys were the first ones off and immediately set about anybody within sight, including the local constabulary that stood in front of them. What an absolute bunch of nutters they were; indiscriminately kicking out at Cologne fans, police dogs and even horses. It reminded me a little of my trip to St James's Park the previous season. United's reputation had preceded us, so the local plod certainly made us feel at home with their long riot sticks, God knows how many police dogs there were, and upwards of thirty mounted coppers. Soon the Cologne fans were nowhere to be seen and the overzealous coppers were the only thing stopping us from running riot and taking over the place. As we squared up to the German old Bill, they were quick to let their ferocious dogs loose, and just like back home the dogs were on twenty-foot leashes. The police dogs showed no fear and were soon jumping up and biting at our mob. The first person to get savaged by the dogs was one of the Flaherty crew, a toothless ginger Villa fan called Whitey. I'm sure the dogs must have sniffed him out because the poor sod had them snapping at his ankles. After the dogs received a few boots from the United mob, the dog handlers came to Whitey's rescue and dragged the ferocious hounds off him.

Whitey's ordeal certainly wasn't over, once the dogs were dragged off him and while still on the floor the German coppers pulled him away and threw him into the back of a German police van. Unfortunately, the police dogs came off the worst, when the German coppers discovered their dogs had bitten a Villa fan, the dogs were immediately put down.

From what I can remember of it FC Koln stadium was very impressive. Although smaller than the 70's Old Trafford, it was cantilevered on all sides with terraces to the lower section and seats above.

A combination of the dreary slow pre-season football, the hot afternoon sun and copious amounts of beer, meant before the end of the first half I was asleep on the terraces. I was rudely awaken towards the end of the game to find myself covered in beer and Mad Dog using my chest as a pillow. Some drunken Red was carrying a few pints across the terraces when he tripped over Mad Dog's prostrate body and soaked both Mad dog and me in beer. As we made our way out of the ground it wasn't only the German police waiting to escort us onto the trams, but also British Military Police. The MPs were apprehending any of the soldiers that had been at the game and the MPs certainly didn't use kid gloves on the unruly army boys. When we returned to the Altstadt it wasn't long before the local bar owners were turning us away. To be fair, we were in a bit of a state.

After visiting several small watering holes in the city centre, we found ourselves in a bar come restaurant that had an Oompah Band playing on a timber bandstand. The clientele were obviously Germans and mostly in their fifties. Being a refined group of young Englishmen, we certainly made an impression as we danced around like a bunch of lunatics. Oddly enough the locals were quite taken in by us and regarded us as a novelty, however, the novelty soon wore off. While we were waltzing around the dance floor, Ged spotted a young attractive woman dancing with a smaller and much older man. She was in her early twenties, blonde, beautiful and about five foot eight inches tall. Her dancing partner was fifty-plus, grey, thin, ugly and about five foot nothing. Ged doing his best impression of an Italian gigolo, slowly danced his way over to the blonde beauty, which was an hilarious sight in itself. Ged was more like Andy Capp than some red-hot Latin lover. Still using his best moves, he resembled a drunken cheetah stalking its prey – two steps forward and three steps sideways! Ged was certainly well hammered, so much so that every now and then his legs would buckle from underneath him, and when he tried to regain composure it looked like he was having an epileptic fit, which was funny as fuck. Not to be put off by his wobbly legs, Ged slowly shuffled around the people on the dance floor until he got shoulder to shoulder with the blonde beauty's partner and cheekily started winking and blowing kisses at her. The older geezer obviously knew what was happening but did his utmost not to make eye contact with Ged.

While the blonde and her old fella were embraced in a snake like seduction, Ged managed to work his way in-between them and gently removed the old fella's arm from around the blonde babe, only to confidently position himself face-to-face with her. With pure cheeky arrogance Ged nonchalantly elbow-shoved her partner off the dance floor and to the amazement of everyone the blonde beauty hardly batted an eyelid as Ged smooched only inches from her and whispered sweet nothings into her shell-like. The old fella was soon back on the dance floor and also adopted Ged's 'dance moves' trying to get his young bird back. After a very amusing round of threesome twisting and turning Ged was soon disposed of, however, not for long. The old Kraut and the blonde bird were by now dancing in a very close embrace and must have thought they'd seen the last of Ged. But as soon as the old Kraut moved a few inches away from his sexy dance partner, Ged was back in pole position like a shot. This time however the blonde babe gave Ged a little wry smile, which only encouraged him more. The only problem was, Ged had one too many German beers and was too drunk to stop his head from flopping backwards and forwards. Funnily though, it looked like he was trying to drop the nut on her.

All this hilarious 'Pepé Le Pew' wooing that Ged got up too went on for some time until the old Kraut finally lost his patience and complained to the bar manager. Not long after, the manager, a man mountain, appeared and stampeded across the dance floor like Big Daddy, eager to thump his opponent with a bone shattering forearm smash. The big fella headed straight over to Ged who was by now in a very intimate embrace with his gorgeous dance partner. With one massive hand, the big German ape grabbed Ged by the scruff of his neck and unceremoniously marched him out towards the exit door. Trying to stop our mate from getting thrown out, we formed a human barrier across the doorway, which at the time seemed like a good idea. However, it was a huge mistake! The no nonsense German was not bothered one little bit by our feeble human barrier and forcibly threw Ged at us like a heavy ten-pin bowling ball, which sent us tumbling over like skittles out through the doorway and into the street. "RAUS! RAUS!" the enormous Kraut screamed at us as he pushed the last few Reds out into the street. After letting things calm down for a few minutes, half a dozen of us walked back into the bar and headed straight for the dance floor. Unlike those Adonis-like Chippendale sex gods, us Reds stood half-pissed on the dance floor, turned our backs on the band and collectively dropped our trousers to reveal our dirty arses. For me, it just had been the most satisfying moonie ever! Like a scene from a movie, the band immediately stopped playing and the bar went deathly quiet - you could have heard a pin drop. I had just finished pulling up my trousers and was about to announce through a smug grin; 'that'll show ya fuckin Kraut wankers', when the silence was broken by a frightening yell. I looked up to see the giant German and a couple of his bar staff steamrolling towards us angrily waving their baseball bats. God knows how we managed to pull our trousers up in time and got out of that bar, but somehow, we did. Luckily, we were a hundred or so yards up the street when they stopped giving chase. I was certain if they had caught up with us, I would've been sipping my breakfast the next morning through a straw at the local hospital.

The night was still young, and we came across a few United who told us that that there were a load of Reds in the bars down by the river. So off we trotted towards the river and it wasn't long before we heard the chants of the United fans coming from the bars nearby. Soon we came across some small bars almost next-door to each other, with what seemed like a couple of hundred Reds milling about, mostly outside and enjoying the beer and generally having the craic. It was certainly a bit noisy and rowdy but nothing more than the usual singing of a few United songs and whistling at the local girls who passed by. The singing was being led by the one and only Mallet, who as usual was pissed out of his head and standing on the tables like a conductor in front of the choir. Although Mallet didn't have a thin wooded baton to keep the boys in order, instead he had an 18-inch long piece of rubber pipe filled with sand.

We had only been there for about half an hour when a mob of Germans appeared. They initially kept their distance and just gave us a lot of verbal abuse, but as soon as a few of our lads walked over to challenge them, they disappeared. We thought that was the end of that but ten minutes later they returned but again kept their distance. When we went to over to challenge them for the second time, they pelted us with bricks. Within seconds of the bricks flying at us, the Reds were charging at the Germans who were soon on their toes. I was with a Cockney Red who was the spitting image of the late 70's New Romantic icon, Gary Numan. At such a tense moment, this bloke had an adrenalin rush and threw his beer bottle at a retreating German, hitting him flush on the back of the head and sending him crashing to the ground. The German was just about to get to his feet when we reached him. The barmy bastard pulled out a knife on us even though he was getting a right 'ol pasting. The knife was easily taken off him, which for us was even more reason to give him a bleedin' good hiding.

As the blows were raining down on the Kraut, two young Manchester scallies turned up and instead of giving the German a few digs, they immediately started rifling through his pockets. To my amazement after they had finished going through his pockets, they removed his shoes and then his jeans. Cheeky little sods! This clash with the Germans seemed to be the turning point for the remainder of our stay in Germany and the rest of that night was filled with clashes between United and Germans. When we went to the Altstadt the next afternoon we came across a few cars that had been damaged and several shop windows had been boarded up. Not surprisingly there was a very heavy police presence.

By early evening there seemed to be gangs of German blokes everywhere. These weren't gangs of young kids; these were tooled up men in their thirties and forties who were roaming the streets looking for United supporters. The atmosphere was getting very tense, so it came as no surprise when the few bars that were open in the Aldstadt area all refused to serve Reds. This situation left us wandering around in search of any drinking hole that would allow us in. We weren't too far from the large cathedral when we came across a couple of United fans, who told us, that they had just escaped from a bar that had been attacked by a large mob of Germans. Apparently about twenty Reds were having a 'quiet' drink when a mob of Germans, all carrying weapons, stormed into the bar and battered the United fans within an inch of their lives. Their injuries were so bad that many of the Reds were unable to get out of the bar and therefore had to wait for the ambulance service to take them to hospital. We all agreed that Cologne was now too dangerous and the next morning we would head off to Schalke where United were playing their next game.

When we met up at the train station the next morning, Ged announced that he had a cunning new plan. Düsseldorf was approximately halfway between Cologne and Schalke and Ged's cousin who was in the British Army was based there. Ged was sure if we could track down his cousin, we would have a place to stay for the night and then travel on to Keele the following day. We hadn't seen Banker since the day of the game while having a drink in a crowded bar. When Banker realised, he was almost out of money he announced that he was going to get some more blood money. But seeing his path to the door blocked shoulder to shoulder by Reds, he jumped out of a small window and that was the last we had seen of him.

After leaving all of our possessions, including our passports and return tickets to Blighty in the lockers at Cologne station, Mad Dog, Ged, Clive, Wilkie, Dutch Pete, Steve from Morcambe and I jumped on the train taking us up to Dusseldorf. Nearly a week on the piss had started to take its toll and so it was agreed that we would wait for the evening before we went back on the beer. So, when we got to Dusseldorf, we decided that jumping on the first tram that came our way and getting off anywhere for a kickabout, would be a great way of passing a few hours. After only half an hour of footy with Ged showing everyone that he was the new Nobby Stiles, we were all knackered and slept in the park for the rest of the afternoon. When we eventually went in search of a bar, we found a gem of a place run by an elderly married couple who didn't any speak any English but treated us like long lost sons and gave us free schnapps and even a free meal. Sadly, just before midnight the old couple indicated that they were closing the bar and it was 'Auf Wiedersehen Boys'.

We had been walking around the deserted streets for about twenty minutes or so when we came across two young girls standing outside a closed bar. Above the bar it seemed as if a party was going on. YES! What a stroke of luck! Not only a place to get a drink but we may just get our heads down for the night once all the merriment had finished. Dutch Pete was the only one who spoke German, so we instructed him to do the business and get us upstairs to the party. Dutch Pete and the German girls exchanged a few words and it seemed as if the girls were beckoning us upstairs while Dutch Pete carried on talking to them. After a few moments Dutch Pete turned to us and said, "There's something strange going on here, I don't think it would be a good idea to go to that party. I don't know why, but these girls are acting a bit funny." Mad Dog immediately snapped, "Fuck off! Are ya mad? This is the only fuckin' place where we're getting a drink around here. For fuck's sake - I'm going up there." Dutch Pete pleaded with Mad Dog. "Please don't, it's not safe." A few more of us were also very keen to join the party but Ged who was the unofficial leader said, "Oh bollocks to it, let's just walk on a bit further, if we don't find anything, then we'll come back." So, well and truly pissed off, we wondered back into the night. Dutch Pete was quick to point out that the two girls were following us. We hadn't walked far, in fact only just a few hundred yards from where the party was being held when we came across a little bar with the lights still on and open for business.

When we entered the bar, we noticed straight away that the walls were covered with football memorabilia, scarves, flags, photos etc etc. There were only about a dozen locals in the bar and much to our relief they made us very welcome. The bar was quite long with uniformed tables and chairs at the far end that doubled up as a little restaurant. The bar counter itself was over twenty feet long and could probably accommodate a dozen or so people sitting quite comfortably. To the right of the bar counter and next to the entrance was an L-shaped bench seating. The atmosphere in the bar was very friendly and relaxed and no one seemed to mind, when around 2am, I decided to make the bench seating into my bed. Because I was knackered, sleeping anywhere would be heaven. No sooner had my head hit the seat, I thought I was out for the night. But what seemed like only a short time, I heard the shouting of a pissed-up German who came into the bar and demanded a drink. At first the barman refused to serve him but after a few words were exchanged the barman gave in and handed him a bottle of beer. Mad Dog, who was sitting next to the pissed-up German, said the guy was so drunk he could hardly stand and couldn't even pour the beer into his glass. Much to the annoyance of the barman, the pissed-up Kraut spilt his beer all over the bar. Muttering under his breath, the unhappy barman took the bottle off the Kraut and poured his beer into his empty glass. The pissed Kraut had been in the bar for only a few minutes when he started chatting to the barmaid. He must have asked if there were any English in the bar because some of the lads noticed the barmaid pointing at them and said, "Ja - Manchester United." With this, the German fella took a few steps away from the bar and was now standing behind Mad Dog and Clive. He then pulled out a handgun and said in broken English, "Englander? Dead!" He was only inches away from Mad dog and Clive, but luckily, he was so pissed the first bullet went way off target and ended up in the wall five feet above my head.

I don't know if it was the sound of the gun or being covered in plaster that made me realise, I wasn't dreaming. The barman who had been collecting glasses when the first shot was fired was only a few feet away from the gunman. He immediately dropped the glasses on the floor and got hold of the gunman's arm and tried to wrestle the gun away from him. While still trying to get the gun, the second shot unfortunately went into the shoulder of the barman. By now I was on the floor crawling my way to the door.

A few locals went to the barman's assistance, but the gunman would not release his gun. I had just gotten to my knees to open the door when the third shot went off. I must have seen too many 'B' movies because when I heard the bang of the third shot, I put my hand on my back and for a few seconds was convinced I'd been shot. Glad to say the third bullet didn't even hit me but instead ended up in the gunman's neck. There were now five locals trying to disarm the gunman, but he wasn't having any of it. As soon as I was out in the street, I ran and took cover behind a nearby car with Ged soon joining me.

We looked at each other in complete disbelief as the fourth shot rang out. The street was completely empty, and the sound of the gunshot echoed around the houses, making it seem as if the gunfire was actually in the street. "Fuck me, he's out here," screamed Ged. Out of blind panic both of us scrambled under the car to escape from the lunatic gunman. We lay under the car for what seemed like an age but was probably less than a minute. After seeing three pairs of legs come running out of the bar, it seemed like the perfect time for Ged and I to make our move. We rolled out from under the car and ran to the end of the street where to our relief, found Clive, Wilkey and Dutch Pete, who was in a flood of tears and almost inconsolable. There were only five of us standing at the end of the street; however, there were seven of us who had originally gone into the bar.

Then like a bat out of hell Mad Dog came bursting out of the bar and ran down the street to join us. Not surprisingly he was as white as a sheet as he'd been only inches away from the gunman throughout the ordeal. His clothes were splattered in blood, he was shell-shocked and scared. Apparently Mad Dog had sat frozen to the spot and couldn't move an inch off his bar stool until the gunman had been totally overpowered. Afterwards we stood in the dark empty street totally numb at what had just happened, staring at each other and shaking our heads in disbelief. After a few minutes I said, "Come on lads, let's fuck off out of here." Everyone nodded in agreement. We were about to leg it, when Ged noticed one of our group was missing. Steve, who had joined up with us at Cologne station was nowhere to be seen. We could only assume that he was still in the bar. Because the way that the bullets were flying around, anything could have happened to him. Against our better judgment we all agreed we would have to go back to the bar and make sure that Steve was okay. So quite apprehensively we made our way back up the street towards the bar. Reaching the bar, we could still hear raised voices, which made me wonder if going back inside was a sensible thing to do? However, I followed Ged and the rest of the boy's back inside the bar where we were greeted by an unbelievable sight, the locals were restraining the wounded barman as he was trying to kick and stamp on the guman who was lying on the floor in a pool of blood. The gunman was in a right state; apparently the fourth shot that we had heard had gone straight through the gunman's cheek and exited just under his eye, that and the hole in his neck didn't make for a pretty sight!

Fortunately, Steve was unhurt because the lucky bastard was in the restaurant area of the bar, checking out the football memorabilia and talking to some locals when all the shit kicked off. Steve said he couldn't believe what he had witnessed, he thought it must have been some kind of big prank like 'Candid Camera' or 'You've Been Framed'. No sooner had things started to calm down when the German old Bill came bursting through the door with guns drawn.

The German police must have thought the gunman was English because we were quickly marched out of the bar at gunpoint and forced to stand spread-eagled. While the German coppers were searching us, a couple of them with machine guns stood only feet away while we were given a thorough and prolonged heavy handed search. While I stood facing the wall with my eyes closed and my heart almost pumping out of my chest, I listened to the loud sirens, the police dogs barking and howling, and no end of people shouting in foreign tongues. Contemplating our fate as I often did, my imagination went into overdrive. *'These bastards are going to machine-gun us!'* I've seen those German war films – *'we're fucking done for'!*

I was quickly bought back to reality when I felt a sharp dig in my back. I slowly turned around and saw a German police officer who started bellowing at me, "Pass, Pass." He wanted to see my passport, which was in a locker in Cologne with the rest of my stuff. *'Oh, bollocks'.* I thought. We're going to get shot now – *'Caught behind enemy lines without papers - The bastards will think we're spies'*! Dutch Pete was the only one carrying ID and tried his best to explain to the German police why his English mates had no passport or any other form of ID.

The local police were not happy with us at all, and soon we found ourselves on our way to fuck knows where in the back of a Kraut paddy-wagon or whatever it's called in Krautland. In the back of the wagon, we were like frightened kids on our way to see the headmaster. Each one of us scaring each other with the thought of what may happen next. I thought they could easily turn the tables on us and make out we were the main suspects responsible for the shootings. I've seen the movies where the guy goes inside for life for a crime he didn't commit. We could be locked up for years like that geezer in the Count of Monte Cristo. Also, these fuckers haven't forgiven us for winning two world wars and the '66 World Cup! Because we were present at the shooting, we were taken to a high security police station, passing several checkpoints along the way. After going through a few heavily secured doors, we were shown into a large open room with lounge seating and asked if we would care for tea or coffee. Half thinking this could be a trap and the Gerry was leading us into a false sense of security. *'They would probably poison or drug our drinks'*, I thought, I declined a drink at first but when the other lads survived their hot beverages, I soon changed my mind and ordered milk with two sugars.

After an hour or so two English soldiers joined us. They were Military Police from a nearby barracks and had come to check out our story and also act as interpreters on our behalf. The first thing the MPs asked us was, "Were we in Cologne at the weekend?" When we confirmed we had been in Cologne, one of them said, "Well, this is probably a bit of karma then. Your lot caused havoc over there." Then the other MP informed us they were also in Cologne on Saturday and arrested nearly twenty of their own army boys. "Gods knows how many of you civvies ended up in German nick", one of the MP's remarked.

Once the ice was broken, the two MPs were quite light-hearted and after we had given them the full story of what had happened in the bar, they even passed around their hip flasks. By the time the German police officers came back into the room, the MPs were convinced that we were the innocent party and we certainly shouldn't be facing any charges. After the German police and the MPs had a chat, we were told that the only issue the police had with us was that none of '*The Englanders*' were carrying any identification, which at the time was an offence in Germany. The two MPs came to our rescue and explained that in England it is not necessary to carry ID cards and there was no sinister motive in our actions, other than naivety. After some friendly banter between the police and the MPs, we were free to go.

We all piled into the back of the MPs Land Rover and they gave us a lift to Düsseldorf train station. Steve was the only one brave enough, or as I thought, stupid enough to travel to Schalke for the match. The rest of us were all in agreement; we'd had a very lucky escape and it was time to head home. I was still a nervous wreck while waiting on the platform for the train to Cologne and every time I saw someone put their hand inside their jacket or reach for something in a bag, I was in fear that they may pull a gun on us. It was a massive relief once we collected our luggage and passports from the lockers in Cologne and boarded the train to Ostend.

A week or so later after we were back home in Blighty, we discovered just how lucky we really had been. Ged got a phone call from Dutch Pete and was told that the shooting in the bar was big news not only in Düsseldorf but also in Holland where the story had made the national papers. Amazingly the drunken gunman was celebrating his fortieth birthday with friends in an apartment above a bar, which was only a few hundred yards from where the shooting took place. In fact, it was the very apartment that the two girls were trying to entice us into! As the story goes, the birthday boy's younger brother was badly beaten up a few days previous by some United fans in Cologne. So, when he heard that Man United supporters were drinking in a nearby bar, he went out to seek revenge. The final twist of the story was that the gunman had died of his injuries a few days after the shooting. I shudder to think what would have happened if we had succumbed to the young girl's charms and followed them up the stairs to the party? It could have easily turned into a blood bath. On reflection, I think Dutch Pete probably saved a few lives that night.

JIMMY'S TONIC

By Kevin James

Cologne 1, Manchester United 1

Jimmy Greenhoff, United unhappy striker, gave himself a tonic and his team a satisfactory start to their German Tour.

The ex-Stoke star who is in dispute with United scored a magnificent goal midway through the first half to give his side the lead against the German League and Cup-Winners.

McIlroy made it possible with a flowing run and pass that gave Greenhoff just enough space to hammer home the ball from the edge of the area.

With fellow striker Pearson due to have a knee operation this week, United might just be tempted to change their mind about a pay rise if Greenhoff maintains this sort of form.

Static

McQueen playing his first match since injuring his knee last May, gave manager Dave Sexton extra reassurance for he played without any obvious discomfort.

The intense heat brought discomfort to every player and the match inevitably became rather static after a first half of subtle touches from both sides.

Greenhoff's goal inspired Cologne to reveal the sort of soccer that had made them one of the most feared teams in Germany.

Full back Kenepka began to attack down United's right flank and it was from one of the runs that the Germans equalized.

Circa '76 - No one, but no one called Pancho a 'Tosser' when Eddie and I were around.

St. Etienne '77 - returning back to Blighty with my 'souvenir's' after my first trip aboard and experiencing the brutality of the foreign riot police. It certainly wouldn't be too long before I received a few more whacks from their long riot sticks.

Cologne '77- Back Row:(from left) Dutch Pete, Sid, Wilkie, Ged. Front Row: Banker & Mad Dog (topless) Me in shades, Big Clive on the deck.

Banker on lookout as I have a giraffe away from Cologne Zoo.

Amsterdam '86 Dutch Pete – Ronald – Ged – Me – Kenny

Amsterdam '86 - **Back Row** *Bowie sitting next to Arthur Albiston! – Jonnie with his beer.* **Front Row** *Me in shorts.* **Sitting on the deck** *Oscar with his infamous Handlebars next to Dutch Pete.*

Rotterdam '91 – Maca – Me – Tim – JC – Big Clive – Mark – Glyn – Colin – Wilkie

PSV Eindhoven '84 a very messy night Colin – Me – Sharky – Dave

BARCELONA MAY 26th 1999
EUROPEAN CUP FINAL

MANCHESTER UNITED 2
BAYERN MUNICH   1
BRUMMIE REDS NEVER FAR AWAY

Taroni – Eddie – Martin – Mickey – Paddy – Me - 'the Boy in the Cup'
Brendan

One of our many – many trips to Wembley in the '90s Maca, Wilkie, Ged, Me, Tim (and his plus one) Colin, Jonnie and Big Clive

Wembley (via Kilburn) May 2011 - Brian & Sean my old mates from J Stand and life savers from Istanbul

Chapter 12.
Spurs '79

10th March '79
Spurs   1 – 1   Thomas   (51,800)

United Line–Up
Bailey, Nicholl, McQueen, Buchan, Albiston, Coppell, Grimes, Thomas, Mcllroy, J. Greenhoff, Ritchie. **Sub** - Jordon

Manager
Dave Sexton

FA Cup, 6th Round

After a late goal from Jimmy Greenhoff, The Reds had seen off lowly Colchester United in the 5th round of the cup, Tottenham Hotspur were pulled out the bag as United's next opponents in the 6th Round.

After seeing off Spurs (in the replay) and beating the scousers in the semi-final, we took on Tottenham's North London rivals Arsenal in the final, that was the Red Devils third appearance in a FA Cup Final in four seasons. Sadly, there was to be heartache in the final. Sammy Mcllroy had dribbled past the Arsenal defence to score a dramatic late equaliser, but a late – late goal from Alan Sunderland gave Arsenal a 3 -2 victory.

Leading up to the Spurs cup game United's league form had been very rocky and the Christmas results were dreadful, The Reds lost 3 – 0 to both Bolton and the scousers, then the day before New Year's Eve West Brom thumped us 5 – 3 at Old Trafford. And here's one for the quizzers, United didn't score or concede a league goal in January but they didn't have any 0 – 0 draws!

In the previous round I had visited Colchester United's Layer Road ground, and I think I can safely say it's still stands as the worst ground I've ever seen. The corrugated metal roof was full of holes, the crash barriers were no more than glorified rust buckets, and the concrete steps were crumbling to pieces. I can also safely say Colchester United had the toughest club stewards I have ever encountered. When they knew the Red Army were going to be visiting, Colchester United's board decided to get an army of their own and enlisted one hundred Paras from the local garrison. The Paras swapped their famous maroon berets for white butchers' coats and basically were given free range on the night. The small mob of Reds that went into the Colchester end certainly had a rough time of things and most of them were thrown headfirst out the ground by the heavy-handed Paras. So, from the ridiculous to the sublime; the next cup game was a visit to the home of Tottenham Hotspur. White Hart Lane has got to be my favourite away Ground. (Well, it was before it became and all seater stadium). Because it was an FA Cup tie, United had received extra tickets from Spurs, which was a bonus. However, I was a little surprised when I discovered that United had been allocated a section in the infamous *'Shelf,'* the three-tiered grandstand that ran the length of the pitch. Tottenham fans that inhabited *'The Shelf'* had a fearsome reputation. For reasons I still don't understand, for big games at White Hart Lane, Millwall fans would travel north of the river and team up with Spurs. In the

'76 –'77 season, Spurs were relegated from the old First Division and a mob of Brummies and Telford & Corby Reds were chased out of '*The Shelf*' by a gang of tooled up, lunatic Millwall fans. The infamous Stilesy from Corby made a heroic one man stand, taking on all comers until the Old Bill dragged him out.

On the day of the cup game the Brummie Red coaches were stuck in heavy traffic as we tried to make our way to White Hart Lane. And as per usual most of us were bursting for a jimmy, so as the coach crawled past a recreation park, half a dozen of us decided to jump off and relieve ourselves in the bushes. As we were doing so we noticed a couple of Spurs fans, so as soon we'd shaken our little willies, we gave chase. They were like Olympic sprinters therefore we soon gave up trying to catch them. When we returned to the main road, the traffic had suddenly picked up and our coach was nowhere to be seen. There was a bus stop nearby so after asking a few locals how to get to Tottenham's ground and waited for the Number 17 to come along.

When the bus turned up, we quickly jumped on, and almost as quickly, jumped off again. The whole bus was packed with Spurs, when they saw us, they were up and out of their seats and at us, it was now our turn to run like Olympic sprinters. After the Spurs fans had given up the chase, a couple of lads who were wearing scarves took them off while we waited for the next Number 17 to arrive. Unfortunately for me I was wearing a United away top and I did my best to cover up the crest as we got on the bus packed with Tottenham. We got to the ground just before kick off which was pretty unusual for us, because we would always stop somewhere for one more pint. We had the motto *'If you've seen one kick-off - you've seen them all.'* That said, in my rush to get into the ground, I went through the wrong turnstile at *'The Shelf.'* I was just about to show the turnstile geezer my tickets when he said the old Bill has just told him not to let anyone in at the moment because it was kicking off everywhere. Then he noticed my United top and snapped, "There's already enough of you cunts in here, so fuck off to your own section." The Spurs fans behind me must have heard me talking with the turnstile geezer, as when I pushed to get back out of the turnstiles, I got several whacks around the head. By now I was on my Jack Jones and as I apprehensively entered the turnstiles to *'The Shelf'* for the first time, I was greeted by Shay F, kicking and screaming as he was being 'escorted' out of the ground by three coppers. As Shay saw me, he shouted out in a drunken slur, "Grange, get these bunch of cunts off me ya wanka." Just as he said it, one of the coppers immediately smacked his head against the wall and another forced his arm further up his back. As I started climbing the steps at the back of the stand the noise from the crowd was deafening and even before I got to the terracing, I could feel the atmosphere was electric. As I walked on to *'The Shelf'* I looked to my right and saw the frightening but very impressive hoards of Tottenham fans, and was in awe at the size and overall length of the terrace, which seem to stretch as far as the eye could see. *'The Shelf'* was packed to the rafters with riotous fans who were singing and moving as one. But the best was yet to come.

When Spurs were promoted back to Division One after only one season in Division Two, they shocked the football world by signing two of the Argentinian 1978 World Cup winning team, Osvaldo (Ossie) Ardiles and Ricardo Villa. The Argie pair were an instant hit with the Spurs fans and *'The Shelf'* started to mimic the Argentinian fans by giving the players a ticker tape reception as they run out onto the pitch. Long narrow strips of paper and large pieces of confetti were wildly thrown into the air as the Spurs players appeared. It looked like a snowstorm for a few seconds, and the Spurs fans in *'The Shelf'* disappeared under a sea of giant white dandruff. What a spectacular sight, and one that I'm sure I'll never forget. But the large mob of Spurs fans that were waiting for us as we tried to leave the ground certainly didn't give us a tickertape send off. There must have been a couple of hundred of them and the Reds at the bottom of the steps were doing their best to keep the Tottenham mob at bay. The sheer pressure from the weight of numbers on the stairs pushed the Reds who were at the vanguard out of the ground and into the middle of the Spurs mob. As more and more Reds poured out of *'The Shelf,'* chaos ensued outside and we soon found ourselves surrounded as literally thousands of the Tottenham fans came rampaging out of the ground. There was little or no chance of the main body of the United mob coming to our rescue as a line of coopers had formed a three-man deep cordon across the road to stop Tottenham getting at the United fans, who had been situated behind the goal in the Paxton Road end. It was only when the pressure of both sets of fans became so intense that it was virtually impossible to throw a punch that plod decided to get involved and separate the warring fans.

The old Bill made a gap in their human wall to let us join up with the Reds from the Paxton Road terrace. A few Tottenham fans mingled in with us and even though it was their turn to be vastly outnumbered they were really up for it and they all went down fighting like fuck. As we made our way back to our coaches we had to contend with small mobs of Spurs, who'd been hiding behind virtually every block of flats in the vicinity attacking us. As well as the older lads and men who were steaming into us, there were a fair amount of young kids, some as young as ten who were ready to stick the boot in or throw bottles and bricks at us. Some of the cheeky young fuckers were even throwing missiles at us from their own balconies.

SPURS ARE FOILED BY THOMAS

By Robert Oxby
Tottenham Hotspur 1, Manchester United 1

Man United pulled themselves together to earn a replay in a breathlessly exciting FA Cup sixth round tie at White Hart Lane, where a 52,000 crowd produced a vintage old-fashioned atmosphere.

For once the old cliché a game of two halves became the most accurate description. United came close to being overrun in the first half but ultimately, they were unlucky not to snatch victory.

Dave Sexton, the United manager urged his side to tighten up the midfield at half time and with Mcllory, the visitor's best player they took control. Mcllory had a splendid match and was shaded by the magnificent Ardiles whose exquisite skills put guilt on the occasion.

Jones gave one of his best performances, Villa worked ceaselessly, and Hoddle no longer unsettled helped his side sweeping passes. It came as no surprise when Spurs went ahead after 38 minutes. Perryman floated forward a free kick and as Ardiles moved in for a header, Bailey made to intercept, hesitated and was undone.

Bailey atoned for this blemish, going to his knees when Ardiles bent a shot around the defence and saving a dangerous header from Jones.

But United so ragged earlier grew in authority and Kendall made a fine save when Coppell followed up his own overhead kick. The goalkeeper also hurried himself sideways to turn away a bender from Coppell.

The ensuing corner bought United 50th minute equalizer when Mcllory floated the ball across Spurs defence and it fell to Thomas to stab the ball over line. Thereafter Spurs had to defend desperately.

Chapter 13.
Liverpool '79

31st March '79
Liverpool 2 – 2   Jordan, B.Greenhoff (52,584)

United Line–Up
Bailey, Nicholl, Buchan, McQueen, Albiston, Coppell, B. Greenhoff,
*McIlroy, J. Greenhoff, Jordon, Thomas **Sub -** Ritchie*

Manager
Dave Sexton

FA Cup Semi Final – Maine Road

United's Cup run was the only saving grace from a
disappointing season – even Villa were above us in the league.
That said, the home game prior to the semi-final, we had
beaten Leeds 4 – 1 with the 'New Boy Wonder' Andy Ritchie
getting a hat-trick. Even though United had made it to the
Semi Final of the FA Cup, a 3 – 0 home win against Chelsea in
the 3rd round was the only real convincing performance. We
needed a replay to see off Fulham and only a late goal from
Jimmy Greenhoff saved our blushes at lowly Colchester
United. As you will have learned from the last chapter, we
needed another replay to see off Spurs. A 2 – 0 win in the
replay at Old Trafford saw United through to the semi-final.

Even before we had left Birmingham, we'd had run-ins with
both Arsenal and Wolves, who were playing their semi-final at
Villa Park. The Wolves fans smashed up a café that a few of
the Brummie Reds were using whilst waiting for the coaches.
As expected, there were loads of skirmishes in and around

Piccadilly and the police sirens seemed to be a continuous soundtrack for the whole of the day. The atmosphere approaching Maine Road was electric and extremely hostile. It seemed every minute or so we would hear 'The Roar' go up as United and scousers did battle. Even as we queued to get into the ground it was continually going off, with both sets of fans attacking their bitter rivals as they stood in line to get through the turnstiles. When 'Dog-leash' gave the scousers an early lead, two twats near to us in the United section of the Kippax started to celebrate. To say that they got battered was an understatement. By the time the old Bill arrived, both were unconscious and covered in blood. When Brian Greenhoff put United 2 – 1 up, a mob of about thirty United fans jumped up behind the Liverpool goal. It went wild in there and coppers didn't restore order until the United fans had been escorted out of the scousers seats and into the packed Kippax. The hostility when we play Liverpool is always extremely intense; so when the bastards equalised with five minutes to go in a FA Cup semi-final, that sent the atmosphere to a completely new level, thousands of Reds came charging out of the Kippax at the final whistle intent on battering any scouser close by.

I had only walked a few yards outside the ground when I noticed a gang of very vocal scousers walking towards us. I grabbed one of them by his scarf and threw him onto the bonnet of a parked car while simultaneously trying to batter him and remove his scarf at the same time. A couple of other Reds soon joined the melee with one of them continually banging the twat's head against the car windscreen. In no time there seemed to be dozens of United fans queuing up to have a pop at them. While the shenanigans were going on, a copper appeared on horseback. At first casually trotting along, then gradually building up speed and charging directly into the United fans. As the Reds scattered, the mounted copper had the choice of at least twenty of us to pursue, unfortunately, I was the unlucky one! The fucker backed his horse into me and crushed me against a parked car. It felt like being sandwiched between Big Daddy and Giant Haystacks in one of their romantic wrestling clinches. Just like a fake wrestling move, I dropped to the floor like a lifeless rag doll but somehow managed to pick myself up from under the horse and staggered into the packed crowd. From his greatly elevated viewpoint, the mounted copper soon spotted me and immediately rode into the crowd after me. Fuck me - that copper knew how to handle a horse! He chased me up and down several lines of parked cars and back into the open ground at the rear of the Kippax and again in and out of the packed crowd. At the same time, I was also dodging the odd copper or two on foot who were giving their mounted colleague a hand. I finally shook off the horse and the copper by diving under an ice cream van. From my prostrate position I could see the horse's legs circling the van, and after he had passed me and started going around the van again, I scrambled out from underneath the ice cream van and with my head kept head down, ducked and dived through the crowd. Luckily for me the ice cream van was parked quite close to the end of the car park so when the mounted copper came back into view, I was disappearing down one of the many ginnels (alleys) surrounding Maine Road.

Later I met up with a few of the Manchester lads, including Bowie and headed off to Victoria Station to make sure the scousers had a good send off. There were only about fifty of us, but just like Leeds a few weeks earlier, we chased the scousers all over Victoria Station. Sadly, the fun and games came to an end after a dozen vans full of coppers had turned up and steamed straight in amongst us. In the late seventies the scousers were amongst the first to adopt the 'Casual' look; wearing kicker boots, straight leg jeans, Pringle sweaters and branded tracksuit tops. With all their parlances for fashion, they stood out like a sore thumb and these scouser gangs were soon being run all over Deansgate. One such individual was standing in a doorway just a few hundred yards from Victoria Station when Bowie and I walked past him. Bowie shouted at him, "Alright mate?" The kid in the doorway, turned his head but didn't reply. So, I then spoke to him, but still no reply. Then Bowie snapped, "Oi, we're talking to you, ya scouse wanker." With this the scouser stared straight back at us and slowly produced a machete from inside his jacket. "Fuck off or you can have some of this," he snarled. Looking wide-eyed at the blade, both Bowie and I decided perhaps it wasn't a good idea to take things further. As we walked away the dipper shouted, "Another time, ya Munich cunts." Those words would come back to haunt him later. We continued walking back towards Deansgate when I noticed a van delivering newspapers had stopped just a few yards in front of us. The driver jumped out and took a bundle of *Pinks* from the back of his van and disappeared into the newsagents. From the sound of the engine and fumes coming out of the exhaust, it was obvious the driver had left it running. Bowie and I looked at each other with big grins and without a word; we scrambled into the van and were on our way. We were probably about fifty yards up the road when the driver came out of the shop and realised his van was missing. In the wing mirror I could see the poor sod chasing after us. To his credit, the driver did his best but had little or no chance of catching us. Looking back now we must have been mad; we were both pissed and had just nicked a motor with a large pink 'FINAL SCORE' logo splashed all over its side. To make matters worse, the old Bill were all over the place, but for young delinquents like us, you just don't think of the consequences when nicking a van on the spur of the moment.

We drove around aimlessly and were laughing so much I could hardly keep control of the van. I then suggested we drive back into Victoria to see what was occurring. We went past the station a few times and it seemed a little deserted. So I thought we should drive the van over to The Nelson pub, just off the Oldham Road to meet up with the rest of the lads. Approaching Deansgate, we drove past a group of scousers and Bowie shouted out, "That's the scouse cunt with the machete." With the van at our disposal, we really needed to take advantage of it. We circled round again and approached the scousers for a second time. Bowie had collected a few bundles of newspapers from the back of the van and positioned himself by the sliding door that was pushed open. There was no time for a dress rehearsal, so we had to get the timing just right. When we were level with the unsuspecting scousers Bowie, although a little tanked up, managed to accurately lob the bundles of newspapers, which knocked two of the scouse fuckers clean off their feet and left the rest of them totally shell-shocked. "Nice one," I said, looking through the side mirrors as we drove off. Bowie was buzzing and wanted to do another drive past, but I thought we had ridden our luck for long enough and drove the van up to Yates Wine Lodge and abandoned it. Being a considerate bloke and all that and for good measure, I put the keys through the letterbox of a locked-up shop.

Just before closing time we went to the Beer Keller in Piccadilly where most of the lads were drinking, but I was so knackered and pissed; I thought it best to find a seat. Although I was sitting next to the speakers, I soon fell sound asleep and I bet the bouncers must have taken a very dim view of this. I must've been completely blotto because I was later told that several times Ged had thrown my beer onto my face to try and wake me up. Even all the pulling and slapping didn't have any effect, by this time the bouncers had lost patience and carried me out of the cellar bar, dragged me up the stairs and threw me out into the street. Being flung out of the door and bouncing off the pavements with a right thud obviously did the trick.

I was staying at Ged's place, so I had to wait around for well over an hour until the rest of the lads came out the Beer Keller. When they finally showed their ugly mugs, I was hoping it would be time for bed, but no such luck; it was off for a Ruby. It was well past 3am when we were ready to leave the curry house and the waiters couldn't get us taxis quick enough. You can only imagine the stick they must have got from our gang of pissed-up Reds in the early hours of Sunday morning? We'll never know if the Indian waiters got their own back on us by gobbing into our curries.

Not surprisingly at that time in the morning our chariot was a clapped-out Nissan, driven by a Paki who only spoke Pigeon English. That said, he seemed to be a decent sort and warmly welcomed us into his taxi as we got into the back seat. Ged was at the time still arguing over the bill and was the last one to leave the curry house. While Ged was paying up, I decided to get my own back on him for pouring my beer over me earlier in the night. I asked the driver if it was ok if my mate sat in the front, he seemed a little surprised by my request, so I explained that my friend got very upset if he was too close to people and he was also an epileptic. From his blank expression, I guessed the driver didn't understand, therefore I pointed out he must be very patient and promise not to go over 20 miles an hour as this could induce my friend into a fit. I explained that even if he shouts at you to go faster, you must drive slowly. The driver seemed genuinely concerned about the welfare of Ged and promised not to drive fast under any circumstances. I patted the driver on the shoulder and thanked him for being understanding. By the manner in which Ged stormed out of the curry house I guess he had little joy in getting any money knocked off the bill. Seething with anger, he flung the passenger car door open and threw himself onto the seat, muttering obscenities to himself. Before Ged had closed the car door, he looked toward the mild-mannered driver who was staring at him like a simpleton with a friendly and sympathetic smile. I suppose the driver was only trying to make Ged feel at ease, but a pissed-up Ged didn't see it that way. "What the fuck are ya looking at Gungadin?" Ged snapped. The driver was true to his word and kept calm. He just slowly nodded his head from side to side and kept the biggest stupid grin on his face.

"What the fucks up with you? You some kind of menc ya fuckin' paki bastard? Just fuckin' get us home ya cunt." Ged continued. Unperturbed, the driver just nodded his head and calmly responded, "Yes Sir – I drive slow!" As we drove off Ged threw all manner of abuse at the poor driver. But like a village idiot, the driver just kept on smiling, nodding his head, and repeating, "Yes Sir – I drive slow!" The sides streets were completely deserted and the fact that we were crawling along at a snail's pace, got Ged even more angry and irate. "Put ya fuckin' foot down, fer-fuck's-sake," he yelled. The driver simply nodded and repeated "Yes Sir – I drive slow!" Red with rage and blood vessels nearly at bursting point, Ged turned around to see the three of us in the back pissing ourselves with laughter, and completely lost the plot and screamed, "What's so fuckin' funny? What are you fuckin' cunts laughing at?" Then immediately turned his abuse back at the driver, "Your taking the piss? Put ya fuckin' foot down ya black bastard." But the driver just kept to a steady 20 miles an hour, even when we drove onto a dual carriageway with no other cars in sight. As we were dawdling along the empty dual carriageway a very aggressive Ged was screaming at the driver to go faster and the driver just kept on repeating, "Yes Sir – I drive slow!" I was laughing so much I thought my sides were going to burst. Ged then spotted a cat slowly crossing the road in front of us. He grabbed the steering wheel and screamed out, "Kill that fuckin' cat! - Kill that fuckin' cat!" The startled driver fought with Ged for control of the wheel and now almost in tears, said "Please Sir, No – No, I drive slow! - I drive slow!" But Ged had completely lost the plot by now and kept repeating, "Just kill the fuckin' cat - kill the fuckin' cat." The drivers attitude finally changed for the worse when in the struggle for control of the steering wheel they hit the curb a couple of times and Ged broke off the indicator stick. Now in tears and with his car stopped in the middle of the dual carriageway, the driver proclaimed in a calm voice, "I know you sick man, but you also madman. I drive slow but you madman. Get out! Get out my car now or I take you to police." Slightly taken aback by the drivers' reaction, Ged replied, "No Fuckin' problem, I could fuckin' walk home faster anyway ya cunt." And with that, Ged got out of the car and slammed the door shut leaving the three of us in the back seat almost dying of laughter. We finally managed to compose ourselves and got out of the car and followed Ged into the night. Every time we thought about the taxi driver, as we stumbled through the empty streets me, Wilkie and Knockers collapsed to the ground in fits of laughter. It took us over two hours to walk back to Gorton and for some inexplicable reason, Ged just couldn't see the funny side!

SENSATIONAL—THIS BATTLE OF GIANTS

By JAMES MOSSP

Liverpool 2, Man. Utd. 2

RARELY can the passion, the fury, the excitement of an F.A. Cup semi-final have reached such towering proportions as the classic confrontation of the great Northern giants.

Four fine goals, a missed penalty, desperate goal-line saves and thee bookings were all crammed into 90 minutes of football that could, without argument, be described as sensational.

Now the show moves to Goodison Park on Wednesday— United fill of the instinctive passion that fills their hearts on the big occasion. Liverpool controlled and patient, still with their ambitious eyes on the League and Cup double.

In the seats below me some famous heads were bobbing. Sir Matt Busby, Bill Shankly, Dents Law. Bobby Charlton—they were kicking every ball.

They may have seen it all before, but I am sure this was a new experience. "That was not game for the heaty." Said Sir Matt as he left his seat at the end.

A mild Manchester afternoon was awash with adrenalin and tension. Nothing grips a footballer or a fan like a semi-final.

Wembley lies around the corner.

Wembley with its glorious heritage and a stage that every young man dreams of stepping upon. This was no different.

In every kick, every tackle, every pass, the importance of the occasion blazed like a beacon.

They spluttered towards finding some kind of composure in the early minutes and almost inevitably the Soothaman Kenny Dalglish stepped onto the frenzy with the patient control of a master and Liverpool were in front.

Phil Thompson brought the ball down on his chest and his pass to the right was collected by Jimmy Case, who wasted no time handing over to Dalglish.

The conjurer unfolded his bag of tricks. With an old-fashioned dribble that I thought went out of the game when Sir Stanley Matthews hung up his boots, he drew the young goalkeeper Gary Bavey and threaded the ball into the bottom corner of the net as though through the eye of a needle.

We were still savouring the neatness of the exploit—and so, I suspect, was Liverpool goalkeeper Ray Clemence—when United hammered back with an equaliser. Out on the left Jimmy Greenhoff pushed a high, looping centre to the far post.

187

Liverpudlians looked for Clemence to gobble up the ball but he stayed transfixed on his line and Joe Jordan jumped to head past him. It looked like a goal from a United practice match.

The drama was not over. They exchanged bruises and they fought for possession and in the 37th minute everyone in the ground stood rooted as referee David Richardson saw Martin Buchan blocking Dalglish.

The referee raced straight to the penalty spot, pausing only to book Gordon McQueen for the fury of his protest.

Terry McDermott, who replaced Phil Neal as Liverpool's penalty-taker, marched forward full of confidence but his shot hit the bottom of the right-hand cost.

Relief

United must have felt like men being led away from a firing squad, and Buchan compounded the overwhelming sense of the relief with a goal-line save from Graeme Souness.

Liverpool seemed strangely laboured in the unfamiliar strip of daffodil yellow.

Where was the flair? Where was the style? Where was the passion Bookings for Phil Thompson and Alan Flansen were ample demonstration of their frustration.

The drive belonged to United and after 56 minutes the went on ordering in for the goal that their fans felt sure would carry them forward to the May 12 glory day.

Jimmy Greenhoff tossed in another centre and Steve Coppell was there to nudge the ball over the area for Brian Greenhoff to steer it home.

Suddenly there could have been many more goals. Clemence soared to tip away a deflected free kick from Mickey Thomas, and Coppell ran clear and screwed wide.

Equally Dalglish could have scored when he found himself alone but lifted the ball over the top while Bailey snatched the ball off Ray Kennedy's toe four yards from goal and Buchan made another goal-line clearance from Souness.

Eight minutes from the end came the ultimate surprise. Phil Thompson led the desperate assault and made a cross from the right. Bailey plunged and his touch sent the ball looping into the goal mouth in a long slow arc for Hansen to side-foot it home.

The battle went on until the combatants must have been exhausted. Liverpool's Steve Helghway. Brought on for Case after United's second goal, stretched Dave Sexton's "bonny little team" and Bailey was producing saves right to the end. They all left the pitch shaking hands—great fighters who had just fought the most honourable draw.

Afterwards, the ice-cool Scottish International defender who stole Liverpool's equaliser eight minutes from the end. Said "I had to do something the way I was playing. I couldn't have had a worse match and I blame myself for United's first goal."

I thought I heard Ray Clemence shout 'Mine' when in fact he shouted 'Away.' I left Jimmy Greenhoff's cross, and Joe Jordan had a free header. He couldn't believe his luck."

Chapter 14.
Villa '79

8th September '79
Villa   0 – 3   Coppell, Thomas, Grimes   (34,859)

United Line–Up
*Bailey, Nicholl, Buchan, McQueen, Albiston, Coppell, Wilkins, McIlroy, Jordon, Macari, Thomas **Sub** - Grimes*

Manager
Dave Sexton

League Position After the Game

P	W	D	L	F	A	Pts	Pos
5	3	2	0	8	2	8	2nd

Just before the start of the season, the fans favourite, Stuart 'Pancho' Pearson was sold to West Ham, and United broke their transfer record by paying £750,000. for Ray 'the crab' Wilkins. Thanks mainly to the 'Blackboard Coaching' from Dave Sexton, the previous season had seen some very dull and unattractive football. United's top scorer, Jimmy Greenhoff had only scored 11 goals in the league and we had finished the season in ninth place (one below villa!) and with a goal difference of 'minus 3'. With two wins and two draws in the first four games of the new season, United had gotten off to a reasonable start, but sadly the style of football was still painful to watch.

For 99% of Brummie Reds, our games against the Villa were as big as a City or Liverpool game. I was looking forward to the game more than usual, partly because I had missed the previous season's 2 − 2 draw after time spent that Saturday afternoon locked up in Steel House Lane nick. I was arrested after a bit of a bother outside the Grand Hotel and was dragged into the back of a Black Mariah; and after a very short ride to Steel House Lane and without any of my details being taken, was unceremoniously thrown headfirst into a cell. At around about 5 o'clock I was rudely awakened and taken out of the cell and placed in a large room where the custody Sergeant proceeded to write up the arrest papers for about twenty young shoplifters. I had been sitting in the room for roughly ten minutes and I noticed that, even though a few coppers were coming in and out with various undesirables, they were only shouting their prisoners' charges to the Sergeant; 'drunk and disorderly; theft; criminal damage', etc. etc., then the coppers would just dump the accused in a chair and exit the room, leaving the Custody Sergeant as the only copper in the room. Even though the room I was sitting in had frosted windows, you could tell we were right next to the street. This gave me an idea; I would try my luck and follow the copper through the door. With the door only a few yards away, I briefly waited then tried the handle. What a fuckin' result - it was unlocked. I opened a second door and spotted the main entrance to the nick, which was just to my right, so, I casually strolled out of the front door and legged it down the road to track down the lads in whichever boozer they were in.

On the day of the game our usual little crew met Ged and about thirty Manchester lads off the early train. As soon as I saw Ged, I could tell he wasn't particularly happy. He soon told me that the infamous 'Spud' had latched himself onto his little mob. The first time we were introduced, I witnessed Spud knocking out two bouncers who had tried to eject him from a nightclub.

When I saw the film Trainspotting, the character Begbie, played by Robert Carlyle instantly reminded me of 'Spud.' What a coincidence that one of Begbie's mates in the film was also called Spud!

As often was the case, Spud had been terrorising everyone including the United fans on the train down from Piccadilly with his favourite, "Have you got 10p mate?" Spud was so mean, moody and menacing that very few people refused. He collected so many 10 pence's which he crammed into his jeans pockets that he walked like John Wayne. Spud was a very handy lad and when sober could be a good craic, but after a few sherbets, oh dear! Later at the bar, Spud asked "So where's all these Villa wankers, Grange?" Thinking on my feet, I told him that Villa didn't come into the city centre when United were in town. Spud immediately replied, "Well, we will go and find them in the Holte End later then." With that he went around the pub telling everyone that we were all going into the Holte that day.

Moving up to one of our favourite haunts, 'The Windsor,' we passed a little trendy wine bar where a few of the boys spotted a very tasty girl behind the bar counter. The look on the girl's face was priceless as forty lads walked through the door into the deserted bar. Soon everyone was ordering big rounds and confusing the girl by continually requesting extra drinks or telling her she had charged them the wrong amount. Also, when bottles were placed on the bar counter, the lads simply took them and walked off without paying. She was in a right state and unsurprisingly threatening to call the old Bill. Spud tried to charm the young girl and he told her to calm down and get him a sarnie, and in return, he would get the money off the lads. She nervously agreed, but the moment her back was turned to make his sarnie, Spud lent over the food chiller and lifted a whole chicken and unceremoniously devoured it like someone in a medieval feast, with bits of chicken all around his mouth and hanging off his chin. Before the girl had turned around to give Spud his sarnie, he quickly threw the half-eaten bird back into the food-chiller but was still chomping on a mouth-full of chicken. The bar girl looked gob smacked as Spud stood to attention as if to say, 'It wasn't me.' Even though there were bits of chicken falling out of his mouth. When she saw the left-over chicken carcass in the food chiller, she gave out a loud scream. For a few seconds Spud tried to console the girl but as she picked up the phone, Spud shouted out, "forget the sarnie darlin', I'm not hungry anymore." Then once again he dived into the food chiller and not only retrieved his half-eaten chicken, but also a couple of quiches as well. When she saw Spud helping himself to food again, she flipped. In one movement she dropped the phone and picked up a water jug and ran around the bar to attack Spud. To our surprise he was out the door like a shot. Normally he would have chinned her, but instead, he ran up Needless Alley holding his chicken and quiches. We later caught up with Spud in The Windsor bar with bits of food still all round his face and on his clothes, demanding that all the United fans in the pub should go in the Holte End; and of course they all nodded in agreement, finished their drinks, and left the pub. Martin S. knew a lot of Villa fans and one of them had wandered into The Windsor and was chatting with Martin for a few minutes, when the Villa fan jokingly said to Martin that being in a pub packed-full of United fans, he thought that by now one of them would have taken a pop at him. Unfortunately for the Villa fan this was in ear-shot of Spud, who responded, "So why would ya think someone would hit ya?" "Coz I'm Villa," came the reply. Wrong answer of course, and without hesitation, Spud nutted him, sending him flying over a nearby table. As soon as the Villa fan was back on his feet, he was out of the door.

Now I'm not sure if that particular Villa fan was responsible for what followed, but not long after he had stumbled out the door, a mob of Villa turned up and smashed a few of the pub windows. Carrying a small bar stool in one hand and a pint glass in the other Spud was one of the first out the door. It went off big style, and to be fair, the Villa fans were very game. Most of the United mob were laden with bottles, glasses and broken bits of furniture and Villa were sent running back down the alley. When we arrived back inside the pub and were waiting to be served, the Villa mob returned, however, this time they were almost twice as many; and not only from the front of the pub, but they also charging in through the small back door. There was now a pitch battle outside in the alley and punch-ups inside the boozer. I was stuck inside and everything that could be used as a weapon was used. Several United fans were behind the bar throwing glasses and bottles and even glass from the broken windows was thrown at the Villa fans.

By the time the Old Bill turned up the pub was completely wrecked and resembled a war zone. The Old Bill steamed in with their truncheons flying in all directions and their dogs were biting anything that moved. Once the law was on the scene most of the Reds headed off to New Street station to get the train to Villa Park. There were hundreds of United trying to cram onto the train, and the Villa fans that were already on it, were given a few slaps and thrown back onto the platform. Partly due to all the excitement at The Windsor bar, United went barmy on the train and even though we were only on it for five minutes, our carriage looked like a bomb had gone off by the time we arrived at Witton station. Seats had been slashed and ripped, all the light fittings had been smashed and a couple of the windows had been kicked through.

After we got off the train about fifty of us made our way to the Holte End and went through the turnstiles in dribs and drabs. I was with Ged and Clive and as we got through the turnstiles Clive said, in the worst Brummie accent I've ever heard, "Where's the programmes?" Right away a dozen or so Villa fans turned around and gave us daggers. When most of us were inside the ground we made our way down to the corner flag next to the Witton Lane where United were seated. As soon as the players came onto the pitch we started chanting, *"UNITED – UNITED."* Then the fun and games began; at first we held our own, but when we celebrated United's first goal a load more Villa surrounded us. For once, I was grateful for the police intervention. If it wasn't bad enough being continually verbally abused and spat at, with the amount of hostile Villa fans around us, it would have been suicide for any of us to go to the khazi. So not long after there were a few steaming rivers of piss continually running down the terraces, which was nice! Towards the end of the game there were so many Villa surrounding us that the coppers were stretched to breaking point. When United scored their third goal we went crazy and so did the home supporters, but obviously for different reasons. They charged through the overstretched police cordon and within seconds we were completely overrun and for the last few minutes, were kicked all over the place. When police reinforcements eventually arrived, we were happily escorted out of the Holte End and into the United section of the Witton Lane seats. At the final whistle we all poured out of the seats into Witton Lane and were greeted by a large mob of Villa; and just like in the Holte, we were massively outnumbered. However, this battle-hardened bunch of tearaways stood their ground and we went toe-to-toe with them. Soon from behind us I heard a massive roar as a large United contingent came running out of the away end of the ground and charged up Witton Lane to join us in battle. As soon as United had superior numbers the Villa mob did an about turn and legged it. Many of them ran back into the Holte End, however, there must have been a couple of hundred of us who gave chase and went charging into the Holte, and soon Villa were run all over the place. A 3 – 0 away win and running the Villa! Double result!

After the game we headed for the City Centre and found 'Sam Wellers', one of the few pubs that opened before 7:30pm and located at the back of New Street station. The pub had two bar counters, but only during the early evening was the front bar manned. The front bar was pretty packed so once we had been served, we went up the small set of stairs to the elevated back bar. It wasn't long before a couple of the Manchester lads commented about the lack of bar staff and Eddie pointed out that bar staff weren't usually in this room until after 8pm. Wonderful, I thought, there's no bar staff and there are goodies openly on display. This was an opportunity just too good to miss; Bowie and Wilkie were the first to jump the bar and soon followed by the rest of us like a plague of locust, consuming everything in our path, swiping all the cigarettes off the shelves and removing all the bottles of spirits from the optics. We also grabbed a crate of Newky Brown and Eddie being Eddie got himself half a dozen bags of crisps. When I questioned him over this and pointed out that he could have grabbed fags or bottles of spirits. He replied, "I'm fuckin' starvin." We nicknamed him Benny after that. Not wishing to push my luck, we hid our booty about our person and headed out of the pub. We made a bit of a noise as we left because most of us had a couple of bottles of spirits that clanked and chinked together as we walked. Eddie didn't have that problem, he just rustled.

After we left 'Sam Wellers', our first port of call was the chippy. Much to the delight and surprise of the two kids serving us, we traded a pack of twenty B&H for pie and chips. After we'd had a little feed, we went back in search of a pub. Frustratingly, we were refused entry from the few pubs we found open, so we strolled up to the Grand Hotel, the scene of my arrest the previous year. Even though the Grand was a bit pricey, this wasn't going to be a problem as we had our own supplies. The normal clientele in the Grand were middle-age couples and theatregoers, all quietly sipping on their G&T's and cocktails. We obviously stood out like a sore thumb and understandably got a look of amazement from the barmaid when we ordered a dozen mixers and loads of ice. While I was waiting for the mixers, I couldn't help but notice one of the bar staff arguing with a well-dressed man in his forties. The bloke was clearly pissed and was insisting on another G&T but his request was falling on deaf ears. When we got our supply of mixers and glasses, we carried them over to a table in a quiet corner so we could top up our glasses with our own spirits. The pissed-up bloke must have been 'eagle eyed' because he clocked us straightaway. He ordered a tonic water and slithered across the room to join our little party. "Hello boys. My name's Roger," he said putting his arms around Bowie and Ged. "Couldn't help but notice the bottles you boys are sharing around. The bastards won't serve me here. Any chance of a top up?" Roger had the style of Terry Thomas and the deepest voice I had ever heard. He made Orson Welles sound like a castrated choirboy. We all gave him a load of stick, but he was very game, and he was determined to get a drink out of us. With a big grin on his mush, he continued, "Okay boys, I will have a bet with you. If I win you can top up my glass, and if I lose you can take me outside and kick the shit out of me," Bowie's immediate response was, "We're going to kick the shit out of you anyway – so fuck off!" After a bit more banter with Roger, we agreed if he won the bet, he could have a drink. Then Dave asked him what the bet was? "I bet I've got a bigger pair of bollocks than any of you fairies" Roger groaned. In a flash Bowie and Dave had their trousers around their ankles, and Bowie said proudly, "Look at these for a pair of a donkey bollocks." Roger slowly pushed Dave and Bowie's shirts to one side so he could have a good view. Then said, "Call them a pair of bollocks? I've seen bigger marbles than those." With that Roger dropped his trousers and produced the most enormous pair of bollocks I had ever seen. We all stared open-mouthed; his bollocks were the size of tennis balls. Seeing that we were suitably impressed Roger proclaimed in his croaky voice, "You've probably just seen the biggest pair of bollocks IN THE WORLD! Now fill up my fucking glass!" Bowie was still in a state of shock and with his trousers still around his ankles, he shuffled over to a couple of old dears and said, "Hey girls have you seen the size of that bloke's bollocks? They're massive!" The site of Bowie's wedding tackle dangled in front of them was too much to bear and they were up and out of their seats like a shot.

Unperturbed Bowie continued shuffling around the room proclaiming that Rogers bollocks were the eighth wonder of the world. Bowie then nicknamed him 'ROGER the BOLLOCK.' Bowie and 'Roger the Bollock' were sipping on their G&T's with their trousers still around their ankles when the old Bill turned up to throw us out of the hotel. "Bleedin' hell mate, you should see the bollocks on this bloke," Bowie shouted over to the coppers as they made their way towards us. At the sight of Rogers enormous bollocks, the first two coppers stopped in their tracks and stared in amazement for a few seconds. These coppers were sound, and judging by their big grins, they definitely saw the funny side of things. The heavy mob who came charging in shortly after were a completely different story. Chaos ensued after they found out we had our own bottles of spirits.

Roger the Bollock managed to pick up a couple of bottles that we had stashed behind some chairs and sneaked them out. Most of the lads were refusing to give up their drink and wrestled with the coppers to keep possession of the bottles. Joe H had two coppers trying to relieve him of his drink but while they struggled with each other, Joe managed to remove the tops and said, "I'd rather throw the fuckin' stuff away than let you bastards have it." He then proceeded to empty the contents of the bottles onto the floor and all over the two coppers. That little act of rebellion resulted in a couple of nights in the cells and a hefty fine when he appeared in court the following Monday morning.

Ged, Bowie and Wilkie were staying overnight at my flat and when we arrived in the early hours of Sunday morning, I found a box of eggs on the doorstep. I'd asked my girlfriend to get me some sausages, bacon, eggs and bread so I could do the lads a breakfast. Seeing just a box of eggs outside my door I thought the silly cow had forgotten the rest of the supplies. Cursing her I tried to open the front door, but initially it would only open a few inches. After putting my weight behind the door, it opened a little wider and I couldn't believe what was on the floor. In her infinite wisdom my girlfriend thought if she left all the food on the doorstep it would be stolen, so she had posted the string of sausages, individual rashes of bacon and slices of bread one by one through the letterbox. I suppose I was lucky she didn't post the bleedin' eggs through as well!

COPPELL SINKS A SITTER!

By Karl Kershaw

Aston Villa 0, Manchester United 3

GOALKEEPER Jimmy Rimmer didn't enjoy meeting up again with old pals from Old Trafford one bit.

United remain unbeaten. Villa nose-dived to their third home defeat in a row—and it all started with a daft mistake by Rimmer.

Nothing could have looked more innocent as Macari hovered on the edge of the Villa penalty box looking in vain for a teammate to pass to.

Finally, he decided to try a hit-and-hope nothing kind of shot at goal. But Rimmer turned it into a winner when he let the ball squirm out of his grasp.

Sprawling

Jordan, handed the simplest of tap chances from only two yards, somehow bungled it and Coppell had to nip in to finish the job.

It was a scruffy mess of a goal—but it was the one that opened a gap between a Villa side desperately struggling for form and a United team who, for long periods of the match, seemed to be playing from memory.

That wasn't the end of Rimmer's hard-luck story. He was sent sprawling the wrong way when Thomas scored United's second from a penalty given when Swain sent substitute Grime sprawling. And in the dying minutes Rimmer was a split second behind the action. Again, when he dived over the top of Grime's shot and sent United home with a score line they hadn't really done enough to deserve.

Villa didn't get a single shot on target for 90 minutes and that must have made the departure of Andy Gray on the same day even harder to bear for their fans.

United had their problems too. They lost Jordon through injury at half-time and Wilkins still hasn't really found a home in their style of play.

McIlroy was still their main weapon in the middle but he was edged out of star rating by the performance in attack of little Macari who provided the one moment of true delight. He caught the ball on his forehead and proceeded to keep it in the air with five consecutive headers as he teased the two Villa players waiting to get in…

Chapter 15.
Leeds '80

3rd May '80
Leeds Utd 2 – 0 (39,625)

United Line–Up
*Bailey, Nicholl, Buchan, McQueen, Albiston, Coppell, Mcllroy, Macari,
J. Greenhoff, Jordon, Thomas* **Sub -** *Ritchie*

Manager
Dave Sexton

League Position After the Game

P	*W*	*D*	*L*	*F*	*A*	*Pts*	*Pos*
42	24	10	8	65	35	58	2nd

*Just 2 points behind Liverpool, United went into the last game
of the season with the slimmest chance of winning the title. All
we needed to do was beat the Old Enemy by a cricket score at
Elland Road and hope that the scousers lost at home to Villa.
United's title hopes looked like a pipedream when back in
March we lost 6 – 0 away to Ipswich. It was The Reds heaviest
defeat since 1961 – but it could have been much worse, if Gary
Bailey hadn't saved two penalties (one of the penalties had to
be retaken – so he actually saved three penalties) Still shell-
shocked no doubt, we only scored one goal in our next three
games following the disastrous result at Portman Road. We
then had a surprise away win at Crystal Palace, where Joe
Jordan, United's leading goal scorer, scored his 9th goal of the*

season. We slipped up again next game, when we lost 2 – 0 at home to Notts Forest. There was a chink of light a few days after the defeat to Forest, when we beat Liverpool 2 – 1 at Old Trafford. Even though United went on to win their next five matches, it would prove to be Too Little – Too Late.

Being the last game of the season we were up for a good day out, so Dave, Speedy, Colin, Eddie, Mad Dog and myself decided to get the early train up to Manchester and join Ged and the rest of the boys to travel to Leeds on the Coach, which was picking up at The Hare & Hounds in Gorton.

We met up at New Street station just before 6am and boarded a near empty train to Piccadilly. Being silly o'clock and the fact that we were all nursing hangovers, meant there wasn't much conversation as the train started to pull away. The atmosphere well and truly changed when a middle-aged train spotter sort walked into our carriage and planted himself in the one of the empty seats next to Dave. As we were the only ones sitting in the carriage and there were plenty of spare seats, I thought this was extremely odd behaviour, "Morning boys," he said in a chirpy manner as he dropped his little shopping bag onto the table. There was no reply from any of us, just looks of suspicion and annoyance. In total silence our unwanted visitor started messing around in his bag and pulled out a flask. He was happily sipping on his tea and flicking through his little black trainspotting book, when unexpectedly he sang out at the top of his voice, 'Sexy Eyes.' He then paused for a few seconds and said, "You don't mind if I sing do you boys? I love Dr. Hook." To our amazement he then continued with

"Sexy Eyes, err-mmm, Sexy Eyes. err- mmm, Sexy Eyes. err-mmm." He may have loved Dr. Hook but certainly didn't know the fuckin' words to the song. "Shut up and fuck off or I'll stick that flask right up your arse," was Mad Dog's critical response. "That's probably what the bent bastard is hoping for," Dave added. Then Dave went into perv mode and showered the Trainspotter with a load of his best lewd and suggestive chat-up lines. "I bet you like a bit of 12-inch cold steel up your arris?" "Have you ever shagged a goat?" "Do you sniff your sister's knickers?" Does your mom put jam or chocolate on your little dick, before she sucks it?". We had all heard these one-liners a hundred times, but the poor bloke was too shocked to reply. He just sat there with a nervous grin. For a minute I thought Dave had finished with him, but he had only just got started. Breaking the uneasy silence, Dave suddenly dived onto the Trainspotter and tried to undo his trousers. "Come on you fuckin' mad old teapot, show us your frilly crotch-less knickers." As the Trainspotter tried to fight him off, he shouted, "I'm wearing Y-Fronts. I'm wearing Y-Fronts. I promise." In the ensuing struggle, the tea spilt all over the Trainspotter's little black book and he went fuckin' barmy. In between trying to dry off his book, much to our amusement he tried to slap Dave round the head. You could tell he wasn't a man of violence because when he attacked Dave, he looked like a mutt doing the doggy paddle. The half-hearted attack came to an end when Mad Dog grabbed his little black book and smacked him around the head with it. In floods of tears the Trainspotter stormed off telling us he was going to report us to the inspector. We were all terrified!

On approaching the Hare and Hounds just before 8am, all we could hear was, "We All Fuckin Hate Leeds!" Even at such an early hour the front door was open, and the place was absolutely packed.

As well as the usual crowd of Ged, Wilkie, Percy, Bowie, Clive, and Knockers being in attendance, the one and only Jonnie Brindley was also there. Jonnie wasn't only a very game lad, but when he was a young boy, he had also survived an encounter with none other than the child murderer, Myra Hindley. There were also a few Blues lads in the pub that obviously weren't going to the game and turned up to wish us well against the universally hated Leeds Scum, and also because they just couldn't miss out on getting an early drink in! After three or four pints, the two coaches finally turned up and for some strange reason about eighty people crammed onto the first coach and about twenty people were on the second. I had been in the Hare and Hounds many times but there were a lot of older, and very handy looking Reds that I had never seen before. I was sure that with this crowd on the coaches, we would certainly be having some fun. As we pulled away from the pub, the front coach had three to a seat and loads of lads were sitting and standing in the gangway - yet the second coach was half empty. We were on the front coach and the atmosphere was fantastic. We sang our heads off and the beer was flowing. It was better than being on the terraces. After an hour or so on the road we had our first pit-stop; a boozer next to Huddersfield's ground. The doors of the pub were just opening as we pulled onto the car park and the landlord initially thought we were away fans planning to go to the Huddersfield game. As we piled up the bar the landlord told us this was Huddersfield Town's top pub and he'll only serve us a couple of pints because it was too early. "You'd better be on your way soon. You don't want to be in here when the boys turn up," He announced. "Even if they are your Top Boys, they will still get a fuckin' good kickin," one our lads replied. After an hour or so about thirty Huddersfield fans turned up and got the shock of their lives. Almost as soon as they had walked through the door they were attacked and immediately retreated outside where they were chased all around the car park. The bar was well and truly closed to us after that. So, it was back on the coach and off to Wakefield. There were loads of different pubs on the High Street, so we split up and went for a wander. About twenty of us went into a big old boozer, which was full of Leeds. You could have heard a pin drop when we walked in. A bit of Yorkshire verbal abuse was soon followed with glasses and bottles being thrown at us. As we rushed back out on to the street there were similar situations in another couple of pubs. It seemed the High Street pubs were full of Leeds. For the next ten minutes there were running battles up and down the street and the Saturday shoppers were all running for cover. There were beaten and bloodied bodies lying on the pavement and almost every pub had at least one of their windows smashed. As we fought on the pavements and in the middle of the street the traffic was bought to a standstill and flying missiles damaged several cars. At the height of the melee three butchers came out of their shop, holding what looked like knife sharpeners, standing on the pavement so they could protect their shop from the rampaging mobs.

The chaos only came to an end when the coppers turned up in force and escorted us back to our coaches. We were all gutted when the coppers insisted on escorting our coaches all the way to Leeds. When we arrived on the outskirts of Leeds, local coppers ordered our drivers to go straight to the ground and park up. As we approached Elland Road, we got the usual abuse from the sheep shaggers. They had their Munich flags, and the odd brick was thrown at our coaches. Every time the traffic came to a standstill a few of the boys would jump off the coach and trade blows with the Yorkshire twats. I had been to Leeds a few times and I knew it was a moody place, but that day the hostility between United and Leeds outside the ground was unbelievable. The coppers were run ragged with the amounts of fights going on everywhere. When we got inside the ground the atmosphere was just as hostile. Besides having a large number of Reds behind the goal, United were also in the side paddocks and small United mobs were dotted around the seats. The only place you couldn't see a mob of United was in the Leeds Kop. Fighting was continually breaking out all around the ground and Reds were climbing fences and jumping from seats into the terraces to have a go at Leeds. These confrontations continued throughout the match and later hundreds were thrown out of the ground. Ninety-two arrests were made inside the ground alone that day. It was some of the worst trouble I had ever experienced inside a football ground.

I must have been going a bit wild because just before half-time I was dragged from the terraces by a couple of coppers and not surprisingly, was roughed up a bit. It was a relief not to be arrested but only ejected from the ground. It was mayhem outside the ground too with loads of United trying to get in. A few of us managed to kick a turnstile door open and get into the seats. After a couple of run-ins with Leeds in the seats, I was thrown out for a second and final time. A large mob of United congregated at the back of the Kop and attacked any Leeds fans that showed their faces. At the final whistle when the Leeds fans left the ground, we charged into them and ran them back into the Kop. When we charged at them a second time, a massive ugly copper punched me straight in the face. The bastard seemed to appear from nowhere and all of a sudden, a big fisted black glove was heading for my face. He didn't only put me on my back; he also made me see stars. A few lads helped me up and I made my way to the main road where there was another small mob of United, which included Coleman and also Bob from Wolves. About forty of them had travelled up from Brum, and after teaming up with a mob of Cockneys, they had walked from Leeds Station to the ground battling with Leeds all the way. In one of the clashes Bob got a brick smashed in his face. Part of the brick broke off and stuck in the bridge of his nose. Amazingly Bob didn't realize that he had part of the brick stuck in his head until one of the lads pointed it out to him. In no time Leeds were suddenly everywhere, but because there were so many coppers around the ground, we decided to follow a bunch of Leeds as they made their way up a steep hill not far from the ground. As soon as the coppers were out of sight, we dived on them and they ran for their lives. Seeing loads more Leeds coming up the hill we retreated to a small side road and some of us waited in the narrow alleys between the houses. When a suitable amount of Leeds walked past us, we ran into them and they immediately scattered and ran back down the hill. We repeated this a couple more times then retreated to the side roads and alleys ambushing them as they passed us. Even though there were only about fifty of us, we were running Leeds ragged everywhere. When we eventually decided to go back down the hill and make our way back to the coaches, we were greeted with more running battles, especially outside Leeds stronghold, The Old Peacock pub. There were more horses there than the Grand National, but these horses didn't have jockeys on their backs; instead they had very aggressive coppers with long nightsticks who were lashing out at anything that moved. Eddie and I got back to the coaches just as they were about to pull out of the car park and we just managed to scramble onto the coach before it drove off into the sunset. I couldn't have complained if they had left us, after all it was well over an hour since the match had ended.

We had to get to the other side of Huddersfield before we found a pub that didn't have cars parked across the car park entrance. This was deliberately done to stop coachloads of United fans from taking over the boozers. We eventually stopped at a pub-restaurant in the small town of Slaithwaite. To say that the stuck up locals weren't happy to see us was an understatement. You would've thought the Vikings had invaded again. Well, in a way, they had! If ever we stood anywhere near the locals, they would give us a look of disapproval and move on to another part of the pub. A few of the lads let them know what they thought of their snobbish approach to us. Then after noticing a sign that was hung at the back of the bar, which read, *'If you are improperly dressed you will not be served.'* Jonnie and Brian (aka The Nutter) decided to take the message literally. So, for a laugh they stripped off stark bollock naked and marched up to the bar and ordered a couple of pints. All of the barmaids immediately left their posts and went in search of the manager who came rushing out with all guns blazing and told us all to immediately leave his pub. He was obviously pissed off with seeing two naked men in his bar. However, there was worse to come. In a parody of Oliver Reed and Alan Bates from the movie, 'Women in Love,' Jonnie and Brian started to wrestle on the pub carpet, with pair of them rolling all over the floor, bollocks and arses flashing all over the place. Naturally, we were all in fits of laughter with a few lads shouting for a tag-team and encouraging the local women to join in. The local gentry were outraged and the blue rinse brigade, were fainting with shock; or more likely excitement. Even though the locals were appalled by this behaviour, none of them, including the manager had the bottle to dive in and separate the two. When the naked 'wrestlers' eventually tired themselves out, we left the pub and boarded the coaches. The locals then got all brave and gave us a load of abuse as the coaches pulled away. Dave let them know what we thought of them by doing a moonie from the back window of the coach.

NOW SEXTON SETS HIS SIGHTS ON 1981

By Richard Bott

Leeds Utd 2, Manchester United 0

MANCHESTER UNITED came to the end of their rainbow at Elland Road, and far away across the Pennines champions Liverpool were collecting the crock of gold again. The goals and the final flourish Dave Sexton's men wanted on the last League Saturday of the season were not forth coming. Instead it was Leeds, after such an unhappy season them-selves, who treated their loyal followers to a crisp, composed performance and a surprise victory.

The men from Old Trafford had not lost at Leeds for eight years and they had galloped in Liverpool's footsteps maintaining the marvellous challenge with a run of six victories.

No wonder the Red Army besieged Elland Road comment that another win was imminent and that the slightest slip by Liverpool would keep their team in contention.

Dave Sexton swallowed his disappointment last night and sent his "warmest congratulations" to Liverpool. "We had our chances, but they didn't go in. We needed the inspiration of a goal." he said.

"But I send out congratulations to Liverpool. The cream always rises to the top." It has been a long race and we have given them a terrific run. "I'd like to finish ahead of them one day—maybe next season."

The hill Manchester had to climb became a mountain when Derek Parlane shot Leeds into a 14th minute lead and then when skipper Martin Buchan retired from the action with a torn leg muscle after 43 minutes.

Striving

Andy Ritchie stepped off the subs bench and Jimmy Nicholl moved alongside Gordon McQueen in the back four with Steve Coppell switching to full back.

They were still running, chasing, striving to turn chances into goals as the minutes ticked away and with their cause lost.

Leeds had seen to it with a penalty, converted by Kevin Kird after 76 minutes.

The chances were there in abundance but with the swirling wind playing tricks with the ball, Manchester could not find their golden touch.

They were on against it from the 14th minute when a simple but neatly executed Leeds move saw the ball speed from Parlane to Flynn, on to Harris and then back across the box for Parlane to score with a low shot.

Whatever was happening at Anfield—and there were enough translator radios in the ground to feed that information—meant nothing while Manchester toiled through the second half without success.

Chapter 16.
Aberdeen '81 West Ham &
Southampton

1st August '81
Southampton   3 – 1 Moran   (10,000)

2nd August '81
West Ham   0 – 1   approx. (10,000)

United Squad
Bailey, Gidman, Duxbury, Nicholl, Buchan, McQueen, Albiston, Moran, Coppell, McIlroy, Wilkins, Macari, Birtles

Manager
Ron Atkinson

Pre-season Friendly Aberdeen—Pittodrie

The prize money for the Pre-season Tournament in Aberdeen was laughable by today's standards – Aberdeen the eventual winner picked up a cheque for the princely sum of £15,000. – the losing finalist Southampton, collected £10,000, and after beating United for 3rd place West Ham picked up £5,000. United got what they deserved, Sweet FA. Becoming United's third Manger in only five seasons, the pre-season games were Big Ron's first look at his new team. And after the shocking performances against Southampton and West Ham at Pittodrie he must have been in no doubt that United needed to buy big and buy quickly!

Only Colin, Speedy and I made the long trip up to Aberdeen. Most of the lads dropped out at the last minute and Paddy being Paddy, missed the train. In later life Paddy progressed from missing trains to missing planes and costing himself a small fortune. Armed with a 24 pack of beer each, Speedy bought along a bottle of Bacardi for good measure and the three of us boarded the train at New Street station and settled in for the eight-hour journey up to the Granite City. We had been jumping (jibbing) trains most of the previous season, but we thought the trip up to Aberdeen would be a bit too challenging and reluctantly purchased second-class tickets. However, always wanting to get value for money, we chanced our arm and took possession of a small first-class carriage. We had been travelling for about two hours and were well into our game of seven-card brag when the clippie finally showed his face, and by then there must have been getting on for twenty empty cans on the floor in the first-class carriage. As the clippie opened the sliding door to our carriage, he looked at the empty crushed beer cans littering the floor; he smiled and said, "Having fun boys?" Without us even replying, he then sat down next to us. The clippie immediately noticed that we were playing with extremely explicit porno playing cards with tits, fanny's and massive cocks splattered all over them. When we had finished playing our hand, he beckoned us to pass the cards over to him. Initially I thought he would want to confiscate them, but wide-eyed he slowly examined every one in detail. When he eventually handed back the cards he said, "I might be back for a game with you a little later." Thinking that he might just be the rarest of things; a clippie who was a good craic, we offered him a beer and closing the carriage door he said, "Maybe just the one." Four beers and a couple of hands of cards later, he finally got around to checking our tickets.

When we gave him our second-class tickets he just muttered, "Cheeky Sods – make sure you take your empties with you." In return we gave him the porno playing cards. Well, it was the least we could do!

By the time we arrived in Aberdeen the floor of our carriage was three deep in beer cans and they spilled out into the gangway as we opened the sliding door and made our way off the train. After eight hours on the piss my legs had virtually turned to jelly, so to try and keep myself upright I commandeered a British rail baggage trolley that had a large sign attached to it stating, *'NOT TO BE REMOVED FROM THE STATION'.* We threw our bags and the last few cans of beer on the trolley and went in search of some digs. As we left the station and started walking around the nearby streets, I was bumping into everything from pedestrians and lamp posts to parked cars and the occasional stray dog. After what seemed an eternity of walking the streets, we came to a road that was lined both sides with B&B's. Colin walked up the steps of first few B&B's but as soon as they saw me slumped over a British Rail trolley, they quickly closed their doors. By the time we got to the last B&B in the street, we decided it would probably be best if I took the British Rail trolley and kept it out of sight. When Colin was told they had availability, I dumped the trolley between two parked cars and stumbled up the steps to the B&B. After paying the landlady upfront, we threw our bags in the room and went in search of a drinking establishment. In the first pub we entered, there was a small gang of West Ham fans. At first, we were very wary and kept our distance as they were very loud and singing West Ham songs. But when they started annoying the locals by singing England songs and a few anti-Scottish ditties, we decided we should join them. The Happy Hammers turned out to be great craic and we had a good drink with them, but there's always one who goes a bit too far. One big ugly Cockney kept repeating at the top of his voice how much he hated the Jocks. I really didn't think this was a very good idea as there were only ten of us in a pub packed full of locals. A few times the barman came over to tell the gobby Cockney to watch his mouth and each time he responded with, "Fuck off you Scottish cunt." It wasn't long before you could cut the atmosphere with a knife and I suggested to Colin and Speedy that it was time to find a new boozer.

The next day we found out that we had left just in time. We had only got a hundred yards up the road when we noticed a gang of locals had followed us out of the pub. We quickened our pace and took the first turning off the main road and ran to the bottom of a narrow side street. Opposite the end of the street was a dimly lit side alley, and to my surprise I noticed an old classic Bentley. It certainly wasn't the sort of motor you would expect to see in the back streets of Aberdeen. In addition to the unusual sight, it looked like the people seated inside were passing around a joint. I looked back up the street that we had just ran down and there were gang of lads making their way towards us. I rushed over to the old Bentley and knocked on the window and it was immediately opened by one of the female passengers. I explained that we were in a bit of trouble and we would probably need an ambulance if the gang of locals caught up with us and was there any chance of a lift. Astonishingly, the girl immediately said, "Yes of course, jump in." I beckoned over Colin and Speedy and we scrambled into the back the big plush motor. The mob of locals clocked that we were in the car and chased after us, but the guy who was driving put his foot down and we were out of sight in no time. "Ooh, that was rather exciting," said one of the girls in an American accent. The second girl then asked, "What did you guys do to upset those ruffians?" I briefly explained about the antics in the pub and told her that we were in Aberdeen to watch Manchester United in a pre-season friendly. "Are you speaking in a foreign language?" she replied and went on to inform us that they were all Canadian and knew little or nothing about the UK. The other girl, then did the official introductions and told us they were heading off to a night club and we could join them if we wished. They may well have known very little about the UK, but they were certainly well known in Aberdeen. We visited three-night clubs and at each one the doormen greeted our newfound friends as if they were celebrities. We walked into each club without paying, and all of the drinks, including ours, were on the house. I got talking to one of the bar staff in the last club we were at and he informed me that one of the girls, Sarah was the daughter of the Canadian ambassador for the UK. As well as her father being an ambassador, he was also a big shot in the oil business and owned a country estate just outside Aberdeen. So basically, Sarah's old man was stinking rich. Sarah and I really hit it off, and when I found out this information, I immediately started to think of all the exotic places she could take me and all the expensive gifts that I would get. Okay, I admit, I was just a gold-digging slag! Sarah soon crossed my palm with silver; she gave me half a dozen fifty pence coins to play a one-armed bandit with her. When Sarah had ran out of fifty pence coins, I thought I would be a gentleman and handed her one of mine and cheekily said, "Here, put this in for me." She promptly gave me a sexy smile and replied, "Grange, I'd put it in you any time!" After exchanging a few corny one-liners, we were in the back of her Bentley with our tongues down each other's throats. I had just managed to get her top off and was having a great time playing with her three-penny bits, when the car door burst open. Sarah's friend had collapsed in a drunken stupor in the club and their driver-minder had carried her out to the car. He then laid the unconscious girl on the backseats and suggested to Sarah that they should take her home. We said our goodbyes and arranged to meet at a hotel in the centre of Aberdeen the following morning. When I eventually woke up the next morning I just about remembered that I had arranged to meet Sarah, but for the life of me, I couldn't remember where or when. My dreams of walking barefoot with Sarah on a desert island beach, strolling romantically hand-in-hand in paradise went straight out of the fucking window. After the disappointment of realising my dream was over and being a kept man, gone forever, I had a nice cuppa and made my way to the ground to buy our match tickets.

When we arrived at Pittodrie ticket office I nearly died with shock. The robbing Scottish bastards were only selling tickets for the whole tournament. We were usually paying around £2 to get into the Scoreboard Paddock for a Man U league game, so I was expecting maybe to pay a quid a game for a friendly. Some hope, the tickets were ten quid. Yes, ten fuckin' quid; that worked out at £2.50 a fucking game. A few years earlier I had only paid £2.50 to see United lift the Cup at Wembley. Very begrudgingly we purchased the tickets and went off in search of a cheap pub. The first pub we came to, we bumped into a few of the West Ham fans we'd been drinking with the previous night. I was stopped dead in my tracks when I spotted one of the Cockneys we'd been talking to the night before had a line of stitches down the side of his face from the top of his ear down to his chin. Shortly after we had left the pub the Aberdeen lads attacked the Cockneys and gave them a good hiding. The Cockney with all the stitches told me a young kid no more than fifteen years old had smashed a pint glass in his face, which resulted in fifty-three stitches and because he had been drinking all day, the nurses wouldn't give him any painkillers. The other mouthy Cockney who shouted out that he hated Jocks, suffered a much worse fate; several locals attacked him with hammers and an axe, and he was still in hospital, with no prospects of going home any time soon. After beating the crap out of the West Ham boys, the locals pushed their calling card into the Cockney's pockets with the message, 'THE ABERDEEN CASUALS SAID HELLO.'

When we got into the ground, I was amazed to discover that Pittodrie was an all seater stadium, however, the seats behind the goal were just simple bench-like seating. It didn't seem right, and I hated it. If someone had told me that this was the future of football, and in less than fifteen years Old Trafford would be all-seater, I would have laughed my head off and said, the men in the white coats are coming to take you away ah-ha. United's first game was the early kick-off against Southampton, and from the way United played they must have drunk more than I had the previous night. We certainly didn't have any interest in the next game between Aberdeen and West Ham but because the bars in the ground were open all day we hung around for a few pints and got talking to a gang of Aberdeen fans. They were singing the praises and wax lyrical about their manager, Alex Ferguson, whoever he was!

Towards the end of the night we bumped into our Scottish centre half - Big Gordon McQueen, and even though he was out with his wife he seemed more than happy to chat with us. He even took it on the chin when we said how crap the whole team had performed against Southampton. Gordon offered to buy a round and out of his trouser pocket produced the biggest wad of £20 notes I'd ever seen. It turned out to be a very good night after all. As the free drinks kept coming and coming we tried to get Mr and Mrs McQueen to dish the dirt on our ex-manager, but all Gordon would say was that he fully understood the fans frustrations regarding Mr. Sexton and he might have been as dull as dishwater, (no shit Sherlock) but he worked tirelessly to try and bring success to United. McQueen added that our new manager, Big Ron, was the polar opposite to Sexton. What a relief!

Not Long after the bell rang for last orders, big Gordon gave Colin a £20 note and told him to get a double round in. Colin trotted off to the bar, but very quickly returned saying the landlord had refused to serve him because it was now after time. On hearing this Gordon pulled out his wad of twenties from of his pocket and handing Colin another £20 note, saying, "Give this to the landlord, that'll make him take the towels back off the pumps." Colin returned back to the bar but once again came back empty handed. Well not exactly empty-handed. He was still holding the two £20 notes. Shaking his head Colin said, "Still no joy!" On hearing this, Mr McQueen jumped up and stormed over to the bar and straightaway started ranting and raving at the landlord, "Don't you know who I am." The landlord's reply was, "I couldn't give a fuck who you are, we're closed." With his face red with rage Gordon shouted over to his wife, "Come on, we are fuckin' outta here." And without a good night kiss or a see you at the match tomorrow, he stormed out of the pub leaving Colin still holding two of his £20 notes. – What a result!

Our game against West Ham on the Sunday was an even more dismal performance than the Southampton game. But the afternoon was brightened up a little when a mob of United invaded the pitch. Most of the Reds sat behind one of the goals and there was a small contingency of West Ham fans in the stand to the right of us. After being goaded by the Cockneys at the end of the game, about forty United tried to scale the fence that separated the two stands. The Scottish Old Bill supported by some heavy-handed club stewards soon pulled the United fans off the fence and tried to eject them from the ground. The old Bill and stewards made the mistake of leading the United boys around the side of the pitch and past the section where the West Ham fans were situated. When the United fans marched past the Cockneys, once again they received a load of abuse. This obviously only aggravated the situation more and it wasn't long before the Reds on the side of the pitch were diving into the West Ham fans. Seeing this, the rest of the United mob behind the goal were soon running across the pitch and chasing West Ham out of the ground. After seeing off West Ham, we turned our attention to the home fans who were congregated at the opposite side of the ground. We tried in vain to get into the Aberdeen end but the old Bill along with a small army of stewards stopped us from getting at the Aberdeen supporters. We were eventually driven out of the ground by mounted police and more dogs than you would see at Crufts.

After running riot in the streets outside Pittodrie we came across a seafront fairground. Even though we were shadowed by a load of coppers, it didn't stop us turning over a few of the sideshow stalls and fighting with the fairground boys. It was Sunderland '77 all over again – All the fun of the fair! As it was our last night in Aberdeen, we decided to go to a club to guarantee a late drink. We had only been in the club a short while when the whole of the United team walked in, minus Mr McQueen. Colin, Speedy and I were all wearing badges and it didn't take long for a few of the players to notice and they started chatting to us. Sammy McIlroy had barely said hello when Speedy launched into him, telling him and Jimmy Nicholl what we thought of their lack-lustre efforts over the last two games. More than a bit shell-shocked, they replied that these were only friendly games, to which Speedy snapped back "Ten fuckin' quid to see that shit!" Jimmy Nicholl had heard enough and turned around and set his sights on an absolutely gorgeous blonde who was strutting her stuff on the dance floor. Within five minutes the jammy bastard was leaving the club with her. Fair play to Sammy, he stopped and listened to us moaning about the price of the train fair, the cost of the match tickets, and the teams' woeful display. To ease the pain, he ordered a double whiskey for each of us.

While we were sipping on our whiskies, we were joined by John Gidman and Kevin Moran. John told us of his nightmare car journey with Dave Sexton and Martin Buchan. He was in a car with them for almost three hours and said they were so boring that at one stage he contemplated opening the door and jumping out of the car while they were doing eighty on the motorway. While John was entertaining us with tales of the boring twosome, who would come and join us? None other than Mr Buchan himself. While the rest of the team were very casually dressed in T-shirts and jeans, Martin was wearing a tie and club blazer. Within a few minutes of Martin joining us the other players quickly drifted away and when I asked him if he was still sending Christmas cards to Gordon Hill, it wasn't long before Martin did one as well. A combination of deafening music and the beer being ridiculously expensive and shit, we decided we would go back to our digs and polish off

Speedy's bottle of Bacardi. Before we left, we asked the barmaid if she would sell us a large bottle of Coke, she readily agreed and placed a bottle on the counter. But before we could ask her the price, she went off to serve some other customers, then disappeared into stock room. We must have waited a good ten minutes but the barmaid didn't return, I was losing patience, "Oh fuck it, we have spent enough money in here let's just take the bottle," I said, so Colin grabbed the bottle of coke and we made our way down the stairs to the street.

We had only walked a few yards when the bouncers came charging out of the club and running towards us. While me and Speedy were straight on our toes and legging it up the street, in a moment of madness Colin decided to throw the bottle of Coke at the doormen. In throwing the bottle he lost valuable seconds in the race to safety and the bouncers soon caught him and dragged him to the ground. The bouncers lost all interest in Speedy and I as they were quite happy to give Colin a good kicking. After being kicked around the street the bouncers then dragged Colin back into the club. Once they had got Colin in the club, they dragged him into a small deserted ground floor bar and threw him on the floor. As soon as he hit the deck a bouncer dived on top of him and stuck his knees in his back, then another couple of bouncers did their best to pull his arms out of his sockets. Colin was already in absolute agony when some kind soul came into the room and trod on both of his hands. The kind soul turned out to be the manager of the club and while kicking Colin in the ribs he said, "So you like our Coke do ya? Well you can drink as much as you fuckin' like."

He then told his bouncers to drag Colin over to the bar. Colin was pinned against the bar counter by the bouncers then the manager forced open his mouth and shoved the nozzle of the Coke dispenser into it. "There ya cunt, drink that," as the Coke gushed into Colin's mouth. When the nozzle was finally taken out of his mouth and the bouncers released him, Colin collapsed in a heap on the floor. As he lay gasping for breath the manager lent over him and growled, "You are the luckiest fuckin' Englishman alive, I normally cut the hands off people who steal from me, but you've caught me in a good mood." The manager told his bouncers to get Colin to his feet and when he was standing upright, the Manager head butted him, "Now show this cunt the pavement," were his final words. The bouncers duly obliged and threw Colin in-between two parked cars. Speedy and I were waiting a safe distance from the club, but as soon as we saw Colin being thrown into the road we went to his assistance. Fortunately, our digs weren't too far away, and we soon got Colin back and cleaned up. While drinking neat Bacardi Colin told us what had happened to him after he was dragged back into the club. He ended his little bedtime story with; "I don't think I will be drinking Coke again, for a very - very long time".

KEEGAN DESTROYS UNITED'S HOPES

By Karl Kershaw
Southampton 3, Manchester United 1

A BRILLIANT one-man show by Kevin Keegan powered Southampton to a convincing victory over Manchester United at Pittodrie yesterday.

Superstar Keegan produced his vast array of skills to the delight of the appreciative North East fans.

Keegan struck in 26 minutes when he dived to a knee-high cross from Steve Williams to head well past keeper Gary Bailey.

United then lost Scottish international centre half Gordon McQueen through injury, and he was replaced by younger Mike Duxbury.

United's re-arranged defence looked even more shaky and Southampton were desperately unlucky not to go further ahead when Steven Moran struck the post after a quick break from defence.

In 35 minutes, Keegan turned goal-maker with a superbly flighted cross which Charlie George headed past Bailey.

However, in the 75th minute Lou Macari almost pulled a goal back form United when he headed a cross from Sammy McIlroy narrowly over the bar.

In a last bid to retrieve the match United threw on Ashley Grimes for McIlroy who had made little imprint on the events.

In the 78th minute full back Nick Holmes crashed in a cross from Steve Williams for the third goal to complete a humiliating day for United.

But in the dying seconds Manchester United gained some consolation when Steve Coppell rifled in a 25-yard drive.

West Ham 1,
Manchester United 0

West Ham claimed third place and a cheque of £5,000 in Aberdeen's tournament thanks to the devilment of Winger Bob Barnes and the scoring prowess at David Cross at Pittodrie yesterday.

In a strangely lethargic encounter, Barnes setup the solitary 57th minute goal with a nicely judged cut-back and Cross responded with the sure-headed touch of the proven finishers.

West Ham showed improvement from Saturday's 3-0 defeat at the hands of Aberdeen, but Ron Atkinson's men fared no better than against Southampton, when they lost 3-1

Chapter 17.
Cov. City '81

29th August '81
Coventry City   2 – 1 Macari   (20,050)

United Line–Up
Bailey, Gidman, Buchan, McQueen, Albiston, Coppell, McIlroy, Wilkins, Macari, Birtles, Stapleton **Sub -** Duxbury

Manager
Ron Atkinson

League Position After the Game

P	W	D	L	F	A	Pts	Pos
1	0	0	1	1	2	0	15th

Even though United had won the last seven games of the previous season, only conceding two goals in the process, Dave Sexton was replaced as manager by big Ron Atkinson. United finished the '80 – '81 season in 8th position and paid out a club record £1 million for the services of Gary Birtles. But once again scoring goals was a problem for The Reds. Birtles made 25 league appearances and failed to score a single goal. Joe - Joe – Joe Jordon was the only player to get into double figures. Sadly, it was to be Jordon's last season with United, as he signed for Italian giant's AC Milan in the close season.

Big Ron replaced Jordon with his first major signing - shelling out £900,000 for Frank Stapleton from Arsenal. Captain

Marvell and Miles Platting born Remi Moses would join United a few months later.

It was becoming the norm that The Reds were well off the pace at the beginning of the season and it wasn't until our fifth game when we chalked up our first victory. Even though Frank Stapleton was looking like a good buy with five goals in seven games, United only scored more than one goal in a match twice in their first twelve games.

I hadn't been to an all-seater stadium before 1981. Then after my trip to Pittodrie a few weeks earlier to see United in a pre-season tournament, I was about to visit my second all-seater ground in just a few weeks. Coventry City became the first English club to introduce an all seater stadium.

Much to the annoyance of the home fans, the then chairman of the Sky Blues, Jimmy 'the wanker' Hill unilaterally took the decision to do away with the terraces. Over the next couple of seasons Coventry City's home gates plummeted and terracing was eventually re-introduced to Highfield Road.

It was becoming the norm to be greeted at away railway stations by hundreds of local plod and escorted to the ground. To avoid this, we took the short journey from Brum in my works transit van. There were so many crammed in the back, I didn't dare drive above thirty because I wouldn't have been able to steer the vehicle. After parking up the van we came across a boozer that was full of United, and amongst them were a few of United boys including Tank and Eddie B. There was a very raucous atmosphere and you could hear glasses being smashed every minute or so. While one of the barmen was cleaning up some of the broken glass, he did a very silly thing and tried to push Tank out of the way. Tank's immediate response was to take a swing at him but fortunately for the barman he missed. Having failed to give the barman a right-hander, Tank then proceeded to chase the petrified bloke around the bar. Everyone present found this extremely amusing, well everyone except the barman of course. While Tank pursued him with a bar stool he ducked, dived and twisted his way around the packed pub until he finally made his escape through the entrance door. Tank was so pissed off he hadn't caught the barman, he climbed up onto one of the tables and took the TV off its wooden shelf and threw it over the bar. A mirror and several bottles of spirits were smashed, immediately followed by barrage of glasses and bottles and a few chairs. All the remaining bar staff wisely ran for cover.

The pub soon emptied and a mob of well over a hundred started making its way towards the ground. Most of the Brummies including, Dave, Speedy, Paddy, Eddie and I were at the back of the mob, but when we approached a pub-full of Coventry fans we were surprised to see 'The Boys' at the front of the mob just walk by. By the time us lot at the back were passing the pub, the Coventry fans inside were going crazy and the bouncers on the door could no longer contain them. They came charging out at us and as we turned around to challenge them, we hadn't realised the main body of United mob had kept on walking and there were probably less than twenty of us facing a pub-load of rival fans. I steamed in and remembered quickly putting a couple of them down. Someone or something must have hit me round the head and knocked me out, I recall coming around and finding myself lying on my back surrounded by half a dozen Coventry fans, all sticking the boot in. The weird thing was it all seemed to be happening in slow motion and it got quite surreal when a size ten Docker made its way towards my face at a snail's pace. I can even remember seeing the sole of the boot before I grabbed hold of it. Then Sha-zam! I was a hundred yards up the road standing next to Speedy and Dave. Seeing the kicking that I had received, they asked if I was ok, to which I replied, "I think so," but I just couldn't work out how, in what seemed like a split second, I managed to get up off the floor, fought off a load of Coventry fans and get that far away from them? To this day it still puzzles me, and all I can imagine is that I'd had a massive adrenaline rush and for a few seconds, must have been like a thing possessed. As we approached the ground it seemed like there was a Paki shop on every corner and small mobs of United were having a field day raiding the local shops and quickly emptying the place of all the booze and fags with the owners not putting up too much resistance. Some also got a kicking and had their windows smashed. It was like the good old 70's had never ended. I'm sure it must have cost the poor shop owners a small fortune.

When we got to the turnstiles it was pandemonium because there were thousands of Reds without tickets. A good few turnstile attendants must have made a packet that day, pocketing cash and letting United supporters jump over the turnstiles. Inside the ground it was just as hectic because Reds without tickets tried their best to find a seat and were standing everywhere, also sharing seats and sitting in the gangways. The coppers and club stewards were clueless and had lost control. So basically, we'd been told to sit wherever we saw a spare seat. Seeing that a load of Reds had already squeezed into the seats in and around where my seat was allocated, I looked around to find an alternative seat. On the back row there were two St John's ambulance men, they had plonked themselves down and had taken up a further two seats with big black plastic bags. I approached them and asked them to move the plastic bags so I could sit down. When they refused, we quickly got into a heated argument and I ended up throwing both of the plastic bags down the gangway. As I was doing so one of them tried to pull the bags off me and I ended up sending him tumbling down the steps too. A copper witnessed what had happened and immediately grabbed me from behind. As we struggled, I somehow ended up throwing him over my shoulder. He hit the floor and another three coppers jumped on me and dragged me down the steps and onto the edge of the pitch. When I was on the side of the pitch each of the four coppers grabbed me by my limbs as if to give me *'a leg and wing'* and carried me around the perimeter of the pitch to the police control point. The copper who I'd thrown over my shoulder was telling me what was in store for me when they got me behind closed doors. I was taken into a small enclosure at the back of the main stand and after being punched in the face several times by a sadistic sergeant I was dropped to the ground, then dragged to my feet and slammed against a brick wall. A few moments later a set of large gates were flung open which led out onto the street and the sergeant yelled out, "officers under attack." All the coppers ran out into the streets to control the rampaging United mob. I couldn't believe my luck. I looked around and there was nobody to stop me walking back into the ground. Feeling extremely relieved, I made my way back around the edge of the pitch and by this time the game had kicked off and I gave the players a bit of encouragement as I walked past them. Quite a few of the lads had seen me being carried around the pitch and were amazed when they spotted me jumping back over the perimeter wall and into the seats. Like me, they thought I was going to get a fuckin' good hiding, a stint in the cells and a visit to the local magistrates for assaulting a copper.

There were plenty of Reds in our section but the tier above us seemed to be entirely filled with home fans and we were receiving quite a bit of abuse throughout the game. One of them stood out as a right obnoxious bastard and besides plenty of Munich chants, the scumbags were continually spitting at us and showering us with their drinks. Just before the final whistle we tried to make our way out of the seats but being so packed with fellow Reds on the narrow-seated steps, it was difficult to get past. A lot of pushing and shoving started while we were clambering over seats and trying to get to the gangway. In the crush a couple of Reds tried to pull Jonnie back and straight away Jonnie elbowed one of them in the face, within seconds myself and Jonnie found ourselves fighting with our own supporters. We were packed in the seats like sardines and it was difficult to get a proper punch in, so fortunately, what could have turned out to be a nasty encounter ended up as handbags at close range and the skirmish was eventually broken up by other Reds.

Outside the ground United mobs were running riot and were having running battles with the old Bill and a few game Cov Boys. We chased a load of Cov into a nearby park but when they came to a pile of building waste, three of them stopped and armed themselves with long pieces of 3 x 2". The United mob also made use of the scattered rubble and as the Cov fans swung their wooden claymores around like things possessed, several bricks were thrown at them, but all missed their target. With the Reds surrounding the Cov boys, they were literally saved by the cavalry. There was such an onslaught from the mounted coppers it seemed like a re-enactment of the Charge of Light Brigade and many of us ran for cover in the alleys of the terraced housing. However, a few of the more belligerent mounted coppers even followed us up there, so a few of us ran into one of the houses backyards, straight through the house and back into the street.

After a few pints, when most of the lads had made it back to the van we decided to head into Brum. But after taking a few wrong turnings we ended up in the City Centre. As we approached the train station, we saw a small crew of Coventry fans, we had stopped at the set of lights and we could see them eyeing up our van, they started walking towards us, Paddy who was sitting in the passenger seat lent over to the lads in the back and said, "Pass me something out of the tool- bag."

Within seconds Paddy was handed an old carving knife. As soon as he had the twelve-inch long knife in his hand, he jumped out the van and screaming his head off like a wild lunatic, waving the knife above his head, he charged at the stunned Coventry fans. The shocked crew stopped in their tracks and as Paddy got closer, they all turned and ran for their lives. With all of us laughing our heads off in the van, Paddy lowered the knife and casually strolled back and jumped into the passenger seat. After a round of applause from the lads Paddy said, "Thank fuck they all turned and ran, this knife couldn't cut warm butter, I might as well have run at them with a rolled-up newspaper."

Still struggling to find our way out of the city centre we drove past a bus stop when Eddie shouted out, "Fuck me! that's the cunt from the ground that was giving all the Munich chants." We immediately turned around but as we got back to the bus stop, the Coventry scumbag was just boarding a bus, so we decided to follow it until the fucker got off so we could give him a good kicking. After following the bus for ten minutes we were all getting a bit frustrated, so Eddie suggested the next time the bus stopped, he and a few of the lads would get on the bus and drag the mouthy wanker off. So, at the next stop I pulled the van in front of the bus and the lads jumped out the backdoors and charged onto the bus. They found the scumbag upstairs who turned as white as a sheet when Eddie and the other lads ran towards him. As they laid into him the rest of the passengers on the top deck quickly ran down the stairs with a few hysterical girls screaming their heads off. The driver soon came up to see what all the commotion was about, by then the horrible Cov cunt was screaming like a pig and had rolled into a ball and was trying to take cover underneath the seat. All this of course made it very difficult for the lads to get at him properly, and when the bus driver said he was going to drive to the nearest police station, the lads had to reluctantly give up trying to get him off the bus. When I saw the lads coming off the bus empty-handed, I was extremely pissed off because he deserved a fuckin' good kicking, and after that, we could have kidnapped him and dumped him back in Brum. Sadly his guardian-angle must have been looking after the horrible bastard.

UNITED FAIL IN MIDFIELD

By Ronald O'Connor
Coventry City 2, Manchester United 1

English soccers first all seater stadium was the ideal setting for Coventry to give Dave Sexton their new manager the perfect start to the season victory over Manchester United at the club who dismissed him for lack of entertaining football was said modestly slightly more satisfying than an ordinary success and ironically it was Coventry who showed more style than United.

From the start with 20,000 spectators settled in their seats only 400 short of capacity it was Coventry who set the pace and after 11 minutes Whitton 20, in his second league game scored a superb individual goal.

Whitton a midfield player converted to a striker and chosen on merit ahead of Englishman Hatley to partner the lively Thompson had an excellent game and made a far greater impression than the disappointing Stapleton, United expensive recruit who had only one attempt on goal -a header which went over the bar.

Ron Atkinson United's manager knows where his problems are and he is concerned about the lack of a ball winner in midfield hence his continued interest in Robson but more worrying on Saturday was Baileys lack of confidence in goal after the adventurous Gidman has provided a fine centre for MaCaris's equaliser, it was a blow from which United despite Birtles encouraging form could not recover.

Chapter 18.
Man City '81

10th October '81
Man City   0 – 0   (52,037)

United Line–Up
Bailey, Gidman, Buchan, Moran, Albiston, Moses, Robson, Wilkins, Mcllroy, Birtles, Stapleton **Sub -** *Coppell*

Manager
Ron Atkinson

League Position After the Game

P	W	D	L	F	A	Pts	Pos
10	4	4	2	12	5	16	5th

With Ron Atkinson replacing Dave Sexton as manager, most United supporters were hoping for a return to the swashbuckling, free flowing football of The Doc. Unfortunately scoring goals was once again a problem for United, even though new signing Frank Stapleton had scored 5 goals and the goal shy Gary Birtles had hit the back of the net 3 times in United's first 9 games of the season. United had only scored more than one goal in a match, once in their first 8 games and only the first home game of the season had an attendance above 50,000. Then in the game before the Derby at Maine Road, the floodgates opened. Roared on by a crowd of just under 47,000 and with the help of a hat-trick from Sammy Mcllroy United battered Wolves 5 - 0 at Old Trafford.

We had got jibbing the train up to Manchester well and truly sussed. Clippie would always start his rounds at the back of the train so when we got on the train at Brum we always sat in the front carriage, then when we got into Stafford we would jump off the train, run along the station platform and get on to the last carriage, thus missing out the Clippie. (Circumnavigating)

When we arrived in Manchester and met up with Ged and the rest of the Manchester lads, I was initially delighted to hear that they had got me a ticket for the game. When I found out the ticket was for the City side of The Kippax, I was a little less enthusiastic. As was always the case, on Derby Day it was chaotic outside the ground, with the old Bill running around like headless chickens trying to separate rival fans who were fighting in the side streets, back alleys, open ground and car parks surrounding Maine Road. It was almost as bad inside the ground as well. There were about twenty of us with tickets for the blue half of The Kippax and once we went through the turnstiles, the City fans put spotters on the lookout for any Reds that they might recognise. If the City fans didn't recognise you as a Blue or if you hadn't got a City badge on your jacket, you had a pretty good chance of being challenged. While I was waiting for the rest of the lads to come through the turnstiles, I saw a few nasty City fuckers jump on Reds as soon as the younger spotters had pointed them out; and of course, it was always five or six to one. About a dozen of us managed to meet up at the bottom of the steps as planned and we made our way to the uncovered part of the Kippax with the city seats to the right. We were hoping that this part of the Kippax might be a little less volatile, but it was Derby Day – there was no chance. After only a few minutes, Bowie lent over my shoulder and whispered, "Get ready for it Grange – we've been sussed!" Sure, enough there was a hefty push and a large gap opened up behind us. There were a few loud cries of *'City'* then a few war cries and the City fans were all over us. We got a right hammering and even blokes in their forties and fifties were giving us a few digs as we tried to escape through the packed terraces.

I lost the rest of the lads and had to put up with watching the first half surrounded by bitter blues, all of them continually slagging off United and singing Munich songs. At half time I went down to the back of the stand to see if I could meet up with any of the lads, but I had no joy. While I was milling about the back of the stand, I noticed a small mob of United asking the stewards that were positioned against the dividing fence if they would open one of the gates and let them into the United section. The stewards were having none of it and signalled to nearby City fans that they were Reds. After informing hundreds of City fans that there were United standing next to them, the stewards casually walked away leaving the Reds to their fate. It was suicide to ask City stewards to let them into the United section, they may as well have swung a red and white scarf above their heads. There was nothing I could do to help my fellow Reds, so I went back into the terraces and lost myself in the crowd. The Second half was just as uncomfortable as the first, with snarling City fans hurling abuse at the United team and their fans. After City had a goal-bound shot saved, all of the City fans surrounding me jumped up in excitement, I of course just stood still. This was noticed by a few young city twats and they challenged me. As soon as I opened my mouth one of them shouted, "The cunts a Cockney Red." The thick wankers had probably never been out of Moss Side. I found myself trying to fight off three or four of them, but luckily a few coppers came to my rescue, and much to my relief they threw me out of the ground. I hung around outside until the final whistle, and not being able to find any of the lads I latched myself on to a mob of United and we picked up where we left off before the game.

There were running battles all over the place and with so many small mobs in action; it was virtually impossible for the law to keep the violence under control. We were a few hundred yards from the ground when we were attacked by a large mob of City. We were definitely outnumbered and after putting one of them down, I found myself pinned up against a car with half a dozen City fans raining punches down on me. I managed to break free, but only got a few yards before being knocked to the ground, whilst trying to escape between a couple of parked cars. I was kicked and stamped on, but I was saved from a really bad beating when another mob of United turned up and ran the Blue twats. For a minute or so I lay between the two cars to get my breath back, and as I did, I could feel a warm sticky liquid over the one side of my body. *'Oh fuck – I've been stabbed'*, I thought it to myself. Then as I pulled myself up onto my feet and checked my body for a stab wound, I discovered that I was covered in oil and grease. One of the local residents must have done a DIY service on their car and tipped the old oil into the gutter. I knew I must I have looked a right state because as I leant against the car several people that passed me, burst out laughing.

Before the game we had arranged to meet back at The Nelson at the top of Newton Street. As soon as I walked in, the place erupted with laughter. "Fuck me, you look like you've been working on a North Sea oil rig." Big Clive shouted.

After a few pints and cleaning myself up as best I could we went on a bit of a walkabout. We hadn't gone far when a few of the lads decided to call into a chippie that we were passing. Already queuing in the chippie was a gang of City fans and within seconds Percy got into an argument with a couple of them. A few insults were passed then Percy hit one with the vinegar bottle and dived onto another one of them. They were soon rolling around the floor and the City fan made the mistake of putting his fingers inside Percy's mouth, the Blue bastard was doing his best to rip open Percy's cheek. Percy was a very game lad and immediately sank his teeth firmly into the foreign fingers that had invaded his gob and the blood immediately started to flow. Even though Percy's mouth was full of blood he wouldn't let go and the City fan was squealing like a pig. After Percy had almost bitten a couple of his fingers off, he stood up and gave the City fan a kicking before heading off to another boozer. It looked like something out of a Tarantino film, the City fan looked like he had a couple of fingers hanging off, and Percy was covered in so much blood he looked like he had been stabbed or slashed.

After visiting a few boozers, we made our way to The Waldorf. Already sitting inside the small bar was one of the locals from The Hare & Hounds in Gorton. He was much older than us, and a gang of City fans had just beaten him up. He told us that the City fans were in the alley at the back of the pub, so without getting any more details a few of us went in search of them, with GS picking up a couple of bottles as he made his way outside the pub. We soon came across a small group of City, all mostly in their teens. GS walked straight up to them with a bottle dangling from each hand, "Are you Blue bastards?" GS yelled. "No – No," a few of them quickly replied. "We're just in town for a drink," one of them added. "Have you been fuckin' around with our mate?" Wilkie snapped. GS followed up with, "You lying bastard, you're all Blue cunts." Then the teenager standing nearest to me said a really stupid thing, "I'm not a City fan - I support Liverpool." I stared at him in amazement for a second, then just before head-butting him, shouted, "That's even fuckin' worse." GS immediately smashed his bottles over a couple of their heads, then stabbed the kid I'd head-butted in the arse.

We walked back into The Waldorf where Bowie and big Clive were having a soda siphon fight and were running around the pub like a pair of kids with everyone getting soaked. Bowie was the first to run dry, so he grabbed a couple of bottles of sauce and proceeded to empty the contents over Clive. This really pissed Clive off and he went one better and grabbed the fire extinguisher off the wall. Bowie was half laughing and was pleading with Clive not to set off the fire extinguisher.

The landlady was hysterical and screaming at Clive to put the fire extinguisher down, but her request fell on deaf ears and Clive sprayed the lounge bar with foam. Whether full of bravado, pissed, or simply didn't give a fuck after all that commotion, we stayed in The Waldorf to finish our drinks. It wasn't long before the pub doors almost flew off their hinges as two van loads of old Bill came charging through the door. There wasn't really any serious damage to the pub and the foam could have been mopped up in five minutes, but it was Derby Day and the coppers waded in without asking any questions, truncheons were flying all over the place and bodies were thrown out of the pub. The landlady and the bar staff were screaming at the coppers pointing out Clive and Bowie as the main culprits, and the pair of them were thrown headfirst into one of the police vans. Annoyed that the Landlady had pointed out a couple of the boys I shouted over to her, "You bleedin' old cow, you should be ashamed of yourself grassing to the coppers." She instantly gave me a mouthful back, and then pointing at me, said to one of the Coppers, "He's another one of them." I was grabbed by two coppers and joined Clive and Bowie in the back of the cop van. Ged and Knockers protested so vigorously about me being thrown in the back of the van, they soon joined us too. Even though I had been up to no good all day I was fuming at the injustice (as I saw it!) of being arrested just for giving the landlady a piece of my mind.

Before we got to the nick, we did a slight detour and picked up a few more passengers at The Portland Bars. The pub had been totally wrecked and there was a massive melee going on in the surrounding streets. Being a bit pissed and very naïve, I banged on the side of the van and called the coppers all the bastards under the sun, and as our van reversed into the nick, I made sure I was right next to the backdoors so as they opened I could immediately protest about the injustice of it all. What a Silly Billy! The second the doors opened I put my head outside the van, and I was just about to say, "You've got it all wrong gov. It's all a big mistake," when I was dragged out of the van by my hair and thrown to the floor. I was whacked a couple of times with the truncheon and kicked several times by at least two coppers. After being introduced to the welcoming committee in the dimly lit courtyard of the nick with a copper either side of me and my arms very forcibly shoved up my back, I was frog-marched into the station and straight into a cell. On the way to the cells my head was accidentally bounced off several doorframes and the odd wall, and as soon as I was hurled into the cell the beating continued. After throwing me around the cell for a couple of terrifying minutes, they dragged me to my feet and made me empty my pockets onto the concrete bunk. I emptied the contents of my pockets as told; I only had a few £1 notes, a bit of loose change and my Walsall bus pass. When one of the coppers noticed my bus pass, he asked me why was I up in Manchester causing all this agro when I was a 'Brummie Cunt'? I did think about correcting him and saying actually it's a 'Walsall Cunt', if you don't mind. But somehow it didn't seem like an appropriate time to crack jokes. Then dragging his hand across the bunk, the copper sent all my belongings flying onto the floor. "Pick it up," he snarled. As I bent down to collect my things the bastard kneed me in the face. Once more I ended up on the floor with two of our trusted boys in blue stamping on me for good measure. They were absolute animals, worse than any football hooligan or street thug. Anyone in a position of authority that abuses their power in that way should be locked in stocks for a week and randomly gobbed at by passers by.

The coppers in the nick were having a very busy night. Every ten to fifteen minutes some poor sod was dragged into the cells and savagely beaten. The noise from the coppers shouting abuse, and their victims pleading for mercy was very nerve wracking. I was on my own in the cell for quite a while and was just nodding off, when the door was flung open and another lad was thrown into the cell. He was followed into the cell by a copper, who grabbed him around the throat then banged his head against the cell wall. "I'll be back to see you later," the copper said to my new cellmate, then after slapping him around the face a few times he left the cell and slammed the door shut. Thankfully, my new cellmate was a Red and he told me that he had been involved in the fights between United and City in the Portland Bars. He confirmed the pub had been absolutely smashed to pieces as both sets of fans smashed up chairs and tables to throw at each other. He had managed to avoid arrest there but was picked up an hour or so later after it went off in Piccadilly Gardens. I think we were both asleep when our cell door was opened and a third lad was flung in, I don't know if the coppers had gotten bored of kicking the shit out of their prisoners, or this particular lad was so pissed that he probably wouldn't have felt a thing, but he wasn't knocked about like me and the first lad that had joined me in the cell. As the pissed-up lad curled himself into a ball on the cell floor, the Portland Bars Red looked wide eyed at the kid's red Kicker boots. "Fuckin' hell, they are a smart pair," he said as he stared at the feet of the prostrate drunk.

Around 5am the cell door opened and a copper shouted, "Grainger! – Out here!" Blurry eyed I made my way to the door, and after the various kicking's I'd received the day before, I ached from head to foot and limped all the way to the custody sergeant's desk. All the other lads from The Waldorf were already in the reception waiting to be charged. We were all eventually charged with drunk & disorderly and criminal damage, and because of my little tête-à-tête with the landlady, I had 'foul and abusive language' added to the two other charges. When Bowie was called up to see the desk sergeant, he had the usual aggravation that he experienced every time he had a run-in with the law. The copper would ask, "Name?" and Bowie would reply. "David Bowie," which was his real name. Bowie always got the same response from the coppers, a kidney punch or his head bounced off the desk, and on this occasion, he got both. I'd told him loads of time to change his name to David Jones or stop getting into trouble with the law.

While I was still waiting to be officially charged, the Portland Bars Red was brought into the room, and as soon as he saw me, he looked a little sheepish. Then with a cheeky smile, he pointed to his feet. The cheeky bleeder was only wearing a pair of red Kickers!

Well, it seems after I had left the cell the little pikey had gone and swapped his trainers for the drunken kid's Kickers. Must have had a bit of scouse in him, I thought!

When we appeared in court a few weeks later, I pleaded guilty to the drunk and disorderly charges, but not guilty on the criminal damage and using foul and abusive language. But as I stood in the dock with the rest of the boys, I experienced a bit of déjà vu. Just as a copper had once said to me when I was in court in my mid-teens and also pleading 'not guilty' to one of the charges, one of the court ushers lent forward and whispered in my ear "Don't try and be a flash cunt, just plead guilty." it's nice to know the great British justice system is consistent.

INTRUDERS HEAD GOLD RUSH

Man City 0, Man United 0

City and United reinforced the mounting optimism about Manchester football by providing in their 103 derby, a match which rose in quality and entertainment value above the usual standard of these tense emotional neighbourhood scraps rights Colin Malam.

As such the game also went some way towards justifying the heavy spending in which both clubs have indulged during the past few years. At the end the 3 million took to put these players on the field did not seem so excessive as it had at the beginning.

Corrigan kept city in the game well United were rampant during the first 20 minutes and Caton aided by Hartford who showed all his old aggression in midfield. on his return to Maine Road lead the fight back.

United's costly signings, Robson, Stapleton, Birtles, Wilkins and Moses quickly began to dismantle the city defence at the centre of which Reid teamed up with Kevin Bond. United football flowed so sweetly in those first 20 minutes that Ron Atkinson's bold decision to relegate Coppell to substitute after a run of 200 consecutive league appearances look to be fully justified.

Robson growing in authority all the time appeared certain to mark his league debut for United with a goal in the 12th minute. Moses and Birtles opened a gaff for him brilliantly but Corrigan managed to trap the ball between his legs when Britain's most expensive player shot.

Corrigan also made to find saves from the revitalized Wilkins in the first half. He was utterly beaten however when McIlroy ran onto a subtle pass from Albiston and bounced his lob on top of the bar.

That was the end of United dominance. In the 26th minute penetrating cross field pass from Caton enabled Hutchinson to pull the ball back across the face of the United goal where neither O'Neill nor Reeves could supply the final touch Coppell in fact worked busily and effectively alongside Stapleton and supplied the final pass from which Robson spinning on the penalty spot drove the ball against Corrigan once more in a second-half less distinguished and eventful than the first

Chapter 19.
Arsenal '83

15th February '83
Arsenal   2 – 4   Coppell 2, Whiteside, Stapleton   (43,136)

United Line–Up
*Bailey, Duxbury, McQueen, Moran, Albiston, Coppell, Moses, Robson, Muhren, Whiteside, Stapleton **Sub** – Wilkins*

Manager
Ron Atkinson

League Cup Semi-Final 1ˢᵗ Leg

After winning the second leg of the semi-final at OT 2 – 1, United were sadly defeated in the final (after extra time) by the Scousers, this stopped the Reds lifting both domestic cups. Arsenal must have hated the sight of United, because we also beat them in the semi-final of the FA Cup. After a replay in the final we lifted the FA Cup for the 5th time. Because of Norman Whiteside's success in the 1982 World Cup finals, '82 – '83 became the teenage sensation breakthrough season and he scored many important cup goals in his first full season with the Reds.

On the league front, we made an unusually good start to the season - only losing one of the first 11 games. But form and results dipped in the New Year and United didn't win a single league game in February.

While we were waiting for the train to pull out of New Street Railway station and take us down to Euston, a big black puff came mincing along the platform. He must have been six foot six tall, skinny as a rake, wearing a crocheted sleeveless jacket with a matching beret and a pink shoulder bag. He looked like he had just stepped out of a seventies sitcom and made John Inman look like The Marlborough Man. As he passed by our windows, we all gave him wolf whistles and a few limp wrist actions and the kinky bastard loved it, so much so that when Eddie gestured him to come into our carriage he did! He entered our carriage from the opposite side where we were all sitting, and bold as brass he wiggled his way up the gangway. When he got to our seats, he said an extremely camp low whisper, "Hello boys," which was greeted with cheers and laughter from the lads, followed by, "Hello sailor" and "Oooh, you are awful, but I like you," and several other camp phrases from popular TV sitcoms of the day. He took it all on the chin and stood there with a coy smile. When all the noise and initial exuberance had died down a little Eddie shouted out, "Go on then which one of us do you fancy." The puff gave a little giggle and said, "Oh, I think you are all very handsome." Dave immediately responded with, "Fuck off, there must be one of us that you would like to bum more than all the others." Looking a little shocked for a few seconds, the black shirt-lifter then gave us all the once-over. Eventually he flicked his limp wrist and pointing at me said, "That one." All the lads were in hysterics and Dave yelled out, "I always knew you were a bum bandit Grange." He then turned to the puff and said, "If ya get your big black cock out Grange will suck it for ya." The Dusky Duckie gave me a big smile and said, "I will be sitting in the next carriage when you're ready." (cheeky cunt) Then with a massive roar of laughter from the lads he minced off back down the aisle. He appeared again about fifteen minutes later on his way to the buffet car and much to the amusement of the lads as he minced passed me, the saucy fucker gave me a little wink. Then, on his way back, holding his little bag of goodies in his limp wristed hand, he stopped in the aisle, turned around and stared at me for a few seconds then beckoned me over by cocking his head and said, "Hurry up, before it goes cold."

The lads may well have thought it was extremely funny, but it was getting beyond a joke for me. Fortunately, that was the last time we saw the Big Black Puff, but it didn't stop Dave and the rest of the lads taking the piss out of me for the rest of the journey.

When we 'jumped' the train in those days we would always keep an eye out for the clippy and either get off at a station stop and run past the carriages where the clippy had already passed through, or we would hide between the seats where there was space to store luggage. To carry out this manoeuvre properly so your feet wouldn't be seen, you had to clamber in backwards and lift your feet as high as possible. On this occasion we decided on the latter and when the clippy was spotted in the next carriage half a dozen of us took up our positions. Unfortunately, I was opposite Dave when the clippy came into our carriage to check the tickets. Standing only inches away from me the clippy spotted Dave's legs sticking slightly out of the luggage space and told him to come out of his hiding place. Dave replied, "Fuck off, I'm trying to get to

251

sleep in here." The shocked Clippy responded, "You can't sleep in there, it's not allowed." To which Dave snapped back "I'm half vampire bat, I can only sleep in the dark – now fuck off and leave me alone." Meanwhile I was just feet away crammed into my own little hiding space trying my utmost to contain myself from laughing. In situations like that when you have to be totally silent for obvious reasons, it's nigh on impossible to stop yourself from bursting out with laughter, no matter how hard you try. However, with huge relief, I managed to quell my laughter as Dave continued to refuse to leave his little bat-cave. Astonishingly, the clippy gave up and eventually wandered off to the next carriage and didn't return.

No sooner had we arrived at Euston Station, we headed to a pub not far from Holloway Road tube station, where a sizeable United mob had gathered for the main attraction; this being three charming erotic dancers, known commonly as strippers. Having paid a quid on the door I was hoping to see a good show. The pub was full of Reds cheering on these lovelies. Pints in hand we had to worm our way through the mass of lecherous overgrown schoolboys, and all for a better look! I had to admit these girls certainly were no innocent Sunday school teachers. They were probably the most game and dirty girls I have ever come across. The first session was quite normal run of the mill stuff like sticking their tits in blokes' pints and rubbing spectacles against their fannies. These erotic dancers really knew how change the tempo and started dancing to a more interesting tune, when an old fella had his tie removed and one of the strippers shoved it right inside her pussy before another pulled it out with her teeth. Just the sort of stuff your missus wouldn't do! After putting on a good show, the girls went around the pub with a couple of beer glasses collecting tips, and that's when it got a bit wild. A few lads from Staffordshire approached the girls and told them that their mate was a self-confessed virgin, and could they sort him out? Without any arm-twisting, they were more than keen to assist. Our innocent virgin mate had just hit the fucking jackpot! The fucker will lose his virginity in a threesome or would it be a foursome? Well, whichever way you look at it, he was going to score big time and in full view of the United faithful. To make it a more intimate and romantic occasion, the girls asked him to lie across the pool table; and like a naughty boy being disciplined, he duly obeyed, with a smile from ear to ear. Once on the pool table, the initiation started with one girl promptly sitting on his face and another quickly made it a threesome by giving him a blowjob. The third stripper, which I suppose would now make it a foursome, soon joined in and started whipping him with a couple of bar towels. She momentarily disappeared into the crowd only to return with a small tin of lighter fuel, which she proceeded to squirt on to the virgins pubes. She then asked the audience for a lighter, and to no surprise was inundated with offers! However, like a bunch naughty of boys, she pouted sexily and shook her finger from side to side at them to gesture a NO. Then like magic, she stuck two fingers inside her pussy and pulled out a lighter. With a ceremonious click of the lighter she lit the flame near to his hairy Niagara's, which set the pub in uproar. I had tears of laughter running down my face and when his pubes caught on fire the roar of laughter and cheering was so loud you would have thought the King of the Cockney's, Gordon Hill was back in the side and running stark bollock naked up and down the wing. With a hot sensation and smell of burning pubes, the virgin realised the initiation process wasn't going to plan as he had hoped. Squirming and wriggling like fuck, he struggled to get the stripper off his face, but luckily his mates threw beer over his flaming bollocks. What an introduction to sex!

The entertainment was rounded off with two of the girls lying across the pool table and taking all-comers, well not exactly all-comers as the third stripper shouted, "We only want blokes with big cocks." It wasn't too long when a queue of lads stood in line to do the dirty deed, however, only if their manhood's measured up. Much to their shame and frustration, a couple of lads didn't have enough length so were turned away like two horny teenagers trying to blag their way into the old Odeon cinema on a Friday night to see 'Debbie Does Dallas'.

When all the commotion had died down, I met up with Jonnie Brinley at the bar. He was completely bladdered but was holding some fancy foreign bottle of lager with a bit of fruit sticking out the top. He slurred at me, "Grange, I've been drinking these fuckers all afternoon. You've gotta have one mate. they're fantastic." I may have confused him with my response and just for the craic, I said, "What the fuck are ya drinking that for? It's alcohol free." His face seemed to sober up immediately and was a picture. Jonnie was so completely pissed, he needed to hold onto the bar to support himself but the thought that he may have been drinking non-alcoholic beer seemed to sober him up just a little. Squinting his eyes and trying to focus on the bottle of beer in his hand, Jonnie replied, "Alcohol free! Fuck!! The bastards have been charging me a fortune for these." Jonnie then staggered forward and spluttered out his lager. He turned his attention to the bar staff and started shouting at the top of his voice, "Oi you cunts, come over here." One of the barmen came over to see what Jonnie's problem was and he reached over the bar and grabbed the barman by the collar and screamed, "Why have you been serving me non-alcoholic beer all afternoon?" Understandably the barman was lost for words and slightly confused because here was Jonnie, struggling to stand up, completely pissed, and fucking complaining that he had been drinking non-alcoholic beer all afternoon. The barman tried his best to reassure him that he had indeed been drinking strong lager and that he was very inebriated. But Jonnie took offence to the suggestion that he was drunk and told the barman he would smash one of the fuckin' non-alcoholic bottles of beer over his head unless he got a full refund. My little fun with a drunken Jonnie was done so it was time to drag him out of the boozer and hope he didn't remember the incident!

About a hundred or so of us walked to the Arsenal ground and after arriving at Highbury, we all piled into the North Bank. We positioned ourselves halfway up the terrace and after a few chants of *"U-ni-ted"* and *"Man-chest-er. La-la-la,"* we waited for the onslaught, but all that happened initially was a large gap formed around us and it seemed to be an age before the Gooners eventually got their act together and had a go at us.

As the fighting gathered momentum and more and more Arsenal attacked us, the gap in the crowd became massive and it wasn't too long before the old Bill came steaming in with truncheons flying everywhere. At first, the old Bill seemed happy to shepherd us over to the far right side of the terrace with a police cordon around us, but by this time there were so many Gooners around us that the coppers were having problems holding them back. They eventually moved us to the front of the terrace and started to escort us into the paddock that ran along the side of the pitch. As we were climbing onto the side of the pitch a few game Arsenal boys jumped over the parapet wall and continued the battle around the corner flag. The old Bill finally pushed them back into the North Bank but in the melee a young Arsenal lad had got himself trapped in the United mob and the lone Gooner ended up in the side paddock with us. I noticed him looking around and searching for any familiar faces, but there weren't any. With more and more Reds piling into the side paddock, the young kid decided it was time for action, and at the top of his voice he shouted out, "I'm Arsenal. - I'm Arsenal you cunts." This was soon followed by, "Come on you wankers. - Who wants it?" Because of his tender years (he didn't look much older than fourteen), we didn't pay much attention to him but still he continued with his verbal abuse and threats and was getting very agitated. Then when he saw a young Red walking up the small terrace, he launched himself at him. The Red didn't know what had hit him. The two young kids were soon rolling around the terrace with the older United boys pulling them apart just as the old Bill arrived on the scene. Much to the objection of the surrounding Reds, they marched off both the younger lads around the pitch. Talk about wrong place, wrong time! We tried to tell the law what had happened, and explained the young Red was definitely the innocent party, but of course it fell on deaf ears.

After the game we joined up with the mass of United who had been in the Southbank and marched back to Holloway Tube station. There were a few skirmishes with small mobs of Arsenal before we got to the tube station but as we walked along Holloway Road, we spotted a large Arsenal mob, which must have been two hundred strong. After throwing verbal insults at each other we had started to cross the road and were about to jump over the dividing metal railings when four transit vans came to a screaming halt next to us, and a bunch of evil and wild bastards (aka the Special Patrol Group) steamed into us. A few of them had standard short truncheons but the majority of them had long night-sticks or baseball bats and their main target seemed to be the head. I'm not exaggerating when I say the aftermath of the SPG's whirlwind attack made Holloway Road look like a battlefield. I have never before, or since seen so many people with blood pouring from their heads. They were as bad, if not worse than any of the European riot police I had seen in action. After counting my blessings that I had avoided a whack around the head and only received a truncheon across the ribs, I jumped on the tube.

We got off at Kings Cross with a small mob of United and started to walk up to Euston. We had only gone a few hundred yards before we were attacked by large mob of Arsenal who appeared from nowhere. There was no shouting or massive roars, they just went for us and within seconds we were completely surrounded. I was totally unaware of their presence until I received a heavy blow to the side of my head. After that it was total confusion and survival mode kicked in. Even though there were fists and boots flying at us from all angles, a few of us managed to fight our way through them, but a gang of them continued to chase us as we ran towards Euston.

We hadn't run very far when we saw another mob in front of us. Fortunately, they turned out to be Reds and our pursuers became the pursued. We ran the Gooners back down to King's Cross but when I spotted a couple of transit vans on the other side of the road, I decided I didn't want to risk running into the SPG again. I headed back to Euston, which turned out to be a good move because Dave, Speedy, Eddie and I got on the last train to Brum by the skin of our teeth.

There was always fun and games on the Milk Train and this trip was no exception. We were only twenty minutes or so out of Euston when the word went around that the buffet car was being done over. So immediately we made our way to the scene of the crime and sure enough the metal roller shutters had been forced open and about twenty Brummie Reds were helping themselves to the well packed shelves. Some of the lads where brazenly sitting in the Buffet car drinking the stolen beer and smashing the miniature bottles of spirits. I was a bit more cautious and took my booty back to the comfort of my seat to consume. As we approached Rugby train station, we had an unscheduled stop and a load of local plod boarded the train. On seeing this we immediately removed the empty cans off our table and did our best to hide them underneath the seats. The coppers walked up and down our carriage a few times and before long a very youthful looking boy in blue asked me if I had visited the Buffet car. Being the cocky sod that I was, I started taking the piss out of the fresh-faced officer and began singing, **"Baby-face you've got the cutest little baby-face."** He was not amused and when he wandered off without saying a word, I naïvely thought I had seen last of him. He soon returned with a couple of very aggressive women sergeants and they immediately told me that other passengers had informed them that I had stolen alcohol from the Buffet bar. Before I could proclaim my innocence, they were dragging me out of my seat and off the train and I was thrown into the back of a police car.

I was left in the back of the police car for quite a while before two coppers turned up and jumped into the front seats. Before doing that though, they opened one of the backdoors and placed two four packs of beer on the back seat next to me. The copper in the passenger seat turned around and told me I was under arrest for criminal damage and theft. Then he added, "Any smart answers to that?" I assumed the beer cans that had been put into the car were going to be tested for fingerprints and used as evidence against me. I thought the possibility of my prints being on them were pretty slim, but I wasn't going to take any chances. When the car started to drive away from the train, I picked up a pack of beer in each hand and said, "Mind if I have a drink officer?" The two coppers went barmy and started arguing and blaming each other for putting the cans next to me. When we arrived at Rugby nick the coppers admitted their schoolboy error and the desk sergeant made the coppers look about 2 inches tall. He gave them a right bollockin' and as you can imagine they were as popular as a turd in a swimming pool.

Not surprisingly, I was thrown into the cells headfirst. I was kept in the cells until mid morning when I was released without charge. On hearing this good news, I said to one of the coppers, "Any chance of a lift back to Brum?" He didn't have to answer as his bulging eyes and distorted face said everything. The coppers did end up having the last laugh though; as I left the cop shop it was raining cats and dogs so I popped my head back inside the station and enquired to which direction the train station would be. The response 'for me to buy myself a fucking map' didn't really help me. After following some dodgy directions, it took me well over half an hour to get to the train station by which time I was soaked to the skin and resembled a drowned rat. To add insult to injury there were *problems on the lines* and I had to wait almost three hours for a train.

WEMBLEY BECKONS RAMPANT UNITED

Robert Armstrong
Arsenal 2, Manchester United 4

Manchester United played with immense fire and determination to inflict a convincing defeat on Arsenal in the first leg of their Milk Cup semi-final at Highbury last night: It was United's first victory at Highbury for 15 years.

United's goal by Whiteside, Stapleton and Coppell (two), have probably put Wembley beyond the reach of Arsenal who will no doubt try to salvage their pride further in the second leg at Old Trafford next Wednesday.

Arsenal supporters will point to the departure of David O' Leary on a stretcher just before half-time as the reason for their sudden collapse. But even before the centre-back's damaging collision with Moses, United looked rampant, having blown Arsenal's cover to take a 2-0 lead. However, goals by Woodcock and Nicholas keep the door ever so slightly ajar.

This setback stung Arsenal's midfield trio of Rix, Talbot and Nicholas, into a more aggressive policy, which bore fruit in providing their strikers.

United's defensive partnership of Moran and McQueen coolly disposed of the series of high balls that Rix and Sansom pumped towards the far post.

When United were unable to contain Arsenal's rather predictable movement by fair means their defenders were often ready to act beyond the permitted laws. Both Robson and Albiston had their names taken by Mr Martin for fouls on Petrovic and Nicholas respectively.

United had the lion's share of possession for lengthy periods, with Coppell always making a threatening impact on the right.

However, Arsenal appeared to be establishing their usual authority in defence when United capped a lengthy period of early pressure with a goal of the highest quality after 19 minutes. Arsenal lost concentration on the right and allowed Moses who had worked industriously in support of Coppell to hoist a high looping ball into the path of the unmarked Whiteside. The young Irishman left Jennings helpless with a fierce low volley from 12 yards.

Chapter 20.
Dundee Utd. '84

12th December '84
Dundee Utd. 2 – 3 Hughes, Muhren, McGuiness o.g. (21,821)

United Line–Up
Bailey, Gidman, McQueen, Duxbury, Albiston, Moses, Robson, Muhren,
*Strachan, Hughes, Stapleton **Subs - ** Wealands, Whiteside, Olsen,*
Blackmore, Brazil

Manager
Ron Atkinson

UEFA Cup 3rd Round 2nd Leg

A few weeks before United played their first ever competitive game against Scottish opposition, United suffered a humiliating 5 – 0 league defeat at the hands of Everton at Goodison Park. Then to add salt to the wounds just four days later Everton knocked United out of the League Cup with a 2 – 1 victory at Old Trafford. After beating Hungary's ETO FC Gyor 5 - 2 on aggregate in the first round of the UEFA Cup, Then the Reds narrowly defeated PSV Eindhoven 1 – 0 on aggregate. United were then drawn against Dundee United. After a pulsating 2 – 2 draw at Old Trafford, United made it through to the quarter- final stages after a 2 – 3 victory at Tannadice Park. In the quarterfinals a 1 – 1 aggregate score resulted in a penalty shootout, which United lost 5 – 4 to losing finalists Videton.

There was a fair amount of violence before and after the first leg at Old Trafford. Before the game there were about 40 of us drinking in The Garrett not far from Oxford Road station, and to our amazement a small gang of very pissed Dundee United fans came charging into the pub and told us they had come to take over Manchester. They were only young lads, and nobody took them too seriously until one of them produced a knife. They were quickly ran out of the pub and chased up the road. I think most of us were a bit shocked at the number of fans that Dundee United brought down to Old Trafford. I personally thought they would only bring a few hundred, but they packed out the Scoreboard. After the game there were a some very mouthy Jocks on the train back to Oxford Road station and few scuffles broke out in our carriage; but it went off big style on the station platform and the Jocks got absolutely battered. As fists and boots were flying around, Jonnie pulled out a blade and chased a few of them off the station platform.

As we boarded the coaches in Manchester at 7am on the day of the return leg, we all thought we would be in for a rough time up in Dundee. One of the lads that had travelled up with us from Brum earlier that day was from the Black Country and called Charlie. He was always strapped for cash and was constantly looking for creative ways of get his hands on a few readies and certainly used all his ingenuity to get the money for the trip up to Dundee. His grandad had a fair few bob stashed away but was fast losing his marbles. Charlie couldn't bring himself to steal directly from his grandad so came up with a cunning plan. He asked his grandad if he fancied a trip to Blackpool to see the illuminations, to which the grandad readily agreed. Charlie of course had no intention of taking him all the way to Blackpool, so he put the old man in his car and drove him around for twenty minutes or so until his grandad had fell asleep. When he was sure he was fast asleep, Charlie stopped the car, lent over his grandad and put his watch ten hours forward, then drove him back home. When Charlie got him home, he immediately told him what a great day they'd had in Blackpool and he easily convinced his grandad that he had been to the tower ballroom, rode on the big dipper and had a slap-up meal in the best hotel in town. He also told his grandad that he had spent a fortune and was well out of pocket, to which his grandad replied, "Let me give you a few quid for the petrol, is £50 okay?" Charlie said, "If that's all you can afford, that's fine." His grandad gave him £100, which was not far off a week's wages back then.

The Journey up to Scotland was just like any other trip to an away game, lots of beer and taking the piss out of each other and of course the poor driver, who must have had a dozen empty beer cans thrown at his head. We were north of Newcastle when the driver agreed to make our first pit stop and our two coaches pulled into a small country pub. It was only just opening time and the look on the landlord's face when we all marched into his boozer was a picture. We got talking to him and he said he had been quiet all week and a hundred people dropping into pub unexpectedly was a much-needed boost. The landlord and one of his staff were working like mad to keep the beer flowing, and then would you Adam and Eve it, another coach pulled up outside the pub. But the coach wasn't full of Reds, they were Celtic fans travelling in

264

the opposite direction. In a strange twist of fate, Celtic were playing at Old Trafford that night because UEFA had insisted that Celtic's recent game against Rapid Vienna had to be replayed at a neutral ground because of the crowd trouble caused at Park Head. The Rapid goalkeeper and a linesman were both hit by bottles thrown from the crowd and several spectators ran onto the pitch and squared up to the Rapid players.

The replay of the second leg that was staged at Old Trafford was definitely not devoid of any violence. The Rapid keeper was attacked on the pitch by a Celtic fan and another Rapid player was kicked in the bollocks by a wild Jock. At the final whistle the Rapid Vienna players were escorted off the pitch by the old Bill. Remarkably, more people attended the match at Old Trafford than the original tie played at Celtic Park! Anyway, there wasn't any bother with the Celtic fans, one of them was wearing a United scarf and if I remember correctly a few of them had the stupid 'half & half' hats. As we all probably still recall, back then, we still had a good relationship with the green and white side of Glasgow, but after all the trouble up in Glasgow following our 1 − 0 defeat in 2006 I don't think a meeting of United and Celtic fans would be as cordial these days. And talking of not being cordial, our welcome into Dundee was none too friendly and we had several bricks thrown at our coaches by young kids. Supporting a rival team and being English I suppose it was only to be expected. Luckily none of the coach windows were smashed.

Egan, a great lad from Aldershot, who sadly is no longer with us, had a brother who ran a club in Dundee and arranged for the club to be opened up for us for the afternoon. The club was called The Beehive and it was three floors of hedonistic delight. All three levels had bars with each level having its own speciality. The ground floor had a couple of pool tables, a temporary blackjack table, and a TV showing the United v Dundee United first leg at Old Trafford. The middle floor had a few TV's that constantly played old United games from the 60's and 70's. But by far the most popular was the top level; besides serving food they also had two large screens showing Hardcore Porn. Within a few minutes of being in there Dave kindly informed me that he could smash concrete with his tool because it was that hard. Hardcore Porn wasn't at a press of a button as it is today. Usually the only way you got to see explicit films like the ones we were watching, was to visit a seedy backstreet sex cinema, or so I was told! Understandably most of the lads were transfixed to the screens and were bulging with excitement. But one young pissed-up Manchester lad that couldn't contain himself got his cock out and said, "Sorry boys, I've just got to have a wank." His trousers were down around his ankles and he unashamedly gave himself a 'Hand Shandy'. Dave was getting a little over excited himself and enthusiastically shouted over to the lad who was pleasuring himself, "You can do me, when you've finished tossing yourself off." The dirty little bastard just carried on wanking until he shot his load. Then in true male style, with cock in hand and spunk all over his shirt, he fell asleep. The sight was too much to take and I left the carnal delights of the top floor and wandered down to the middle floor to watch some of the old United games. I had only been in there for a few minutes when I heard someone shout out, "Fuck off you Munich bastards." It was a bitter Blue who had travelled up on our coaches with his so- called mates. A bit of an altercation immediately followed, and a few Reds grabbed hold of the mouthy Blue from behind and held his arms while another Red wrapped his arm around his neck in a strangle hold. While being restrained, one of the Blues' mates went eyeball to eyeball with him and a few insults were exchanged. The United fan then continually head-butted him for what seemed like an age. All the time the City fan was getting nutted, he was shouting out, "You're fuckin' dead when you get back to Manchester - Fuckin' Dead!"

When he finally stopped nutting the bitter and now battered Blue, his face was in a right mess. Soon the lads had to let him go and he just crashed to the floor like a sack of shit. All the time I was there, nobody went to the aid of the City fan and just left him lying on the floor, moaning and groaning.

Not long after this incident some of the Reds who hadn't got tickets went in search of any spares and soon discovered that Dundee could be a bit of a moody town. We entered quite a few packed pubs that soon went deathly quiet as we stood at the bar. Understandably with that sort of welcome, we immediately did an about turn and walked straight out again. For some unexplained reason half the pub followed us out and chased us up the road but were fortunately saved when a vanload of coppers filed across the road and stopped our pursuers from kicking the crap out of us.

We eventually found an English-friendly pub and even managed to pick up a few tickets, however, not at the United end. Not too far from kick-off time we left the pub to make our way to the ground with one of the bar staff pointing us in the right direction. But to our dismay it was going to be a good twenty minutes' walk. We were all a bit worse for wear after a few jars and to cap it off, the weather was fuckin' freezing cold. We asked the barman to call us a few taxis, but he informed because of the heavy traffic on match days, taxis wouldn't go anywhere near the ground. Very reluctantly we started our gloomy trek towards Tannadice Park. We hadn't gone very far when Colin pointed out an ice cream van and commented, "Only in Scotland would you find a fuckin' ice cream van in the middle of winter." With every intention of taking the piss out of the bloke in the ice cream van, several of the lads wandered across the road and were soon having the craic with him. He turned out to be quite quick-witted and when one of the lads said, "I bet you haven't sold many in this weather," he replied, "Na Bovva – I double up as a taxi." With that, he was asked how much to the ground? To which he said it would be £1 a head. After confirming that he was serious, ten or more of us scrambled into his ice cream van and with the repetitive tinny music playing, away we headed off to Tannadice Park. Of course, within seconds we were behaving like five-year-olds and making ourselves ice cream cones and shoving them into each other's faces. When we came across a small mob of Jocks, we threw cans of pop at them and all the driver said was, "You'll be paying extra for that!" We were fucking around so much in the ice cream van it's a wonder it didn't topple over. When we arrived at the ground, we were all covered in ice cream, as were the windows of the van. We all piled out of the ice cream van with some using the serving hatch and others through the driver's door, the old Bill stared open mouthed and in disbelief at what they had just witnessed.

Even though we only had two tickets between us most of the lads jumped the turnstiles without any problem. We were in a small Paddock along the side of the pitch and of course surrounded by the jocks. Everything was ok until Hughes put United 1 – 0 up. Naturally we cheered, which resulted in a few punches flying around, which were quickly broken up by the coppers. Following Hughes' goal, Harry from Cannock ran on the pitch to help Hughes celebrate his goal. For his bravado, Harry was immediately arrested and subsequently spent the night in the local nick. When Harry was up in court the next morning the Judge must have been a Dundee United fan because for the simple care-free crime of running onto the pitch, he sentenced him to fourteen days in a Perth prison. Instead of turkey and all the trimmings, Harry ended up having porridge for Christmas dinner.

The atmosphere in the small Paddock remained hostile for the rest of the game, but it really got nasty after the home team scored their second goal. Charlie had gotten himself a pie only a few seconds earlier and when they scored, one of the Jocks got right in Charlie's face as he celebrated the goal, so when the Jock turned around to face the pitch, Charlie rammed his warm pie into the back of the Jocks neck. "What the fuck is that!" Screamed the Jock. "You've got on my tits so much, I've just been sick all over you," Charlie shouted back in the Jocks ear, then kicked him in the back, which sent him flying. This incident then led to a mass brawl with the coppers' truncheons soon raining down on us. By the end of the game there were more coppers around us than in our little mob and the fuckers then kept us in the freezing stadium like prisoners in a Gulag. We were only allowed to exit the stadium when the home fans had left.

Unfortunately, the ice cream van was nowhere to be seen when we came out of the ground, so we had the long walk back to The Beehive in the bitter cold. To keep our minds off the freezing weather, we started speculating as to what pleasures may be waiting for us. More Porno movies, maybe a couple of strippers, even a lesbian act perhaps? When we arrived back at the Beehive we were stopped in our tracks and got the shock of our lives. In the ground floor bar were big hairy bodybuilders with big black (bum-tickler) moustaches, wearing leather waistcoats and caps. Mincing down the stairs together was a six-foot-tall pink rabbit who was holding hands with an old bloke dressed as goldilocks. It's not something you see every day in Walsall, let alone in Dundee! The Beehive was a woofters club, and here we were, all red-blooded hetro's, standing in the doorway of a bar frequented by chutney ferrets. To say we were wide-eyed and speechless is an understatement.

After the long walk back, and being finally out of the cold, having a beer was the only thing we were concerned with. While it was playing on our minds what fudge-packers get up to, we didn't notice the bouncers coming over to see us. "Sorry gentlemen. - No Jeans." We turned around in unison and saw two big fuckers standing there with their legs astride and arms folded. "No Jeans! – What! No Fuckin' Jeans," Ged exclaimed in shock. "There's blokes walking around dressed as pink rabbits and goldilocks and you don't allow fuckin' jeans?" One of the bouncers gave Ged a cold stare and replied, "They're regulars." "I suppose the Three Bears and the Village People are also regulars?" Ged replied sarcastically. "Fuck off! - You're not staying!" came the bouncer's instant response. So, off we went back out in the cold looking for a late-night pub that wasn't full of pufters.

Soon we came across a Chinese restaurant and decided to go for a nosebag. The waiters were clearing up as we entered the restaurant and we were told they were closed. But after a few words with the manager and promising we would be on our best behaviour he said we could stay. Because it was late, we were only offered limited choices off the menu, that wasn't a major problem. The most important thing was that they were serving us with bottles of beer. Probably because the Chinky waiters and other restaurant staff wanted to go home, the waiters were rude and arrogant, and the food was awful. When the bill was presented, we complained to the manager, but he simply said we were lucky to find somewhere to eat that time of night. After a bit of toe-to-toe arguing with the manager all the waiters stepped forward towards us, all tooled up with kitchen utensils. I've seen a few Kung Fu films and thought one should never underestimate a Chinky, they're all like Bruce Lee; small, but quick as fuck. We had settled the bill and the rest of the lads were leaving when trust me I needed a jimmy, while the rest of the lads exited the restaurant, I quickly popped into the bogs. When I came out a couple of minutes later, the restaurant was empty, so I wandered around for a few seconds then looked through the porthole in the kitchen door and saw all the staff huddled around eating. Still fuming about how the manager had treated us, I was looking for ways to inflict some revenge on the little shit. I then noticed two massive ornamental vases that stood at the top of the small set of stairs that lead down to the street. *'Them fuckers will do,'* I thought to myself. I marched across the restaurant and pushed the first vase, which just toppled over and spilled out its soil. *'Fuck that! I'll put a bit more elbow grease in the second one'* so I gave it an almighty shove. It hit the floor with a loud crack and snapped to pieces. Job done! I rushed down the steps to the front door and to my dismay the door was bolted and deadlocked. After initially pulling, banging and kicking the door without any sign of it opening, I went in search of an alternative exit from the restaurant. Unfortunately, there wasn't one, so the only thing I could do was to go to the kitchen and ask if any of the Chinkies would open the door and let me out, hoping that they wouldn't notice the vases lying broken on the floor. Some hope! I gingerly walked into the kitchen and for several seconds stood staring at all the noisy staff rabbiting away. As soon as they noticed me in the doorway, the chattering suddenly stopped, and they all gave me daggers. I quickly explained that I'd been in the toilet when they were locking up and could one of them come and open the front door for me. After a brief discussion between themselves, one of them picked up a set of keys, and still chomping on his 'beef and brokkerie', walked towards me. I led the way through the restaurant and all the time I was thinking to myself, *'don't notice the vases - Don't notice the vases.'* When we reached the top of the steps, I tried to stand in front of one of the vases, while the Chinky continued chomping his meal. Walking down the steps I thought for a second he hadn't noticed the vases. But as he took a second step he suddenly turned around and did a double take and shouted, "ne gugga bi ginn quin tan fooo," which roughly translated to, "You Cunt!" I told him I had nothing to do with the vases being pushed over, but he just kept shouting at me in Mandarin or whatever language he was using. Yelling at me at a hundred miles an hour was bad enough, but when he started walking back up the steps, I was a bit flustered and in a bit of a panic for a few seconds. Then I thought if he goes back into the kitchen and gets the rest of the yellow peril out here, I will probably end up part of next weeks' chow mein take-away. So, I made a grab for his keys and we were soon wrestling on the steps. After only a few seconds I got my forearm against his throat and he let go of the keys. I had released the bolts off the door when I first tried to leave the restaurant so all I had to do was unlock the door, but while I was trying to find the correct key the Chinky jumped up and was screaming his head off and he ran back towards the kitchen. Fortunately there were only two deadlock keys and I managed to open the door before the Kung Fu army could practice their Origami on me. I fell into the street and ran as fast as my little legs would carry me. I took a glance back and saw them standing at the front of the restaurant and feeling immense relief that they hadn't given chase.

On the Journey back to Manchester we stopped at a service station, when I got back on the coach, I noticed the City fan was sitting a few seats behind me and he looked like the Elephant Man after a crazy night on the piss. Sitting next to him was the lad that had caused the damage to his face and they seemed to be in a deep and reflective conversation. I later found out that the City fan was one of City's top boys and the United fan who had rearranged his face may well have been in danger of his life when he got back to Manchester.

IT'S DEFLECTED GLORY AS MUHREN GOAL SINKS SAD DUNDEE

Dundee Utd 2, Manchester United 3
Aggregate, 4 — 5

VETERAN Arnold Muhren sweet-swinging left foot last night powered Manchester United uneasily into the quarter finals of the UEFA Cup.

Only then, as last as the 78th minute of the pulsating match, when Muhren's deflected shot flew past goal keeping magician, Hamish McAlpine, dare United remotely relax.

It was Muhren's first goal in his second come back game in place of Jasper Olsen. That can now be raised as a gamble with a handsome pay-off United prepare for another big cash-in next spring.

A tension packed and scrappy second leg could have gone either way and even into a penalty shoot-Despite their uncertainty in defence, and their slices of good luck, Ron Atkinsons's side showed a resolution, even if they failed to produce football of a high calibre.

It was scrappy, uncreative—and nerve-wracking.

Strike

The chance to settle down and elevate the tie to a higher level came in the 12th minute with a rapier strike by Mark Hughes, thanks to Gordon Strachan.

That lead lasted just 13 minutes when the unmarked David Dodds beat Gary Bailey with ease and then the Scots had to survive a horrendous own goal five minutes short of half time.

A retaken Strachan corner was flicked on by the ever-eager head of Hughes and the ball flew into the net as Gary McGinnis desperately tried to head it clear.

But the local heroes equalised yet again in the 55th minute, when Gordon McQueen failed to cut out a free kick and Paul Hegarty was there with a powerful header to make it 2-2.

It had always seemed unlikely that United would beat McAlpine after his brilliant diverted dive to stop the deflected shot by the ever-busy Remi Moses in the 72nd minute. But six minutes later came the Muhren magic. His shot apparently flicked off McQueen on its way through a packed goalmouth barring McAlpine's vision.

It was, at last, all over for a desperately relieved Manchester United.

Chapter 21.
Chelsea '84

29th December '84
Chelsea   1 – 3   Hughes, Moses, Stapleton   (42,197)

United Line–Up
*Bailey, Duxbury, McQueen, McGrath, Albiston, Muhren, Robson, Moses, Strachen, Hughes, Stapleton. **Sub -** Brazil*

Manager
Ron Atkinson

League Position After the Game

P	*W*	*D*	*L*	*F*	*A*	*Pts*	*Pos*
20	11	5	4	41	25	38	3rd

Over the Christmas period The Reds won both their home games 3 – 0, but the attendances at Old Trafford were very disappointing with less than 37,000 turning up for each game. In January we lost all of our home league games, but then went on an unbeaten run until mid-April. A disappointing end to the league season resulted in a 5 -1 thrashing away to Watford. But all was not lost! A good cup run saw United take on the role of Scouse Busters once again, and a wonder goal from Big Norman saw us lift the FA Cup for the second time in three seasons, and of course stopped Everton doing the League & Cup Double. The FA Cup final victory was bitter – sweet for star defender Kevin Moran, as he became the first player to be sent off in an FA Cup final at Wembley.

Ever since the Sun newspaper printed a load of crap in the late seventies about the hatred between United and Chelsea, the encounters between the two clubs had become battlegrounds for rival supporters. When Chelsea turned up in massive numbers at Old Trafford in '77 (the first fans to do so in many years!) thousands of United fans battled with the police before and after the game to get at the 'Chelsea Rent Boys'. However, the extremely heavy police presence meant United couldn't get anywhere near the invading Cockneys. The Chelsea mob were escorted to the ground and they were all safely marshalled into the Scoreboard well before 2pm. It was getting on for 6pm before the coppers felt confident enough to open the gates and let the Cockneys fuckers out.

Because of the expected trouble at Stamford Bridge, and the high possibility of their trains getting wrecked, British Rail had cancelled 'The Specials' so most of the Manchester lads travelled down to London by coach. Burnsy, Jonnie, and a few of the Gorton lads had booked on coaches organized by the infamous Eddie B. They had agreed to pick me up, along with a few of the Brummies including Dave and Mad Dog at Hilton Park service stations on the M6. When Eddie B. booked the three coaches, he informed the coach company that they would be taking a hundred and fifty young girls to see The Osmond's at the Victoria Theatre in London. So, you can imagine the look of horror and dread on the driver's faces when they turned up at the pickup point in Manchester and saw a large mob of United supporters waiting for them.

The coach that we boarded at Hilton Park was a right old nail and I questioned whether it would be able to make it all the way to London. Sure enough just after passing Coventry, the coach started to overheat, so we had to stop at every other service station for water. On the journey the driver had so many empty beer cans thrown at him, he stopped the coach on the hard shoulder and announced, "next time anything is thrown at me I'm going back to Manchester." The immediate response from one of the younger lads was, "If you're going back to Manchester you old cunt, you will be walking because we'll take the fucking coach." With that said, we didn't hear any more complaints from the driver.

We finally arrived in London at half past two, and probably because of all the abuse the driver received on the journey down to 'The Smoke,' he refused to take us to Stamford Bridge and insisted he would drop us off at the theatre in Victoria as per the initial booking details.

After getting the tube to Stamford Bridge I had just about managed to get into the United end. The turnstile gates were closed behind me and most of the lads were locked out. Mad Dog, Dave a few others manage to get into The Shed, but they had a very rough time of it. The Rent Boys inside the ground were waiting at the turnstiles and questioning any strange faces coming through. Mad Dog managed to get past the turnstile mob, only because they were battering a couple of Manchester lads who had just gone into the ground before him. There were also small mobs of Chelsea wandering all over The Shed looking for stray Reds, and after witnessing a few more Reds getting a good kicking Mad Dog left the ground at halftime.

In the United end, we were having our own fun and games. At halftime, a mob of about twenty had come out of the main stand to our left and jumped into our section, they were led by a massive mixed-race geezer. I thought they must be United but, as they mingled into the crowd, the old Bill must have recognized a few faces or seen them entering the large open terrace. Either way they were soon surrounded and in doing so, the little mob started chanting, *"Chel-sea."* There was an immediate rush towards the Chelsea mob but with truncheons drawn the coppers made sure the Reds couldn't get anywhere near them. The liberty takers were then escorted back into their seats without any major incident.

After the game we made our way to Fulham Broadway tube station and started piling onto the platform. No sooner were we on the platform, the Chelsea fans were attacking us and mainly because of their sheer numbers, they chased us back up the stairs, but as more and more United started coming into the station we soon ran Chelsea back down the stairs and along the platform. At the end of the platform there was another set of stairs leading to a footbridge, we certainly had the momentum and pursued the Chelsea fans up the stairs over the linking bridge and down the steps to the next platform. As the Chelsea mob disappeared up another set of stairs, I was thinking how easy it was running them on their own patch, but, as we raced along the platform after them, we stopped dead at the bottom of the stairs. The Rent boys had made a stand at the top of the stairs and as we started to make our way towards them, missiles rained down on us. We backed off a little and I guess they probably sensed that by now they may have regained the upper hand. The Chelsea mob came charging down the stairs at us and chased us back over to the adjacent platform. Then, when we were at the top of the stairs leading out to the exit, we made a stand and it was The Rent Boys turn to do one. We chased Chelsea back and forth along the platform and this little masquerade continued for quite a while and became quite farcical like a scene from the Keystone Cops. The game of cat and mouse kept flipping one way and another and when the coppers eventually turned up, about fifty of us managed to avoid being caught up in an escort by jumping on a train.

There were a few Chelsea in the carriage we were on and the adjoining carriages were full of them, but they didn't look as if they were looking for any trouble, unlike like the mob who were waiting for us at next station.

Pulling into West Brompton, we saw the platform was packed with Chelsea, and as soon as they clocked us, they started banging and kicking the outside of the train. Fortunately, the driver didn't open the doors, but we weren't completely safe. The Rent Boys in the adjoining carriages got brave all of sudden and part of our little mob fought with them through the small linking doors to stop them getting into our carriage.

The noise from the banging on the outside of the train became deafening and I was hoping and praying the train driver would get his finger out and move away from the station. But no such luck. The noise became even more frightening when the first window went through and a metal rod was menacingly brandished into the carriage. When the window next to me was smashed I threw myself on the floor and covered my head. The screaming from the Chelsea mob was terrifying, and as more and more windows were smashed, I was joined on the floor of the train by most of the other Reds in the carriage.

We were almost certainly saved by a few lads who were much braver than us. They somehow managed to stop the tooled-up Chelsea from climbing through the broken windows. As I lay on the floor with my hands over my head, I could clearly hear the United lads yelling at each other to push back the Cockneys who were hell-bent on getting into our carriage. When the train finally pulled away from the platform the carriage looked like a bomb had gone off in it and one of the Reds that had helped to keep the Chelsea mob at bay had blood streaming down his face from a nasty wound to his forehead.

We all got off at the next tube station and walked down to Sloan Square. This was 'Yuppie heartland' so quite a few innocent bystanders got whacked and a few shop windows were smashed and looted. But the most outrageous moment was when a group of Reds tried to break the window of a jewellers; several objects were thrown at the window, but they just bounced off, so three of the lads tried to pick up concrete waste bin but struggled with its weight. A few more lads came to their assistance and once the big lump of concrete was balanced, they charged at the window with such force the concrete bin went straight through it and there was a free for all to grab as much bling as possible. They didn't get away without any confrontation though. An old dear who was standing on the pavement and had witnessed the vandalism repeatedly called out, "Phone the Police," while waving her walking stick around, hitting anyone who was in striking distance. She was definitely a game old bird and even tried to apprehend a couple of the lads as they made their escape. Thinking this was all getting a bit heavy and the old Bill would be on the scene very shortly, I decided to make my way up to Victoria and hopefully find the coaches. I left just in time because after walking just a few hundred yards, four riot vans with their sirens screaming speed past me. When I got to the coaches, I was surprised that only about twenty lads, who included Dave and Mad Dog, had made it back.

The rumours were that the rest of the lads had headed straight for Euston, no doubts to have 'The Row' with other rival fans.

The coach drivers were getting very pissed off waiting for the rest of their passengers to turn up and announced they weren't going to wait any longer, so with less than ten Reds on each coach we started to make our way out of Victoria. They say lightning doesn't strike twice, well, it definitely did on this occasion. The coaches had only travelled a very short distance when we passed a large mob of Chelsea. To avoid any eye contact as soon as I spotted them, I immediately moved to the opposite side of the almost empty coach, Mad Dog, who had been sitting right in front of me not only decided to stay in his window seat, he also decided to wind up the Chelsea mob by giving them the fingers, then banging on the window while chanting, "**Uni-ted!**" If that wasn't bad enough, when our coach pulled away, Mad Dog went to the back of the coach and continued to hurl abuse at the angry Chelsea mob.

When our coach turned the corner, we lost sight of the baying mob and thought that was the last we'd see of them; how wrong were we? We had only gone a few hundred yards and we hit a wall of traffic, and in no time a hundred or so Chelsea fans surrounded our coach. One of them opened the exit door next to the driver and had just started to make his way onto the coach when the quick-thinking driver jumped up and kicked him in the chest, sending him flying back onto the pavement. The driver then pushed the door shut and held onto the long door handle for dear life. As the Chelsea mob kicked and thumped the door the driver screamed out for help and thankfully a couple of the lads sitting at the front of the coach went to his assistance. The two lads took charge of holding the door handle while the driver got back behind the wheel. By now the Chelsea mob were going crazy and kicking lumps out of the coach, a couple of them had climbed onto the front bumper and had ripped off the massive windscreen wipers.

Even though the traffic in front of us had started to move, we couldn't go anywhere because there were about twenty of them standing in front of the coach and continually banging on the windscreen. With the exit door almost flying off its hinges because the Cockneys were now using a couple of old dustbins as battering rams, I was starting to think the bastards are going get in here any minute now. We were outnumbered by at least ten to one and there was literally no place to run and no place to hide. My heart sank and my bottle definitely went as I heard a loud bang and a brick smashed through one of the large side windows. That was the signal for the driver to take some positive action and it was like a scene from a Hollywood movie. Fuckin' and Blindin,' the driver rammed the coach into reverse and crashed into the car that was parked behind us, he then drove forwards and swung the coach across the road and drove down the opposite side of the street into oncoming traffic, sending most of the Chelsea mob diving for cover as he did so. As the driver swerved to avoid the on-coming traffic, he sent the front wing of one of the cars flying into the air. Then as the coach sped towards a set of traffic lights, which turned to red. "DON'T STOP," we all yelled! We approached the lights with the chasing Cockneys clearly visible in the drivers wing mirrors, so the driver stuck his fist on the coach horn and drove through the red lights. We didn't hit any more vehicles as we sped across the junction but several cars going through on the green signal ended up mounting the kerb or crashing into the back of each other. With this madness and chaos behind us, I went over to Mag Dog, smacked him across the head and said, "You caused all that fuckin' pandemonium and agro ya twat!" Mad Dog just grinned at me and replied, "I know. – Great wasn't it?"

ROBSON'S SWITCH INSPIRES UNITED

Chelsea 1, Manchester United 3

BRYAN ROBSON'S inspired captaincy turned impending defeat into crucial victory, enabling Manchester United to end a damaging away run and re-ignite their Championship campaign at the cost of Chelsea's defeat in nine matches, writes **Roger Malone**.

Yet United were fortunate not to be reduced to 10 men for all of the second half, because Mike Duxbury, the England right-back was guilty of an offence which, in many observers' eyes merited his being sent off.

That incident apart, United's attractiveness class in attack—Strachan's wing play. Hughes and Stapleton in the spearhead roles—merited their victory after three successive away defeats.

After Davies' goal rewarded Chelsea's fast-moving start in which United were penned in, and might have fallen further behind, Robson, as assistant manager Mick Brown explained afterwards, decided to alter his team's midfield set up.

Goal-line scramble

He moved himself forward from the withdrawn areas Chelsea's pressure were forcing him into—not all the way forward to a front-line role, but far enough, and wide enough to gamble on Chelsea's markers having to come with him.

It succeeded, with Robson positioned to begin all of the moves which led to well-taken goal by Hughes (22min). Moses three minutes later and to the one after 23 minutes which Stapleton will claim, although there was a suspicion of an own goal by McLaughlin in a goal-line scramble.

Yet a different final score might well have developed if Duxbury had paid the price law requires for violent conduct or serious foul play. As Dixon, later to make a costly penalty miss after 78 minutes, broke clear, shortly before half time, Duxbury grappled him to the ground in the manner of a rugby tackle.

Torquay referee Lester Shapter merely booked Duxbury. Ian McNeill, Chelsea's assistant manager, said afterwards: "A couple of years ago, that was an ordering-off offence. Mr McNeill was referring to the clamp-down by referees, which appears this season to have eased off, but surely soccer justice will be better served if rugby tackles lead to marching orders.

Chapter 22.
Amsterdam '86 Ajax & Dynamo Kiev

August 8th '86

Dynamo Kiev 1 – 1 Blackmore, won 4 – 1 on pens (27,500)

August 10th '86

Ajax 1 – 0 (23,000)

United Squad

Turner, Sivebaek, Hogg, Moran, Blackmore, Albiston, Duxbury, Strachan, McGrath, Whiteside, T. Gibson, C. Gibson, Olsen, Hanrahan, Stapleton, Davenport

Manager

Ron Atkinson

Amsterdam Tournament—Amsterdam Olympic Stadium

The Amsterdam Tournament started in 1975 and Ajax were runners up for the first three years, finally winning the tournament for the first time in 1978. They then went on to win the tournament a further nine times. This was United's second appearance in the competition and would eventually add the trophy to their already overflowing trophy cabinet in 2006. The last Amsterdam Tournament was played in 2009 and won by Portuguese giants Benfica.

On the home-front, the previous season United had won their first ten league games and only conceding two goals in the process. We looked odds on to win the league title, alas 'the wheels fell off the bus' and The Reds finished the season in 4th place! Having lost six of their first eight games of the '86 / '87 season, in early November, Ron Atkinson was replaced by a certain Mr. Alex Ferguson. And as they say - the rest is history!!

After experiencing a gale force nine storm on my return from Eindhoven a few years previous, I swore I would never do that sea crossing again, therefore I paid an extra few quid and boarded a little ten-seater City hopper from Birmingham to Amsterdam. Arriving in Schiphol, I headed for Central railway station where I had arranged to meet up with Dutch Pete and the lads who were travelling over on the ferry and were scheduled to arrive at Amsterdam Central roughly the same time as myself. When I spotted Dutch Pete, he was with a bunch of teenagers and strangely it seemed he was inviting one of them to punch him in the stomach. As I got nearer one of them did strike him in the stomach but not with a fist but with the boot. Dutch Pete didn't flinch and told the local teenagers, "If you think I'm tough, you wait until the proper Man United supporters arrive. They are men not boys, now go home." And without another word being spoken the gang wandered off. After saying our hellos, Pete told me he had spoken to several gangs of young Ajax fans on the station that morning and gave them some sound advice: 'basically, that the Man United fans are in a different league so fuck off out of here or you'll get your head kicked in'.

We waited at the station for almost two hours but when the lads from the ferry didn't turn up, we decided to go and have some light refreshments! As it turned out I missed all of the excitement not because the North Sea ferry was battered by a hundred foot waves, but because of the running battles on the decks between United and a West Ham mob lead by one of their top boys, The Colonel. Ged and the Manchester Boys along with The Flaherty's little crew were all on board and all confirmed it was absolute pandemonium on the ferry with the West Ham fans barricaded at the top of one of the staircases and literally fighting for their lives. When all of the trouble started, most of the terrified holidaymakers on the boats had retreated to the lower and car decks to safety. On the upper decks the Reds who were fighting their way up the stairs to get at the Cockneys were met with a multitude of knives and broken bottles, and quite a few of the United boys were slashed or stabbed. While all the fun and games on the stairs continued, the bars and duty-free shops were all being ransacked. The last time there was this level of violence and destruction on a ship was when Captain Morgan terrorised the Spanish Caribbean. With the crew unable to stop the looting and violence halfway across the North Sea the captain decided to turn the ferry round and head back to England. When the ferry docked back in Blighty there was an army police waiting for them. Countless number of arrests were made and after a lengthy court case a couple of lads that I knew both ended up with eight year stretches.

As the ferry sailed to Amsterdam for a second time, I was with Dutch Pete and a few of the lads still enjoying a few relaxing beers at Dutch Pete's local, The Royal Taste, which also served as our hotel and was conveniently located in the red-light district. It wasn't until late afternoon that the lads from the ferry finally showed up and Ged and the boys had just about enough time for a quick pint and to throw their bags in the room before we headed off to the game. What a disappointment that turned out to be, boring lack-lustre nil- nil draw; Just what you didn't want to see after being stuck on a ferry for almost twenty hours. Pissed off and in search of some excitement after the game we headed back into the Red-Light district and Dutch Pete showed us a few of the sights. There was everything on offer in the narrow tall display windows from model material to roly-polies and old grannies and everything in between.

Once we had finished with the window-shopping, we went into a seedy little sex club on a fact-finding mission. There were a couple of very tasty strippers, who were a bit tame, but definitely worth an ogle. Then from the sublime to the ridiculous, with a deafening fanfare playing in the background, a big Black Momma, or 'The Silver Back' as Tony called her, came bouncing onto the stage and the whole room seemed to shake. She was about five foot tall and five foot across and must have weighed well over sixteen stone. She was dressed as a tennis player and carried a tennis racket with a large dildo strapped to the end of it. After quickly stripping off, she got down to business and started ramming the big dildo into her fanny. As she pleasured herself, she got very animated and her massive tits were flying around so wildly, I thought she would end up with a couple of black eyes. Very erratically she stopped using the dildo tennis racket and shouted out that she wanted a volunteer. Tony's hand was up in a flash. She ignored Tony's enthusiasm and from the stage she scoured the room for a more suitable volunteer/ victim. She looked around the audience for a while, but Tony was still waving his arm and seemed like the only one game enough to get on stage with her. Seemingly unimpressed with Tonys' insistence, she walked down the steps from the stage and started to prowl around the room.

A couple of the lads and I were sitting on the front row and I was mightily relieved when she initially walked straight past us and eyed up the boys behind us. But she had led me into a false sense of security and when she appeared in front of me thirty seconds later and held out her hand and beckoned me on to the stage with her. I immediately shook my head and said "thanks − but NO THANKS"! Unfortunately, she wasn't taking no for an answer and grabbed hold of my hand and tried to pull me out of my seat. I held on to the back of the chair for dear life with my free hand. I managed to pull my other hand free from her grip and then with two hands holding onto the back of my chair, as hard as she tried, she couldn't move me. When she finally gave up trying to pull me out of my seat, she reluctantly took Tony up onto the stage with her.

Tony, the dirty bastard had a smile from ear to ear as the outrageous looking tennis player gently positioned him on his knees. She then laid back on a low sofa and slowly pushed a banana into her pussy. The banana was only pushed half in, and the skin of the exposed piece was seductively peeled back by the shameless stage temptress. When the peeled banana was revealed she beckoned Tony to eat it from her pussy. Before getting stuck in, Tony twisted round and to a loud cheer he gave the thumbs up to the lads, he then returned to the job in hand.

The lads champion lent forward and was just about to take the first tentative bite of the banana, when the Silver Back quickly crossed her legs and with a vice like grip trapped his head between her massive thighs. To roars of hysterical laughter, Tony's arms and legs were flapping about uncontrollably as his captor twisted and rolled her hips and tossed his head from side to side. When she released him, he immediately fell to the floor gasping for air. She then hastily dragged him to his feet and turned him around to face the applauding audience. Due to the lack of oxygen and the heat generated between the Silver Backs thighs, Tony's smiling face was as red as a beetroot, the banana squashed all over his mush and his wobbly legs just added to the surreal incident. The audience clapped and cheered the Big Black Momma who by now had lifted up Tony's arm in an act of triumph and yelled to the crowd, "Do you think he deserves a blow Job?" Tony excitedly encouraged the lads to agree, which of course they did, and a deserving Tony lay down on the sofa as the Silver Back gave him his reward for being such a good sport.

After leaving the sex club, Dutch Pete took us to a small quiet little bar in the back streets. It was a nice old fashioned bar and one of its main features was a shiny brass trumpet hanging next to the optics. After a couple of drinks Dutch Pete pointed out the trumpet, and casually announced that if anyone could play a tune on the trumpet then he and all of his friends would have free beer for the rest of the night. "Give the fucking thing here," Jonnie replied "I was in the boys' brigade, this will be a piece of piss." So Dutch Pete had a word with the landlord and he duly handed Jonnie the trumpet. Jonnie was taking it all very seriously and slowly he positioned the trumpet to his lips and adjusted his posture slightly, he then took a deep breath as the rest of the room fell silent. After a few tense seconds Jonnie blew with all his might and immediately disappeared in a cloud of black soot. Unbeknownst to all of us, with the exception of the landlord and Dutch Pete, the trumpet was full of soot. When the black cloud dispersed and Jonnie became visible again, he still had the trumpet to his lips and his face and hands were covered in soot. He resembled a miner coming out of the pit shaft just after he'd finishing a shift. "Bastards! I was going to play, "Onward Christian Soldiers." Bible-Bashing Jonnie angrily yelled. I'm not sure many of the lads had heard him say this as the noise of the laughter was so loud and quite a few of the lads were doubled up. Jonnie soon saw the funny side of it, he didn't bother cleaning the soot off his face for the rest of the night, he also didn't have to buy another beer.

The next day we were all a bit jaded from the previous night's exploits and we were having a few quiet drinks in the Royal Taste. A few lads and I were playing cards outside and watching the world go by, and what a world it was. After a couple of hours, we got bored with Three Card Bragg and Pontoon and someone suggested that if we all put in five Guilders, we would have enough money for a brass. All the lads agreed, and we decided to have a knockout game of cards, with the winner having a Lady-of-the-Night for a quid. The excitement quickly grew and there were plenty of moans and groans and of course cheers and celebrations as individuals were knocked out or went through to the next round. An overjoyed Jonnie was the eventual winner and he jumped around as if he'd just scored the winning goal for United.

Dutch Pete immediately said he'd take Jonnie to see the Swedish Twins – They never forget the 'bolls.' "Don't Forgot the Bolls," (the balls) became the catch phrase for the rest of the trip. As tempting as the Swedish twins sounded, Jonnie already had his eye on a Brazilian beauty who was only a few minutes' walk from our hotel. "She's fuckin' gorgeous," Jonnie exclaimed as he marched off with over twenty lads following him. Wilkie was in charge of his winnings to make sure he didn't bottle it, and God forbid, spend the money on anything other than a Good Time Girl!

When we arrived at the young ladies' room, Jonnie banged on the door and after a few seconds a woman opened the door. Understandably, she was a bit shocked to see a large gang of lads outside her door, but she took it in good humour. Jonnie was right, she was a stunner she had long black curly hair, a beautiful smile, a body you would die for and it looked like her tits were made from marble. Wilkie handed over the readies and with bellowing encouragement from the lads, Jonnnie entered the dusky maidens' boudoir. While he was inside having the time of his life, the rest of us stood in the street and chanted Jonnies' name. After only a few minutes the brass from next door flung open her door and shouted, "I'm entertaining! Keep quiet or I will call the police." Of course, we took no bleedin' notice of the young ladies' request and with us continuing to sing and chant, Jonnie's brass wasn't long in making an appearance herself. As she stood in her doorway she said, "Your friend cannot fulfil his duties with such a noisy crowd - please go home!" This got a tremendous roar of laughter from the lads and just encouraged us to chant even more lewd and suggestive songs.

A large gang of very boisterous, louds lads in a small narrow street soon attracted quite a bit of attention and other tourists stopped to see what all the commotion was about, this included a bunch of bewildered Oriental types who weren't shy in pushing their way to the front of the crowd. When the door finally opened again, Jonnie looked like the cat who had just got the cream – the lucky bastard. He got a great cheer from the crowd and the beautiful brass held up his arm in triumph then gave him a round of applause followed by the thumbs up to the lads. Not wanting to miss such a momentous occasion all the Orientals started to take loads of photos. There were more flashes than on a red carpet.

Following another heavy night on the piss we were walking back to our hotel when Jonnie suddenly decided to strip off and as we walked along the busy narrow streets, Jonnie left a trail of clothes behind him. Luckily for him we were picking up his discarded garments as he dropped them. When we arrived at the Royal Taste, Jonnie brazenly walked in and ordered a round of beers. The bar staff didn't blink an eye at his naked body.

Jonnie was staying in the hotel next door to us so, when our bar shut at 4am, and still stark bollock naked Jonnie staggered round to his hotel and banged on the door, then rang on the bell, then banged on the door again until finally the landlady came down and opened up. As soon as she appeared in the doorway Jonnie sighed, "I know I'm naked – I know I'm drunk - I know you hate me, but I just want my bed." Without a reply the landlady slammed the door in his face. So Jonnie wobbled his way back to our hotel and spent what was left of the night curled up on one of the bench seats in the bar.

The next morning I went down to the crowded breakfast room and as I stood in the doorway looking for a spare seat I saw Jonnie waving his hand, "Over here Grange," he shouted and as I walked towards him I noticed he didn't have a top on. '*Fuck! – He can't still be naked*'? I wondered. But of course, he was! Very apprehensively I sat down next him and tried my hardest to just focus forward and keep a safe distance. But as I sat down Jonnie put his arm around me and said, "what a great craic we had last night," and acted as if sitting in a hotel breakfast room in the buff was an everyday occurrence. It seemed like it was for the young girls who were serving and clearing the tables, they had obviously seen it all before and didn't give Jonnie a second glance.

At United's first game against Dynamo Kiev we hadn't seen any trouble at all. However, as we made our way to the ground to see United take on Ajax there were mobs of local lads and Turkish gangs all over the place. We had several skirmishes and were happy when we bumped into a larger mob of United and teamed up with them. The Ajax fans we had previously come across were only using their boots and fists, but the Turks were a different matter, and as we were drinking outside a bar a small gang of them turned up, all of them were brandishing knives or long sticks.

The Turks were certainly game fuckers. They must have been outnumbered five to one, but they still had a go. They were all waving blades about, but there wasn't really a toe-to-toe encounter, instead they were seen off by a barrage of glasses, bottles and barstools. Within minutes of seeing off the Turks a small army of riot police surrounded our bar under a heavy escort, which included horses and dogs and we were marched off to the ground.

Oscar, a well-known character from Manchester was at the front of the United mob and he had spent the whole weekend walking around Amsterdam with an old pair of discarded bicycle handles. The Dutch old Bill, obviously not understanding the English sense of humour were very perplexed as to why he would be walking around holding a bicycle handle in front of him. Oscar soon clocked the strange looks he was getting from the Dutch coppers, so he said to one of them, "I fuckin' hate walking, that's why I take my bike everywhere with me." The coppers must have thought Oscar had come from the Funny Farm. Although after what happened next, we all thought that Oscar should have been locked up in the Funny Farm.

Being at the front of the mob the police horses were only a few feet away from Oscar, and when one of the horses started having a massive shit, Oscar passed his bicycle handles to one of his mates, then ran forward and put his hands underneath the horse's arse and caught one of the steaming turds in his hands. He then casually squeezed all the liquid out of it and rolled the turd into a ball. With the startled coppers looking on in amazement, Oscar yelled, "In my country, we call this an onion bhaji." He then put the ball of horse shit up to his mouth and pretended to take a bite out of it. A couple of the coppers were so disgusted with Oscar's antics that they immediately gagged and almost threw up. On seeing this Oscar burst out laughing and threw the 'onion bhaji' at the horse's arse, startling the horse so much it almost unseated the rider. This was the final straw for the plod, and they duly frog marched Oscar over to one of their vans. As he was being led away, he was laughing his head off and shouting out. "Can I bring my bike with me." He was thrown head first into the back of one of the vans by two of the biggest coppers I had ever seen.

Once again, the action on the pitch was dire and the only entertainment we got was playing up a couple of darlings who were sitting in the adjoining stand. Unfortunately, there was a ten-foot fence between us, but still all the lads were giving the girls plenty of attention and they were loving it. After loads of wolf whistles and lewd suggestions we started singing, "Get your tits out for the lads." To our amazement and delight after a minute or so one of the girls lifted up her top and exposed a beautiful pair of 'Bristols'. After 180 minutes of football, plus a penalty shootout at the Olympic stadium, the sight of a pair of tits was definitely most memorable and enjoyable.

This being our last night, the lads and myself decided instead of visiting one of the many seedy little sex clubs in Amsterdam, we would go a little upmarket and pay a visit to a Sex Theatre. The establishment that Dutch Pete took us to certainly had a grand interior, with its plush carpets, Rococo architecture and newly upholstered seating that you would expect to see at a ballet or a classical concert rather than acts of debauchery.

Most of the lads were happy to sit at the front of the theatre but after my experience with the Silver Back, I decided I would play it safe and sat a few rows back. There were a few traditional acts like a girl pulling the flags of Nations from her fanny, another young lady blowing smoke rings out of her money-maker and a couple of gorgeous lesbian girls getting stuck into each other. This followed with a slightly more unusual act. The large red curtains opened and there on stage was a young woman tied to a timber stake, and a man dressed as a Victorian baddie was pretending to beat her. The whole thing was starting to look a bit pathetic and boring when the music suddenly increased in volume and there were bright searchlights focused on the back of the theatre. I turned around and I couldn't believe what I was seeing, walking down the aisle was a six foot-six black geezer, top half dressed as Batman and he was hung like a carthorse.

In the style of the early black and white films, Batman strode onto the stage, proceeded to give the baddie a ridiculous fake punch on the jaw, he then untied the damsel in distress. After a few hugs and a thank you kiss from the grateful girl, Batman picked her up and carried her down the steps. He proceeded to walk up and down past the front rows with his massive cock almost hitting his knees as he walked. While still safely in Batman's arms, the rescued girl was busy eyeing up the punters in the first couple of rows and after a minute or so, she indicated to the caped crusader to walk up the aisle separating the seats and as he did so, the girl scoured the audience for a victim. To my dismay I made eye contact with her and when I saw her nod to Batman, then turn back and smile at me, I knew I was in big trouble. I was sitting on the end seat with someone sitting next to me; so, my only escape route was to run up the aisle. But before I had the chance to do that Batman and the rescued damsel were towering over me. She nodded once again, and the black Goliath lowered her onto my lap. I was just about to say, 'what's a nice girl like you doing in a place like this', when Batman ripped open her flimsy dress and exposed her beautiful form. Then to my utter embarrassment Batman shoved his massive tool inside her and while she was still lying across my lap, he proceeded to give her a good rogering. To say I didn't know where to look, or where put my hands was an understatement. The girl was rocking backwards and forwards as the giant cock was going in and out of her and I could feel myself turning as red as a beetroot. I was thankful for small mercies that the theatre was dimly lit, and the rest of the audience couldn't see how flustered I was. I suppose it

299

could have been worse, Batman could have carried me up onto the stage and given me a good seeing to as well!

While still getting over the shock of Batman and the Damsel in distress, I was sitting outside the Royal Taste with Ged when a very drunk Shay F and his little entourage came walking towards us. Shay was very insistent that I went for a drink with him and his boys. Several times I told him I was completely shagged and several times he said, "you're coming for a drink with us" There were lots of, "No I'm not," and "Yes you ares," thrown back and forth. Then Shay's patience ran out and he dragged me out of my seat and threw me over his shoulder and walked off up the street. Protest was futile. As we wandered through the streets, Shay's mates seemed to be taking a swing at almost everyone that walked past, and it wasn't any better when we went into a bar. Before we had finished our first drink, we were shown the door.

The next bar we went into was empty except for four lads playing pool and one of them was wearing an Ajax top. When Shay noticed this he was quick to show his displeasure and after giving him a load of verbal, he said to me "we should do these bastards", and once again I told him I was completely knackered and wasn't really interested in battering up a few teenagers especially when we outnumbered them by four to one. For a while Shay calmed down, but it didn't last long. Just I was getting myself another pint, he walked over to the pool table and took a couple of balls off the table. He then walked away and when he got near to the door he turned around and threw the balls at the pool players, Shay then strolled out of the bar followed by the rest of his mates. I remained sat at the bar shaking my head and thinking *'I don't need any more agro, I'm staying here'*. I was just taking a sip of my beer when I felt a tap on my shoulder. I turned around and one of the pool players rammed the end of his cue in my face. I received a few more kicks and punches, then I was thrown out into the street. So much for saying I didn't want to batter any teenagers!

I made my way back to the Royal Taste and when I arrived, I found Coleman sitting at the bar with Ged and the landlord Fran. I needed to be at the airport by 6am and naïvely thought I might get to bed for a couple of hours. Some chance. We were chatting about cabbages and kings and various past adventures while following The Reds, and before I knew it was 4am and Fran was calling last orders. Because I only had an hour or so before I needed to head off to Schiphol, Fran poured us half a dozen small beers each on the house before he disappeared off to bed.

When my taxi arrived to take me to the airport, I was literally poured into it and immediately fell asleep on the back seat. When we arrived at the airport the taxi driver needed to ask a copper to help him wake me. My Bambi-like legs were only just about keeping me upright as I made my way to the boarding gates. I had to pick up speed a little when my name was called over the PA system and I was told to go to Gate 44 immediately. I was moving as fast as I could as I approached my gate and when the stewardesses spotted me, they started waving their arms and beckoning me forward. I noticed the stewardesses were standing in front of Gate 43. *'I could have sworn the PA announcement said Gate 44, oh well, must be a mistake'*, I thought. The stewardesses were very animated and when I tried to hand them my boarding pass, they refused to look at it and shouted at me to "just get on the plane because they were waiting to take off". (Can you imagine that scenario today?) Waiting for me at the bottom of the air-tunnel was another animated and inpatient stewardess who pulled me through the door and yelled, "Quickly, quickly we need to take off." As I entered the plane, again I tried to show my boarding pass, but the stewardess said, "Just take the first seat you see, we really have to take off or we will miss our slot." As I looked around for a seat and the stewardess started to close the door, I thought it was strange that I had travelled here on a ten-seater rubber band job, and this flight must have had well over a hundred passengers on board and they all looked like family holiday makers. I turned to the stewardess and enquired as to where the plane was going and was a little gob-smacked to hear her say, "Majorca", Yes, Fucking Majorca! "I'm on the wrong bleedin' flight." I yelled. And much to the crew's annoyance they had to open the plane door and let me off. I somehow managed to run up the air-tunnel, across the concourse, down the Gate 44 air-tunnel and onto the correct airplane just in time.

I slept like a baby the whole flight and when we arrived in Birmingham, a stewardess shook me violently and helped me out of my seat. She told me I looked like death warmed up and I honestly felt like death warmed up. I could hardly keep my eyes open as I handed over my passport and I was as white as a sheet and had a bruise under my eye where I had been hit with the pool cue It was no surprise that when I got to Custom Control I was approached by an officer and after being asked a few questions, I was escorted into a small sparsely furnished office.

When my bag was searched and my lesbian porn book discovered, I instantly thought *'thank fuck I didn't buy that Animal Hotel book'*, which had one of the most offensive pictures of a bloke fuckin' a chicken I had ever seen! It put me off eating eggs for ages! Even though nothing but a bit of soft lesbian porn was found in my bag, the officer informed me he was going to perform a strip search. Under normal circumstances I would have kicked up a right fuss, but I was so tired and desperate for my bed I just let him get on with it. After every inch of my clothing was meticulously examined and I was standing totally naked, the officer spoke those words that no red-blooded male wants to hear, "Bend over sir!" When I saw the Customs Officer putting on his rubber gloves, I have to admit my stomach did turn over and I thought to myself *'NO!'* I then shouted out. "You're not sticking anything up my arse – I'm not a fuckin' puff you know!" In a calm but commanding tone he replied, "We can do this the easy way or the hard way – it's your choice." I was starting to sober up fast and feeling a bit aggressive by then, so I yelled back, "You're not sticking your finger up my arse." With that he hit a button on the wall and a few seconds later three burly officers came charging into the room. There were no formal introductions or chit-chat. Two of them immediately grabbed my arms and pulled me across the table and at the same time another officer seized my ankles and spread my legs apart while the one who was wearing the rubber gloves did the unthinkable! When they were finally convinced that I wasn't carrying any drugs they thanked me for my time and told me I could keep my lesbian book!

Some weeks later a group of the Manchester lads along with their wives and girlfriends were all out for a drink together, and as usual the girls were all chatting amongst themselves while the lads were holding their own conversation. Kenny a wannabe David Bailey and tour guide was boring everyone showing them all his photos of Amsterdam and relaying a few soppy stories, but the girls weren't really paying much attention as he passed round his pictures. Before too long the girls were virtually ignoring Kenny, that was until he came out with the classic line, "Yes, and I was only one who didn't go with a prostitute!" All the girls immediately stopped in mid conversation and stared wide-eyed at Kenny. Then as one, they all glared at their relative partners. The lads in turn gave Kenny daggers. Realising that he had dropped the lads right in the shit, Kenny started to backpedal and in a nonchalant and indifferent manner said, "Oh, of course Ged didn't and of course Clive didn't and I'm sure Bowie didn't," and on and on he went until he exonerated everyone present. Needless to say, all the lads got some very heavy earache from the girls when they got home. NICE ONE KENNY!

BLACKMORE TO THE RESCUE

From John Bean:
Dinamo Kiev 1, Manchester United 1
United win 4—1 on penalties

HARD SHOOTING Clayton Blackmore hammered the pride back in Manchester United here in Amsterdam last night as they collided with the best from another continent for the second time in three days.

The young Welsh mid-fielder, a second-half substitute for Jon Siveback, bulleted United back into a tournament that was being brilliantly ruled by Dinamo Kiev, who supplied the bulk of Russia's World Cup effort in Mexico.

The 30-yarder, crashing in off a post, sparked a final 30-minute United comeback that hauled them through to a victorious penalty shoot-out and a place in tomorrow's four-team tournament final.

While Colin Gibson, Petr Davenport, Gordon Strachan and—hittingly—Blackmore kept their nerve in the Olympic stadium, the Russians palpably lost theirs in the spot-kick stakes.

As Ron Atkinson's side again strained for impact up front, Igor Belanov could have put the match beyond United's reach.

In the 16th minute he pulled a penalty wide of Turner's goal after

Kevin Moran had tripped Alexander Zavarov.

And even after Belanov neatly converted a perfect through-ball for Kiev's 25th minute goal he went on to spurn a much easier effort before the interval.

Ajax 1, Manchester Utd 0
From Alex Potter

MANCHESTER UNITED surrendered their pre-season unbeaten record to a nimble and aggressive Ajax side in the Olympic stadium last night.

Luckily for United, Paul McGrath was in the kind of form to suggest he will become one of the most important players at Old Trafford this season,

The republic of Ireland international began as a willing midfield stand-in and finished by shoring-up a defence that never happily contained the Dutch attack.

Gordon Strachan and fellow Scot Graeme Hogg were booked when frustration set in.

United seldom suggested they would climb back into contention after Danny Blind opened the scoring.

Chapter 23.
Montpellier '91

19th March '91
Montpellier   0 – 2   Blackmore, Bruce   (20,500)

United Line - Up
Sealey, Blackmore, Bruce, Pallister, Irwin, Ince, Phelan, Robson, Sharpe,
McClair, Hughes. **Subs** *– Walsh, Martin, Donaghy, Wallace, Robins*

Manager
Alex Ferguson

Cup Winners Cup—Quarter Final 2nd Leg

Before the trip to Montpellier the Reds hadn't won in the league for 7 games, losing 3 and drawing 4. The 4 draws in the league all ended 1 – 1, as did the 1st Leg against Montpellier. Both the club and supporters were relieved that UEFA had lifted the ban on English teams playing in European competitions after the Heysal disaster in '85, and United could take part in the Cup Winners Cup after lifting the FA Cup the previous May.

It had been a mixed season for United, so they could have done without being deducted 1 point and fined £50,000 after a total of 21 players were involved in a mass brawl on the Old Trafford pitch after the Arsenal game.

The home draw against the French side may have been disappointing but at least there was a decent crowd at Old Trafford, the previous home games in the Cup Winners Cup had seen very disappointing gates with less than 30,000 in attendance for the games against the Hungarian side Pecsi Munkas and Wrexham. After beating Legia Warsaw in the semi's, The Reds would go on to win the Cup Winners Cup for the first time, by beating Barcelona 2 - 1 in a rain-soaked Rotterdam. Lifting our first European trophy for almost 25 years, went a long way for making up for the disappointment of losing 1 - 0 to Sheffield Wednesday in the League Cup final at Wembley.

I had recently bumped into an old mate of mine, Tom, who went to the games with me in the mid-seventies. He hadn't seen United for well over five years, but when I told him I was going to Montpellier in a weeks' time to see the Reds he excitedly said he would come with us. Ged knew a travel agent who had said he would sell us train/ferry tickets to get us to the South of France and if we returned without getting the tickets clipped, he would give us 50% back.

We had planned to get an early train from Liverpool Street station on the Sunday morning so to avoid silly early starts, a few of us, including Tom, travelled down to London on the Saturday afternoon. Because he was late confirming he was coming on the trip Tom couldn't get into the same hotel as me and the other lads and all of the hotels in the immediate vicinity were also full. Being totally relaxed about the situation Tom just shrugged his shoulders and said he would find something later and we should go and have a few pints. As was the norm when in London we met up with a few Cockney Reds that we knew and had good old pub-crawl with them. As the night went on Tom got talking to Alex, one of the Cockneys, he was a man mountain and originally from the Isle of Sheepey and he was a man you wouldn't want to upset. When he found out that Tom was without a bed for the night, Alex immediately offered to put him up and even though Alex lived in south London Tom gladly took him up on the offer. After a skin full, Tom and Alex made their way back to south London and as a way of expressing his gratitude to Alex for putting a roof over his head for the night Tom suggested they should go for a Ruby, and of course a few more pints. When they finally got back to Alex's place in the early hours of the morning Tom was instructed to be very quiet as he hadn't told 'her-in-doors' that he was bringing someone home to stay the night, so Tom took off his shoes, tiptoed into the house and crashed down on the sofa and immediately fell asleep. Alex crept upstairs and into bed and also immediately crashed out. A few hours later Alex's missus was awoken by the sound of bumping and banging downstairs. Alex was snoring his head off, so she decided to go and investigate herself. When she got halfway down the stairs, she saw Tom, who she assumed was a burglar pissing up her kitchen door. She ran straight back upstairs and violently shaking Alex she shouted, "Quick, quick there's burglar downstairs." Alex had been dead to the world and was very startled and disorientated to be woken from his slumber by his panic-stricken wife. As his wife's words started to sink in, he dived out of bed and ran downstairs to confront 'the burglar'. Tom was making his way back into the dark living room when Alex jumped him from behind and with his Mrs screaming at him, "Kill the fuckin' slag! Kill him." Alex had totally forgotten that he had bought someone home with him and proceeded to give Tom a fucking good hiding. With Tom lying spark out on the floor and Alex still kicking shit out of him, his missus switched on the living room lights and noticed Toms bag, and then saw the blanket and pillow on the sofa. Fighting with Alex to stop him battering Tom she shrieked, "What the fuck is going on? Why is there a blanket and pillow on the sofa?" Alex was frozen to the spot and reality-hit home as he realised that he had just battered his new mate. When Tom finally came around Alex and his wife did their best to clean him up, but a large deep cut on his head needed hospital treatment so Tom was bundled into the car and her-in-doors drove him to A&E. Tom had several stitches in his head wound, suffered a couple of cracked ribs and couldn't see out of his left eye for a couple of days. Beware of Greeks bearing gifts Tom and send us a postcard if you ever do make it to the South of France.

We were a little late docking into Calais and missed our scheduled train, but at least we hadn't had our tickets clipped and Ginger had managed to board the ferry without a ticket or a passport. Having the afternoon to kill we split our time between the bars of Calais and various Bureau de Change. GS was selling moody tenners for three quid each, so we were all keen to get our special exchange rate as soon as possible. With our pockets bulging with French Francs we eventually boarded the train that would take us to Montpellier. Not until the French clippy came along did we realise that we were on a sleeper train and we had to pay an extra eighty Francs each for the luxury of having a bed to sleep in. Luckily, we had our special Franc to Pound exchange rate, and fortunately once again our original travel tickets weren't clipped or stamped, and again Ginger managed to avoid payment and grabbed himself a spare bunk. When the French train inspector stressed that we must stay in our own carriage and not to wander into the forward carriages we all thought that he didn't want a mob of English football hooligans roaming up and down his train, understandable I suppose. However, a little later we would discover the real reason why he hadn't wanted us to move from our carriage.

After we had been travelling for a couple of hours, we pulled into a station that had several small glorified trolleys on the platform selling food, and more importantly alcoholic beverages. We all piled off the train and got the necessary supplies for the long journey ahead. When the whistle was blown to indicate the train was moving on again, Morse was a good hundred yards up the platform, so a few of the lads shouted for him to get back on the train and because of his location he got on one of the train carriages that was two or three in front of our carriage. Once on, Morse sat himself down in a first-class carriage, scoffed his grub, had a beer then started to make his way back to our carriage. He strolled through a couple of carriages until he came to a locked door. Hoping he could attract our attention he lent out one of the windows and he was just about to start yelling when to his dismay he discovered he had reached the end of the train and there were no more carriages. The train had split at the previous station and as Ged, the rest of the lads and I were happily swigging our beer and choo-chooing down to the South of France, Morse was on his way to gay Paris with only a French baguette and a few beers to keep him company. And that's why the Froggy clippie had told us not to move out of our carriage!

When we eventually discovered that Morse had gone on his own little adventure, naturally our first reaction was to piss ourselves laughing. When we informed the Guard of the mishap he confirmed that Morse would indeed be heading to Paris and he asked Ged to hand over Morse's passport and wallet so he could contact the inspector on the Paris train and make sure that his possessions got to Paris before he did. On the surface that seen a semi reasonable idea but what no one had taken into consideration was Morse's ingenuity and guile. Being stuck on a foreign train with no money, no ticket and no passport, Morse dodged the French clippy for the whole journey and as soon as he arrived in Paris, he boarded the first train to Montpellier thinking his money and passport would be waiting for him there.

We arrived in Avignon in the early hours and got the small commuter train to Montpelier. The train was full of locals making their way to work but their regular ablutions were seriously disrupted due to twenty hairy arsed United supporters stinking out the two bogs on the train. The Froggies who wanted to use the toilet would open the door and close it as soon as the disgusting stench hit their nostrils, one brave girl must have been extremely desperate and ventured inside the toilet from hell, when she came out she was as white as a sheet and had a hankie over her nose and mouth. On seeing the girl in such distress, using his very limited French, Clive shouted out. "You French don't know what a good shit is." Apparently, that was the sweet talkers' total French vocabulary.

Once we had sorted the hotel, Me Colin and Taff tossed our bags into our room and decided we would go on the piss for the day with the rest of the lads. As we were about to leave the hotel Clive and I were approached by a couple of French reporters who wanted to know 'how many United fans would be travelling to Montpellier and would there be many of our infamous hooligans with them'? Just for the craic Clive dived in and laid it on really thick, "We are bringing at least ten thousand maybe even fifteen thousand and we're going to run riot, we're going to wreck your poxy little town – kick fuck out of your coppers and rape all your women, whether they are young or old." The two journalists stood open mouthed and were visibly shocked. After a few seconds they started to quietly mutter to each other, I've no idea what they were saying but it looked like they were crapping themselves and were probably planning on getting the next train out of town. Glaring at the two frightened Froggies, Clive couldn't contain himself any longer and he burst out laughing, "We're only playing you up." Clive said, "We're the heroes of the night and we'd rather fuck than fight, we're the heroes of the Stretford Fusiliers." Obviously, the reporters didn't have a fuckin' clue what he was on about and were totally bemused, "Pardon" one of them said inquisitively and Clive shouted back, "We've come to party you twats!" He then went on to explain that he was singing a United football song. On hearing this the journalist's eyes lit up and they asked if we knew anymore songs? Anymore Songs! Clive probably knew more songs than Pete Boyle, so for the next ten minutes Clive and I reeled off song after song while the two Froggie's recorded us. When we had finished, the journalists and the hotel staff who were in the reception area gave us a rousing round of applause. Just as we were about to finally leave the hotel the manager stopped us and told us that our songs would be on the local radio show at 10am the following morning.

Thinking nothing more of what had been said, we went in search for the rest of the lads. It was the day before the game, but the main town Square was already full of Reds and we had a great craic drinking and singing in the warm French sunshine. All was going tickety-boo until we went back to the hotel in the evening. Ged was waiting by the hotel entrance and he told us that a couple of rooms had been broken into, and two young scumbags from Openshaw were the prime suspects. A well-known taxi driver 'M' was the one who had the most stolen and even though he was of diminutive stature he had a fearsome reputation. He broke into the Openshaw lads' room and soon discovered his stolen items, which included various designer clothes and other valuables. So 'M' and a few of the lads positioned themselves in the bar opposite our hotel and waited for the two young thieves to return. They didn't have to wait long, and as soon as the two kids came into view 'M' shouted over to them and asked them to join him and the lads for a drink. The cocky little sods strolled over and sat themselves down and immediately started laughing and joking as if they hadn't a care in the world. Their laughing and joking soon came to an abrupt end when 'M' put a knife to the throat of one of the kids and the rest of our lads surrounded his mate.

'M' applied just enough pressure so that the blade caused a bit of blood to run down the young thief's throat. Initially both kids tried to plead their innocence but when 'M' told them of the stolen items he had found in their room they both went white with fear. The pair of young toe-rags must have been on the rob all day, because when they were forced to empty their pockets, they had over £500 between them in English and French notes. They were quickly relieved of their cash and given a few digs but really, they got off very lightly. 'M' had already thrown their bags out of the hotel window and in no uncertain terms they were told they needed to find somewhere else to kip. With Montpellier being so busy hopefully they ended up in the gutter.

Talking of ending up in the gutter Tom, Coleman and Shay (The Flahertys) almost had the pleasure of sleeping on the streets having failed to find a hotel room after a full day and night on the piss. They mooched around one of the bigger hotels in Montpellier and thought their luck was in when they found an unlocked broom cupboard. Straight away they crammed themselves inside the 4 feet x 3 feet room and were in the land of nod in no time. Unfortunately, one the hotel staff got the shock of their lives when they opened the cupboard door in the early hours of the morning and discovered three pissed up Brummies' farting and snoring their heads off. The three of them were rudely awakened by being repeatedly prodded with a broom and once awake they were unceremoniously pulled out of their luxury suite by the scruff of their necks and shown the door. Luckily for The Flahertys they soon came across a late – late bar and stopped in there until dawn. For the next few days the lockers at the train station became their changing room and makeshift hotel. I was a bit surprised to learn that they needed lockers to store their bags. I went to PSV Eindhoven with Coleman in 'October!' '84 and he was in his shirtsleeves the whole time. He didn't even take a gansey with him!

After seeing the two scumbags on their way me and a few of the other Brummies' went for a wander about; we had only visited a few small backstreet bars when Jon, Mark and a few others decided they were going to find some grub. This left Colin and I propping up the bar in a seedy little dive, knocking back the small beers quicker than the barman could pour them. Because of the pace of the old barmen we 'hummed and 'erred about finding another bar, when two gorgeous young women walked into the bar and came and stood beside us, it only took a few seconds for them to start talking to us in broken English and asked us to buy them a drink. I made it clear from the start we weren't going to be buying any expensive bottles of champagne and they happily agreed to a glass of house wine each. The drinks turned out to be as cheap as chips, especially taking into account 100 Francs was only costing us three quid! We had gotten the girls a few drinks and I thought we were really getting on well with them and this could be our lucky night, when one of the girls suddenly enquired 'would we like to fuck them'? Both Colin and I nearly choked on our beer. Too fuckin' right we would! But before we could respond she added 100 Francs for sucky-sucky AND fucky-fucky. We were both wide eyed as her friend announced, "It would cost you much more if you were to buy us drinks all night and take us to a restaurant."

Colin and I just looked at each other both hoping the other one would make a decision. While the beautiful young women were stroking our legs and trying to kiss our necks, I whispered to Colin, "Come on let's go for it, in real terms it's only going to cost us three quid!" As he nodded in agreement the girls took us by the hand and lead us out of the bar. We had walked less than a minute from the bar when the girl stopped at a shabby old tenement building and opened a large knackered old wooden door that looked like it was just about to fall off its hinges. Once inside the building she led me up several flights of a dimly lit staircase until we came to her front door, which was almost as tatty as the entrance door. Holding me by the hand she led me into the apartment and I almost died with embarrassment, as I walked through the door, I was led straight into a living room and sitting there was the whole family, granddad, grandma, mum, dad, brothers and sisters, all watching TV. Still leading me by the hand the girl walked us past them all and into the bedroom and not one of other family members seem to blink an eye. I was shell-shocked as the girl closed the door and pointed to the bed. But worse was yet to come. As I was sat on the bed, I couldn't help but notice just like the living room, how sparse the brasses boudoir was. There were no carpets or curtains and no lampshade over the dim lightbulb. My attention was soon taken away from the austere decor when my lovely French host joined me on the bed and proceeded to undress me. As she was removing my trousers, the bedroom door swung open and in walks grandma with a bowl of warm water and a towel thrown over her arm. The frail old lady gave me a forced smile, placed the bowl and towel on the bare floorboards, turned around and left the room. The French Belle washed me, then she washed herself before she got down to business. The grandma must've been watching through the keyhole or some other type of spy hole, because as soon as the dirty deed was finished the old lady entered the room again with another bowl of water and a clean towel. I got dressed and eyes firmly focused ahead I walked past the indifferent and motionless family in the living room. As I went back down the stairs, I wondered how many hundreds if not thousands had made the same journey as me?

Colin and I got back to the hotel just in time to see a very, very intoxicated Bowie receiving a bit of karma. He had collapsed in a chair in the reception area and an earthquake wouldn't have woken him. He would have been the first to violate or defile anybody who was too pissed to know what was going on. Shaving someone's eyebrows off or write 'I AM A CUNT' across someone's forehead was the least you could expect from Bowie. If you were unlucky you would wake up to find his little dick in your ear or being pushed up against your nostril. Now the boot was firmly on the other foot; Bowie's eyebrows had gone, and the lads had removed his trousers and pants and much to the amusement of the night porter they were shaving his pubes. Ged then asked the porter for a marker- pen, the porter happily obliged. Ged then set about drawing a skeleton all over Bowie's chest and arms. For good measure Jon tied Bowie's ankles together so when he did finally wake up and tried to walk, he would have gone arse over tit. After leaving Bowie in the reception with his trousers screwed up in his lap, most of the lads wandered over to the bar near the hotel but I was too pissed and starving to join them so decided to head to bed. When I got to my room and much to my delight, I saw what I thought were small packs of chocolate on each of our pillows. Being so hungry I grabbed the small sachets off the pillows and ripped the tops off all three of them and shoved them straight into my gob. I was so pissed, I had chomped on the chocolates for a few seconds before I realized something was wrong and spat the contents of my mouth all over the floor. It wasn't chocolate! it was fuckin' white soap!!

It was just getting light and me and Colin were dead to the world, but we both jumped up in bed when our door was wildly swung open and Taff appeared trying desperately to steady himself in the doorway, "Morse is here and he's just had some bird rub her tits all over his bald head," he said. With that he slammed the door shut and tried to make it to his bed without putting on the light. He had only taken a few steps when there was a bang and a 'fuck' from Taff. Then it was quiet for a few seconds then crash - bang – wallop and another 'fuck' from Taff. In the near pitch black of the room Taff headed back to the door, flicked on the lights for a few seconds to get his bearings and for a second time tried to make it to his bed. But it was exactly the same outcome as his first attempt he bounced off the wardrobe, fell over the chair and crashed onto my bed - there was another round of 'fucks' and a few 'oh bollocks' and 'you cunt' before he made his way back to the light switch again. Colin and I were tittering like a pair of schoolboys as the pissed-up Taff quickly switched the light on and off to help him get his bearings and for the third time he attempted to get to his bed. Once again, there was lots of bumping - banging and clattering about as he rebounded off the wall and various pieces of furniture, and of course there was lots of effing and blinding but it was third time lucky for Taff as he finally crashed down onto his bed. Whilst we were having breakfast the next morning, I got to hear the full story of Morse and his tit rub.

After jumping the train from Paris and searching almost every bar in Montpellier Morse finally tracked the lads down in the early hours of the morning, they were in a little bar opposite our hotel. He had only been in the bar for a few minutes when one of the waitresses came over and started stroking and kissing his shaven head. In a sexy French accent, she told Morse, "I think your shaven head is so very sexy and because you are an Englishman this turns me on even more." She then quickly turned around to see if the barman was looking her way, luckily for Morse the barman was busy pulling pints, so the waitress quickly undid the buttons of her blouse and

319

dropped her tits onto Morse's napper. Jammy Bastard! I've shaven my head now for almost ten years but I'm still waiting for my bonce to be christened by a big pair of bristols.

While still having breakfast, the manager came charging in and beckoned Big Clive and myself into the reception area. The two of us strolled into the reception and were greeted with the radio blasting out the United songs we had performed for the reporters the day before. A few of the lads wandered into reception to find out what was going on and as soon as they appeared the excited manager informed them that it was Clive and I, they could hear singing on the radio. They weren't impressed, both Ged and Bowie instantly shouted out, "You Wankers" and they continued to take the piss out of us for the rest of the day. Definitely a case of green-eyed monster!

United didn't just take over the main square it seemed we took over the whole of Montpellier. It was definitely a case of 'Reds are here – Reds are there – Reds are every fuckin' where'. There were so many Reds in the town centre we didn't see any Montpellier fans until we approached the ground. We were a short way from the ground when a mob of United came walking towards us and they informed us they had just been attacked by a large gang of Arabs and a couple of Reds had been stabbed. We all waited around for a while until we built our numbers up, then marched up to the ground. We were soon spotted by the local Arabs and as we got closer to them I noticed a few of them were carrying sticks and bottles, but as we charged at them most of them turned on their toes. The riot police quickly rescued the few who stood their ground. Very quickly the riot police got heavy-handed and their long batons and hobnail boots were flying all over the place. We were herded towards our section of the ground and as we approached the turnstiles you could have cut the atmosphere with a knife. The riot police were extremely jumpy and any wrong move or even shouting would result with a whack of a riot stick.

There were about twenty lads in front of me queuing to get through the turnstiles and there was only the slightest of pushing, but this was enough for the riot police to wade in and crack some heads. The bastards went wild and as a few of the Reds fell to the ground after being whacked with the long batons they were kicked repeatedly. As the crash helmet wearing coppers lashed out at anyone within striking distance most of us nervously edged our way backwards and all we could really do was to look on in disgust, it was one of the worst cases of police brutality that I had ever witnessed.

After the game we had the long, long walk back to town and the Red Army had a police escort all the way; well not all the way for me and the lads. To break up the United mob there were two or three coppers positioned in between every sixty or seventy of us, this meant we had little or no chance of stopping for a drink before we finished the hour plus walk back to the town. As we approached a bend in the road that also had a steep incline. I noticed a small alley way and slowed the lads down a little and let the French coppers in front of us disappear around the bend of the hill. With the other coppers lagging behind us, we all raced down the small dark alleyway. As the lads all piled into a nearby bar, I couldn't resist wandering along an adjacent road and spying on the local plod. The front and the rear guard had met up and were standing at the top of the hill looking like a load of totally clueless Keystone Cops. As they scratched their heads and scratched their arses it was pretty easy to tell they were totally perplexed as to where almost a hundred United supporters had suddenly disappeared.

When we finally started making our way back into town, we passed a Vietnamese restaurant and me and JC, decided to go in for a late night nose bag. Like rest of Montpellier the interior of the restaurant was shabby, in fact it was bordering on downright dirty, but it was late, and we were hungry so we thought we would take a chance. There were only a few other customers; a table full of miserable looking Chinkies. We were soon getting stuck into a couple of large bowls of noodles and washing it down with some decent Vietnamese beer when the table full of Chinkies started to get rowdy and were giving the waiter quite a bit of aggravation. The waiter was called over to the table several times, shouted then gestured to go away. The waiter finally snapped, and a stand-up row ensued, it quickly got very heated and the waiter soon found himself surrounded. JC was always quick to don his white sheriff's hat and took it upon himself to try and calm things down. As he stood up, I stressed to him it would be for the best to keep out of it because it had nothing to do with us. But he took no notice. JC's presence only seemed to make matters worse and verbal disagreements escalated into a bit of pushing and shoving. Then two of the yellow peril started punching the waiter.

When JC tried to separate them, another one of them pulled a knife on him. If it hadn't had been so serious it would have been an amusing sight. JC was a big-built bloke and well over six foot. His attacker was five foot nothing, as thin as a beanpole and looked about twelve years old. As the knifeman slowly walked towards him, JC was steadily backing away with his hands up in submission and firmly repeating for him to put his knife down, but his adversary just steadily followed him around the restaurant. Hearing the commotion in the restaurant a couple of the kitchen staff came running out and luckily for JC one of them smashed a chair across the back of the knife man's head. That was the start of the real fireworks, plates, glasses, chairs and tables were soon being thrown around the restaurant and so were a few of the Chinkies. While all of this was going on, I was standing in the doorway, shouting to JC to get the fuck outside. I think he was just about to turn around and make his way towards the exit when he was hit around the head with a glass water jug. JC went down like a ton of bricks and was lying unconscious on the floor. With the restaurant still resembling a battleground I thought to myself 'that's just what I fuckin' need', having to go back into the thick of it! I dashed over to JC and somehow managed to drag him outside without getting stabbed or having my head caved in. When we were out in the street and I was dragging him away from the restaurant JC regained consciousness and I asked him if he was okay. He obviously wasn't, because the first thing he said was "Did you pay the bill"? When I snapped back that "I fuckin' hadn't" he suggested we should go back and pay it. The barmy bleeder must have been in shock!

When JC and I got back to the little local pub opposite our hotel, we found a Polish geezer was in deep conversation with a few of the lads. The Pole was working in Montpellier but regularly travelled back to Poland to see his team Legia Warsaw; a team who was also in the quarterfinals of The Cup Winners Cup. For an Eastern European the Pole spoke good English, which he put down to watching Match of the Day whenever he could. As the drink flowed, he proudly informed us he was a top football hooligan back in Warsaw and his dream was to test himself against English hooligans, especially Manchester United and he was praying that Legia Warsaw would beat Sampdoria and United would be drawn against his team. He was very knowledgeable about English and Polish football and when we were finally kicked out of the bar, he asked me and a few other lads if we wanted to have a drink at his flat, which was just around the corner and added he had some videos he wanted us to see, so we made our way round to his flat. As I walked into his living room, I was taken aback at all the weapons he had hanging on his walls. Besides loads of knives and a few swords, he also had a couple of axes and several baseball bats with nails and screws sticking out of them. He was a great host and we were soon downing his beer and Polish vodka and watching his prized videos, I was half expecting to see football videos or even porn, but to my amazement the videos were of him and his crew back in Poland kicking the fuck out of rival fans. Excitedly he gave us running commentaries of his battles and paused the tape, to point at himself, whenever he came onto the screen. There were lots of weapons used in the many confrontations and in one video they battered the Polish coppers on the platforms of Warsaw railway station. Legia Warsaw had beaten Sampdoria and of course, United played the Polish side in the semi-finals. I travelled over to Warsaw for the game but I'm glad to say I never bumped into my Polish friend and his fearsome mates. I am also glad to say, most of the lads and myself managed to get back home without getting any of our tickets stamped and therefore got our 50% refund. Not proper Jibbing I know – but at least we saved a good few quid!

By David Lacey

MANCHESTER United are in the semi-finals of the Cup Winners' Cup for a second time because they refused to allow intensity hostiles French crowd to treat the, like a lorryload of English lambs. At the end of last night's return leg of their quarterfinal in the Stade de la Mosson it was Montpellier who looked Sheepish.

A free kick from Clayton Blackmore in a stoppage time at the end of the first half and a penalty by Steve Bruce two minutes into the second brought Alex Ferguson's team a 2-0 victory which took them into the last four 3-1 on aggregate. Juventus, the conquerors in the 1984 semi-finals, Barcelona and the holders Sampdoria, all of whom play tonight, may well join them there. Montpellier were punished for a cautious approach which suggested they had set too much store by the 1-1 draw achieved Old Trafford and had overestimated the value of an away goal. Had Montpellier gone for a straight win last night and led their attack with Xuereb from the start instead of bringing him off the bench when they had gone two down, United might not have survived that poor performance in the opening match. As it was, they kept their heads, retained their composure and hit the post.

The post in the second half after the opposition had again had a player sent off.

Hughes remains the common factor. At Old Trafford, Baills had been dismissed for shoulder-charging the Whelshman after play had stopped for a free kick. Montpellier, and especially their president Louis Nicollin, was infuriated because Hughes had gone down holding his face, which had not been touch. This, they reckoned, had sent they're right back to an early shower and rules him out of the return game.

That night Hughes hardly had time for reaction let alone over reaction. Thetis took his legs from under him in the 70th minute and was shown the yellow card. Two minutes later he tackled and saw red. So, in all ways but one it was a particularly satisfying conclusion for United. The exception was Bryan Robson's booking which had put the captain out of the first leg of the semi-finals.

Having been cautioned at Old Trafford for a first-half foul on Baills, Robson saw another yellow card last night after he had brought down Colleter 10 minutes before half-time. The Austrian referee controlled the second leg with fussiness of a town clerk but overall was even-handed with his discipline.

Chapter 24.
Galatasaray '93

3rd November '93
Galatasaray   0 – 0   (40,000)

United Line - Up
*Schmeichel, Parker, Bruce, Irwin, Giggs, Ince, Phelan, Robson, Keane, Sharpe, Cantona. **Subs** – Sealey, Martin, G. Neville, Butt, Dublin*

Manager
Alex Ferguson

Champions League 2nd Round 2nd leg

After waiting twenty-six long years, fans and players were still on a massive high after winning the League the previous season. Unfortunately, United's first appearance in the Champions League, which had replaced the European Cup the season before didn't go the way we would have hoped.

A crowd of only 35,000 turned up to see The Reds first home game in the competition, a 2 – 1 victory over Hungarian side Honved, a 3 – 2 away win in the second leg gave us a 5 - 3 aggregate victory. When United went into an early 2 – 0 lead in the home tie against Galatasaray in round two, the signs were very promising, but, halfway through the second half the Reds were 3 – 2 down and it took a late goal from King Eric to save our blushes. That unexpected score-draw at Old Trafford would make the away trip an uphill battle. A scrappy and frustrating 0 – 0 draw saw the Istanbul side progress to the Group Stage of the competition courtesy of the away goals rule.

Fortunately, the rest of our domestic season went from strength to strength. United led the Premier League table from the fourth game onwards and ended up winning the league with 92pts - eight points ahead of their nearest rivals. At one stage we led the rest of the pack by 16 points. In his first full season Eric scored 25 goals in all competitions and was rightly voted PFA (Player of the Year) and crowned King of The Stretford End. Giggs, Sharp and Kanchelskis also hit the headlines with their brilliant and sometimes breath-taking performances. Attack – Attack – Attack - Attack – Attack! United topped off the season by winning their first Double after crushing Chelsea 4 – 0 in a one-sided rain drenched FA Cup final. Amazingly the FA Cup final would be the last time three of United's stalwarts would been seen in a United shirt. Ince, Hughes and Kanchelskis were all sold before the start of the new season.

The only real blight – no, make that disastrous! part of the season was losing The League Cup final to the Villa Slags, thus preventing us from doing the first ever domestic treble.

'WELCOME TO HELL' – was the banner that greeted the United players at Istanbul airport. Fortunately, the players had armed guards to protect them but we, the travelling support weren't so lucky. However, the armed guards did nothing to stop hundreds of Galatasaray fans from hurling abuse at the players as they made their way through the arrivals area and the police looked on with smiles on their faces as the local lunatics bricked the team coaches as it left the airport.

The shocked and knackered United players and staff might well have thought that they would be safe once they arrived at their luxury hotel on the banks of the Bosporus, but when a couple of players smiled at one of the young bellboys the evil little bleeder ran his finger across his throat and spat on the floor. Throughout his stay, goalkeeper Peter Schmeichel had his sleep disturbed by constant calls that were put through to his hotel room.

The stewardesses on our Turkish Airlines flight were a bit more welcoming than the bellboy. Well the ones with beards were. I've never seen such a bunch of ugly women in my life, every one of them had at least one tooth missing, a couple of them were starting to go bald and they were all bordering on being Roly-Poly's.

The interior of the plane made your local tacky Indian restaurant look like a five-star joint, and the noisy and unruly Turkish passengers that boarded the aeroplane appeared to carry on everything but the kitchen sink, throw a crate of chickens into the mix and you would have had a scene from a Marx Brothers film.

The P.A. system sounded like the staff had put a bit of mesh over half a dozen empty cans of beans and the crap tinny music they played sounded like a couple of tomcats having their Niagara's cut off. The unrecognisable food was cold, and the warm beer tasted like soggy cardboard. Besides all that, the flight was tickety-boo – Oh, except for the fact one of my fellow Reds vomited all over me.

I was travelling with my mate Colin G., a Red who also travelled with me on many England games in the eighties and early nineties. John McG. and twenty or so other Brummies had chosen to fly with Scotty's UF Tours, but because Colin and I wanted to have a few days to look around the famous walled city of Istanbul after the game, we decided we would make our own way to Asia-Minor.

There were fifty to sixty other Reds on the flight, most of them Mancs, and a few of them were sitting behind us swigging a bottle of vodka. I don't know if it was nerves or one of them was pissed, but he was throwing up after every gulp of vodka and making a right horrible racket. His two mates found this hilarious and were continually laughing their heads off. I wasn't so amused and decided to go to the toilet for a jimmy and get a break from the human fountain of sick. As I opened the toilet door to get out, the vodka drinking puker tried to push past me but we got stuck in the narrow doorway and he ended up throwing up all over me.

After a very unpleasant five-hour flight the last thing we needed was to be greeted by Turkish immigration officers. All of the United fans were lined up and made to wait, while all other passengers quickly made their way through passport control. As we were waiting our turn a very moody and shabbily dressed Turkish copper started walking along the side of us and demanded £5 off each of us. Thinking the payment was going to be for an entry visa, most of The Reds handed over the cash without too much fuss. But when we saw the dodgy copper stick the money into his pockets and walk straight past passport control alarm bells started to ring. When the first few Reds were beckoned towards the immigration officers it soon became apparent, we had all just been officially mugged. The fact that we had all handed over a fiver fell on deaf ears, and the immigration officers insisted we pay for our entry visas in Turkish lira. Those who didn't have Turkish lira with them, which included Colin and I, were told we had to pay £10 sterling, which was double the fee we should have legitimately paid. Robbing Bleeders! It seemed they'd missed out the words 'Rip Off' on the banner 'Welcome to Hell'.

When we finally got through customs and into the arrivals area, we were greeted by a mob of screaming Turks who were throwing their arms all over the place. For a few moments we thought we were in big trouble, that was until we discovered they were local taxi drivers touting for trade.

Colin and I had reserved a room at the Hilton for a couple of nights, but what we didn't know was there were three Hiltons in Istanbul, and just our luck, our taxi driver of course took us to the other two Hiltons before he finally dropped us at the correct hotel almost two hours later. We were both amazed at the size of the city and as we were driving around the busy streets of Istanbul, the taxi driver informed us it had a bigger population than London. It certainly was a sprawling metropolis.

Before booking into the Hilton we had to change a few quid at the reception desk so we could pay the taxi driver and it felt very strange to hand over millions of Turkish liras for our taxi ride – the Turkish lira was basically fucked!

Having clocked the moody streets of Istanbul while we were driving around trying to find our hotel, Colin and I decided to leave the bulk of our money and our plastic in our hotel room and only went out with 10 or 20 million lira each. With the help of the hotel staff we instructed a taxi driver to take us to an area where we could find a few bars.

We were dropped off in an affluent looking area that had plenty of designer shops, fancy hotels and apartment blocks. But the few bars that we had found were all connected to casinos or restaurants and were all a bit up market and plastic for our tastes, so we decided to get off the main drag and went for a mooch about in the backstreets.

We had only been walking for a few minutes when we were approached by a respectable looking Turk. He muttered something to us in Turkish and when we spoke to him in English a beaming smile immediately appeared on his face. He shook our hands and replied, "Hello my friends are you English? Welcome to Istanbul!" The Turk seemed genuinely excited to meet us and he certainly had me fooled from the start. He walked alongside us for a few hundred yards and with him rabbiting on in English at a hundred miles an hour we could hardly get a word in edgeways. All we managed to say to him was that 'we were in Istanbul to see Manchester United and we were looking for cheap bar'. The Turk who by now was walking and talking even faster assured us he could take us to a reasonably priced bar and asked if he could join us, so that he could continue practising his (already excellent) English. This seemed a reasonable request and we happily followed him through the back streets.

What a pair of Muppets Colin and I were!

The rambling local led us to a shabby old door that led us into an even shabbier and seedy little club. Just inside the door there was an old man sitting behind a cashier's desk and he looked so old and decrepit I wouldn't have been surprised if he had dropped dead on the spot. Our new 'friend' spoke to him in Turkish then turned to me and Colin said, "there is no entrance fee for my friends". The club was dimly lit with a very low ceiling and there was a small dance floor and stage to our left. It seemed the only other people in the club were the three or four badly dressed, and very unenthusiastic musicians who were sitting almost lifeless on the stage. They were all covered in cuts and bruises and looked as if they had just been dragged off the street and press-ganged into the band. Opposite the stage was the row of booth-type tables and fitted seats.

Hurrying us along our host directed us to the back of club, then with a knowing smile he invited Colin and myself to take a seat and insisted we sit opposite sides of the table to each other, thus hard against the wall. As we sat down Colin said, "What the fuckin' hell is the craic here?" The Turkish motor mouth immediately sat down next to me boxing me in against the wall. His smile had now disappeared, and with a very serious look on his face he said to Colin, "I don't understand your English, please explain." Before Colin could reply three beers were delivered to our table by a very plain looking, skinny and scantily dressed young girl. As soon as she took the drinks off of her tray and placed them on our table, she sat down next to a very nervous looking Colin. He looked over at me and in almost a whisper he said, "We have dropped a right bollock here!" A sudden noise from behind me made me glance round and to my horror I saw three of the biggest and ugliest gorillas coming towards us and one of them was carrying an ice-bucket with a bottle of cheap bubbly in it, another one of the gorillas was dragging along a rickety old chair. I looked on wide-eyed as they approached the table and proceeded to open the bottle of bubbly. As soon as they lifted the bottle out of the ice-buckets I shouted out, "There's no way we are paying for that." The Turkish twat sitting next to me totally ignored me and continued to make small talk as the bouncers poured the bubbly into glasses and handed them round the table. A second girl then suddenly appeared, and the Turkish motor mouth quickly moved onto the old rickety chair so the girl could sit next to me. As the two girls sipped from their glasses, I pushed mine and Colin's glass of bubbly away from us and continued to repeat, "We're not paying for that fuckin' bubbly.' Colin then added "We don't want any of your shit bubbly and we don't want anything to do with these two ugly tarts – so we'll be on our way now."

"You mean you want bill?" the smarmy Turk replied. "We want the bill for the two beers," I snapped. The Turk nodded at one of the girls and she instantly left the table, but soon returned with a scrap of paper in her hand and gave it to the smiling Turk. He in turn handed it to me and the cheeky cunt had the nerve to say, "I hope you enjoyed the girls' company and your drinks." I looked at the small piece of crumpled dirty paper that was supposed to represent the bill and all I could see was row after row of zeros. I handed the bit of paper to Colin and after the bit of impromptu maths, we agreed the bastards were asking for almost £200!

As me and Colin whispered to each other across the table discussing how the fuck we were going to get out of this, one of the gorillas grabbed the empty bottle of bubbly and banged it on the table, then while holding the bottle in a very menacing manner started to shout very aggressively at the mouthy Turk. After a short exchange between the two we were told, "We take American Express if you don't have the cash." I replied, "There is no way we are paying that sort of money for a couple of beers." The smirking Turk calmly responded with, "The beer is free, you are paying for the girl's time and the bottle of champagne." After a few seconds, he added, "You English are very rich this will be no big problem for you." Colin proceeded to point out to him, "When we first met you, we told you we were looking for a cheap bar, that was because we only have a small amount of money, we are only here to watch the football and leave Istanbul as soon as the game finishes tomorrow night." As the Turk translated this to the heavies, they quickly dragged the pair of us from our seats and started rifling through our pockets. All the Turks were visibly outraged that we only had the equivalent of £30 on us and no credit cards.

After another heated debate between themselves the angry Turk turned to me and snapped, "You get a taxi back to your hotel and return with more money or credit card, your friend will stay here until you return!" He definitely wasn't happy when I immediately replied, "I haven't got any money for a taxi you have taken all of our money." Colin added, "There is no more money at the hotel, we are not businessmen, we are only in Istanbul for one full day to see a football game, and then we return home." This was translated back to the three bouncers once again, then one of them grabbed me around the neck and threw me to the floor, it seemed like I was in for a good kicking, but the other two gorillas came to my rescue.

When everything had settled down a bit Colin and I were pushed back into our seats and the four of them had a reasonably quiet conversation amongst themselves and to add a bit of surrealism to the situation, while they were rabbiting on the band suddenly started playing. The biggest and ugliest of the heavies was quick to show his disapproval and threw the bottle of bubbly at them. With all the band members being showered with broken glass they looked more nervous and uncomfortable than myself and Colin did. When they had finished talking, motor mouth said to us with a big smile on his face. "Ok no problem, you can leave now." And then to our amazement he added, "Before you go do you want a beer on the house"? What the fuck was this barmy cunt all about, him and his goons had just mugged us and now they wanted us to sit and have a beer with them. He'd got no bleedin' chance

Shaking our heads in disbelief we declined his kind offer, the cheeky bastard had more front than Sainsbury's.

We made our way out of the club at double speed, legging it to the nearest taxi rank and headed straight back to our hotel. As soon as we arrived back at the Hilton, we dived straight into the bar and hit the top shelf, and just to even the score a little we booked the massive bar bill onto someone else's room. Well to be fair, we'd have probably done that whether we had just been turned over or not.

Meanwhile on the other side of town, John McG and the rest of the Brummies on Scotty's UF Tours were having an even more harrowing and traumatic time than Colin and I had experienced in the seedy back street club. Not surprisingly Scotty had booked his party into a modest hotel in a very moody part of town and during the day the Brummies and a few of the Mancs had several running battles outside their hotel with the local boys. Apparently, it all kicked off when a few Reds burnt a Turkish flag, whether this really did cause all of the violence no one is really sure, but what can't be disputed was, the Turks started the violence by attacking innocent bystanders in the hotel lobby.

By late evening most of the trouble had subsided and the Reds that had been involved in the fighting with the Turks thought that was the end of it. The only thoughts they had when they finally hit the sack was what kind of breakfast would be served up in the morning.

But none of them ended up having breakfast that morning, because around 3am the loud banging on their bedroom doors woke everyone in the hotel. Many of the Brummies were on the lower floors and they were the first to be dragged from their beds by armed police, then thrown into the back of waiting police vans and driven off to local nicks. The heavy-handed marauding Turkish police resembled a SS raid from World War II. Neither women or teenagers were spared the rough treatment, as they were marched, and sometimes pushed down the hotel stairs, then bundled into cop vans and driven off to various police stations around the city.

When most of the Reds arrived at the police stations around the city, they discovered other United fans were already banged-up. Many had been detained on the flimsiest of pretexts, some were beaten, almost all of them had their possessions stolen or were forced to hand over United shirts, hats, badges and match tickets. And as was the case in a cell full of petrified women supporters, they were made to hand over cash and jewellery in exchange for being allowed use a clean toilet instead of the stinking hole that was situated in the floor of their cell.

After a lot of the locked-up Reds had been in the cells for six to eight hours without food or water, they paid the guards to get some grub for them and amazingly some of the boys were let out of the cells and pointed in the direction of the local kebab shop. Of course, they were expected to bring meals and drinks for the Turkish prison guards while they were out buying food for themselves and their mates.

Without any real interrogation or questioning most of the United fans were released as suddenly as they were dragged out of their beds earlier that morning. They were escorted back to their hotels, allowed to get their luggage then they were taken directly to Istanbul airport and put on a plane. It was later reported in the 'Daily Telegraph', one plane was carrying 209 United fans back to Manchester, and none of them had got to see inside the Ali Sami Yen stadium.

You may be thinking the 209 got a raw deal. There were six Reds back in Istanbul who would have given their right arms to be on that plane. Scotty and five of the Brummie Reds were detained on jumped up charges and were banged up in a Turkish prison for several weeks before being released without charge.

Back in the safety of the Hilton, Colin and I had no way of knowing what had happened to the boys on the UF Tours, we were still kicking ourselves and couldn't believe that we had been so naïve to allow ourselves to be turned over as we were the previous night.

Determined that we wouldn't get caught out again we set out to take a look around the famous old city of Istanbul. We were grateful to discover that our taxi driver spoke a little English so we quizzed him as to where Galatasaray's ground was and he offered to drive us up to the ground and wait for us while we had a look around, he would then show us the rest of the sights. We agreed a fixed price for his services and headed for the infamous Al Sami Yen stadium. We arrived at Galatasaray's ground just after 11am and was stunned to find a massive crowd milling around outside, it was like being outside Old Trafford at 2.50pm on a Saturday afternoon. There were literally thousands of Galatasaray fans already queuing up to get inside the ground. With the memories of the previous night's incident very much at the forefront of our minds we gingerly got out of the taxi and started to have a nose around, even though it was over eight hours before kick-off, we could already feel the atmosphere building up. Colin and I were both starting to think they may had brought the kick-off time forward, but we certainly didn't feel comfortable about approaching any of the home supporters to confirm this. As we started walking around, we received plenty of strange, even menacing looks. We weren't wearing any colours, but we stuck out like a pair of sore thumbs with our fair hair and white skin. We had been to well over a dozen countries watching United and England, but we had absolutely never experienced anything like this before.

When we got back into the taxi the driver confirmed the large crowd outside the ground was a normal occurrence on match days and the barmy Galatasaray fans were let into the ground five hours before kick-off, he also told us some of the more fanatical fans even slept outside the turnstiles the night before a big game, as it was a great honour to be one of the first fans inside the ground.

Being a bit shaken about our experience at the ground Colin and I decided we needed a drink, so we asked the driver to forget the sightseeing trip and instead to drive around the bars and hotels where he thought United fans would be congregating.

After over two hours of driving around and around the sprawling city we finally came across a bar with about a hundred rowdy Reds happily drinking away. All the lads in the bar were Mancs on an organised trip and they had coaches laid on to take them to, and more importantly, from the ground. As the afternoon passed we were getting on really well with our new found friends and a few of them assured us they would get us onto their coaches, this seemed like a great result and we relaxed a little in the knowledge that we didn't have to make our own way to and from the ground.

The coaches turned up as planned and we all piled out of the bar and started to board our transport to the Al Sami Yen stadium, unfortunately Colin and I weren't the only Reds trying to get free ride to the ground and there were already half a dozen lads sitting in the gangway of the coach. When people who had booked on the official trip started complaining that they hadn't got a seat, the stewards who had organised the trip soon appeared with a clipboard and commenced checking off the names of the legitimate passengers, all jibbers were quickly shown the door.

There were a few taxis knocking around so me, Colin and four Reds from Miles Platting squeezed into a cab and headed off to the ground. We had been chatting with these Reds in the bar and they seemed like sound lads, but as soon as the

Galatasaray stadium came in to view, they suddenly jumped out of the taxi and did a runner, as they did so the Turkish taxi driver grabbed me by my arm to stop me jumping out of the front seat (if any of the Miles Platting Four read this book – you owe me a fiver! ya mongrels).

The fact that the Mancs did a runner without contributing to the taxi fare wasn't really a major issue, but the fact that Colin and I now had to walk around the ground on our own wasn't something that that we were looking forward to. It was dark as we walked towards the ground and even at several hundred yards away we could clearly hear the war cries from insane Galatasaray fans and of course with darkness it now seemed even more threatening and intimidating than it did earlier in the day, the dimly lit narrow side streets and tower blocks that surrounded the stadium looked extremely menacing and definitely a no go area.

With less than half an hour to go before kick-off there were still thousands of Turks milling around outside and with no signs in English and the atmosphere being extremely tense, we cautiously approached a group of local coppers and produced our match tickets in the hope they would point us in the right direction. When one of the scruffy coppers aggressively snatched the ticket from my hand for a few seconds, I feared the worst and thought the bastard was going to nick it, but he just quickly examined the ticket for a few seconds, pointed to the other side of the ground then pushed the ticket into my chest.

We walked in the direction that the copper had indicated and as we did so the lights towards the back of the stadium got dimmer and dimmer then non-existent. As we approached the darkness, we noticed a small group of Reds who were understandably very apprehensive about walking into the unlit part of the ground. We had just began having a chat about what we thought would be our best option, when a few bricks were hurled at us. I looked up at the direction the bricks had come from and standing on top of a large earth mound I could see the silhouettes of a group of coppers who were shouting abuse at us and hurling missiles in our direction. And just to make the situation that little bit more interesting behind us was a large group of Turks heading in our direction. I felt we had little or no choice but to head into the darkness and grabbing Colin by the arm and we started to jog away from the Turkish mob behind us.

After a few moments we were relieved to see in front of us a small light over one of the turnstiles and what looked like a group of riot police, when they noticed us coming towards them a few of them immediately brandished their long batons, on seeing this our jog quickly turned to a slow walking pace. As expected, we were jostled, pushed about and searched in a very vigorous manner, all coins and of course a few notes were taken off us before we were allowed through the turnstiles. I entered the stadium to a load roar of disapproval and deafening boos and jeering – the United team had just trotted out onto the pitch to do their warmup routine and the home supporters did all they could to intimidate them. As well as a torrent of verbal abuse there were loads of flares lit up around the ground, the flares made so much smoke that at one stage it looked like the massive terrace behind one of the goals was on fire. In the hostile atmosphere some of the United players seemed visibly nervous or maybe they were just totally astonished by the noise and the spectacle that the Galatasaray fans had created inside the stadium.

After the game Mr Ferguson stated 'it was definitely the most incredible atmosphere he'd ever experienced at a football ground' that's some statement considering some of the English and Scottish derby games he had been involved with.

The Galatasaray fans maintained the partisan atmosphere for the whole game and at the final whistle the crowd went wild at the 0 − 0 result, the noise was tremendous. The Galatasaray players with their spoiling tactics, time wasting and the fans with their continual hostile chanting had both played their part, but now it was down to the Turk riot police to intimidate and anger the United players. After Cantona was sent off at the end of the game he became the target for the Turkish coppers, and while he was in the tunnel, he was struck several times with riot batons, and when Bryan Robson came to his assistance he received the same treatment from the Turkish thugs. When Cantona got back into the dressing room he went crazy saying he was going back out into the tunnel to find the Turkish fuckers that had attacked him and Robo. Eric was so wound up it took Brian Kidd and several players to restrain him.

While the players were having fun and games in their dressing room, Colin, the rest of the 1,500 or so Reds and I were locked inside the ground waiting apprehensively to be let out, wondering what kind of reception we would be getting from the deranged home supporters once the gates were opened.

As we started piling out of the ground, we were greeted not only by riot police but also a cordon of armed soldiers who quickly charged off any Galatasaray fans that came anywhere near the coaches. All the coaches we could see had large 'Airport' signs in the front window, not fancying a four or five hour round trip to the airport and then back to the hotel about 20 of us stupidly tried a few escape routes to get away from the ground, but from every direction we were chased back towards the stadium by mobs of crazed Turks. Seeing that there was no chance of escaping safely on foot from the ground and that our situation was starting to get pretty serious, Colin and I started to ask around the coaches that were heading for the airport to give us a lift, most of the coaches we approached were organised by the club and even though we explained our predicament and how hostile it was around the ground, none of the miserable bastards would give us a lift. We even asked a couple of the United stewards just to let us on the coach so they could drop us off a mile or two away from the ground, but again this fell on deaf ears.

As coach after coach drove away from the stadium, I was starting to fear the worst. Then as if heaven sent, I heard somebody banging on the window of the coach that was positioned just behind us. I turned around and to my utter joy

345

there was Sean and Brian O'Connor, the London lads I sat next to in J Stand. With a smile on my face from ear to ear I gestured for the boys to open the emergency door at the back of the coach and Colin and I scrambled aboard. Once we were safely on the coach, I gave a massive sigh of relief and hugged both Sean and Brian and told them that they were probably life savers! The coach was full of Cockneys and just a few Mancs and had been organised via their hotel, which we were now heading for. We got plenty of abuse as we drove past the Turkish hordes, but we had no real bother because amazingly we had a police escort back to the hotel which had been sorted out by one of the lads on the trip who somehow had connections in the Istanbul police force.

We sped through the streets of Istanbul not stopping for anything, which included red lights, of course, we were all loving the special treatment, and for most of the journey the atmosphere was very upbeat on the coach.

That all changed as we approached the lad's hotel. Our coach had just turned off one of the busy main roads on to a wide and affluent looking Boulevard, when Sean turned to me and said, "Our hotel is just down here Grange." "Oh right, which one is it," I replied. I was a bit surprised when Sean didn't answer me and I was just about to ask the question again, when he pointed forward and with a startled look on his face said, "It's that one with the massive mob outside it!"

I could clearly see the mob congregated outside the hotel. As soon as the local boys spotted our coach, they became very animated. As the coach came to a stop the mob immediately surrounded it and started banging on the bodywork and windows. There must have been getting on for three hundred of them. The majority of the Turks that were surrounding the exit door were only teenagers, but there was an awful lot of fuckin' teenagers! While the Turkish mob were battering the coach and making a right racket the tour guide stood up in the gangway and announced the bleedin' obvious, "Apparently there's a very big crowd of local men outside your hotel – so when we get off the coach, I suggest that YOU RUN!"

A few punches were thrown by the first few cockneys off the coach and a little passageway soon opened up in the crowd so we could all get into the hotel, which because of the extra wide pavement was about 30 yards from the roadside. I think most of us got a few kicks and whacks as we trotted from the coach to the hotel, but it could have been much, much worse.

As soon as we were all safely in the hotel the very anxious looking manager locked the doors behind us. The hotel lobby had a full glass frontage which must have been 60 yards long and getting on for 4 metres high, so as we all stood at the bar in the lobby we were on full view to the Turks out in the street, and even though they were making a lot of noise and continually banging their fists on the large glass panels we weren't really paying them a lot of attention. We were more interested in getting a few beers down our necks. After quickly knocking back a few drinks the petrified looking barman pleaded with us to take our drinks into the restaurant, so that we were out of the view of the Turkish mob. Several of us were winding him up and assuring him that everything would be ok, when one of the lads pointed out "I'm sure that mob is getting bigger. Look at 'em there spilling onto the road". We all glanced round and without any real concern, agreed that the numbers had certainly grown.

As we returned to our drinks there was a loud bang that sounded like an explosion. Our first reaction was to dive for cover behind the bar. It fell deathly quiet for a few seconds before a few of us popped our heads over the bar and saw that two of the large panes of glass had been smashed. As we stood up to get a better view several missiles were thrown at us, so we retreated into the stock room behind the bar where we discovered row after row of shelves with bottles that would have kept us happy for a week. I had just helped myself to a second beer when a couple of security guards came into the stock room and hurried us out, leading us to a basement recreation area.

Brian and a few of the other lads took this opportunity to go back to their rooms and got stuck into their bottles of vodka and whiskey.

When we realised there was no chance of a drink down in the basement, Colin, Sean and I made our way towards Brian's room. As we approached his room, we were surprised to see Brian and an Aussie geezer sitting in the corridor drinking vodka. Before we could ask Brian why he was sitting outside his room he shook his head and said, "Where the fuck have you brought me? If I'd wanted all this shit I'd have gone to

Beirut!" Brian went on to explain that he was sitting on the bed taking a swig of vodka when a brick came flying through the window, he rushed out into the corridor and the Aussie in the next room had also retreated there after having his window smashed too.

Very cautiously we wandered inside Brian's room and looked out at the Turkish mob below us. They had been joined by four coppers who were stood smoking cigarettes and chatting to the mob in front of the broken windows. On seeing this Sean said sarcastically, "I see the old Bill's here, that's alright then, we'll be safe now." Of course, the Turkish coppers were about as much use as a chocolate fireguard and our concerns were heightened when we saw a few fires being lit on the pavement.

We had decided by this time it might be a good idea to go back downstairs and find out what was going on. When we arrived down in the lobby a few of the other Cockneys were already remonstrating with the useless local coppers and in good old Anglo-Saxon they were telling them to sort out the wankers that had started the fires. The sight of the Reds standing in the window arguing with the coppers was like a red rag to a bull and the Turkish mob got very vocal, with few of them tried to get into the hotel. The local plod were making a half-hearted attempt to stop them, when two loads of riot police turned up and waded straight into the local boys. They were that aggressive you would have thought the riot police were battering United fans not their own local boys, I can only imagine that how heavy handed the coppers were being they must have been FC Fenerbache or Besikta fans.

As the riot cops were getting the Turkish mob under control a large open backed truck pulled up outside the hotel, besides a few Turks hanging off the narrow foot plates on the back of the truck there was 70 or 80 of them packed in like sardines. One of the passengers in the truck jumped out and started having a heating argument with a few of the riot police and as the argument got more intense, the Turk pushed one of coppers in the chest, and to my amazement none of the riot police retaliated in any way. The mad Turk continued to have a go at the coppers until one of the other Turks in the truck intervened, dragged him away and forcibly pushed him back into the cab of the truck.

The truck drove off only to appear again a few minutes later and for the next 10 or 15 minutes it repeatedly drove slowly past our hotel. On a couple of occasions there was a loud bang as they did so, we all thought this was just firecrackers as the Galatasaray fans were celebrating the favourable results. What we found out the next day certainly made me think twice about the loud bangs being fireworks.

The heavy-handed treatment from the riot squad had caused most of the Turkish mob to disperse, leaving only 20 or so Turks hanging around outside our hotel. When we pointed out to the hotel staff that the worst was probably now over, and asked them to re-open the bar, they flatly refused to serve us. This upset Big Kevin that much that he said to the hotel manager, "Well fuck you then, I'll go and find a drink somewhere else." Then with the manager pleading with him not to go outside Kevin stormed off. As he marched towards

350

the small mob of Turks that were still on the pavement, he yelled at them, "I'm goin' for a fuckin' pint! Have any of you cunts got a problem with that?" Looking on wide-eyed the Turks were totally shocked at Kevin's swaggering bravado and Kevin strolled straight through them without a word being spoken.

After pestering the hotel staff for nearly an hour to get us a taxi to take Colin and I back to our own hotel, one finally arrived. Jumping into the back of the rickety old cab, I couldn't wait to get back to the safety and comfort of the Hilton bar. I was also hoping and praying we didn't have a welcoming committee waiting for us.

By now it was almost 2am and for the first 10 minutes of our journey the streets were virtually deserted, but as we approached a large bridge, we could see the traffic building up in front of us. The taxi slowed down, and because of the heavy traffic drove at walking pace onto the bridge. We had got almost halfway across the bridge when the traffic came to a complete stand still, to my horror as I looked out of the window, I could see a tidal wave of flag bearing Galatasaray fans coming towards us. The over excited and extremely noisy mob were not only surrounding all the vehicles on the bridge and banging their fists on the windows and roofs of the stationery cars. They were also clambering over some of the cars and dancing on the roofs.

When the demented Turks got to our taxi, they swarmed around it and pressed their wild-eyed faces against the side windows. One of them even dived on the bonnet and threw his arms and legs around in such wild abandonment he looked like he was doing an upside-down Dying Fly. As the balmy bleeders continued to bang their fists on the roof and windows both Colin and I dropped so low in our seats we were practically in the foot well and even though we were almost kneeling in the back of the cab, we looked straight in front as to avoid any eye contact with the delirious mob. If the mad bastards celebrated a 0 – 0 like this fuck knows what they would be like it if they actually won the European cup!

When the last few stragglers passed our taxi I slowly sat up in my seat and started to look around to confirm the coast was clear, looking through the back window I was glad to see the crazed Turks disappearing into the distance. As I turned around I heard a very loud horn being sounded several times, and as I glanced out of the side window, I saw a Black Maria driving slowly the wrong way down the opposite carriageway and hanging out of the back of the large vehicle were several coppers bawling their heads off and waving an enormous Galatasaray flag. I sat opened mouthed for a few seconds and thought to myself *'when is all this madness going to end'*.

Once the traffic had started moving again on the bridge, we came off at the first exit and drove down a quiet and dimly lit street. As we drove down the deserted street I was just starting to relax a little when in the distance I saw what I thought looked like a horse plodding along the street, as we got nearer I could clearly see a large carthorse which was draped in Galatasaray flags and scarves, sitting on the horses back were two young teenagers riding bare-back, and standing up, sandwiched between them was a child of no more than three to four years of age. I shook my head in disbelief as we drove past them. A flabbergasted and shell-shocked Colin touched my arm and whispered, "Did I really just see three kids riding a horse?" I gave a massive sigh and nodded to confirm that he had indeed just seen a horse and its riders casually making its way down the street.

When we woke the next morning, I very timidly opened the curtains and was half expecting to see a mob of Galatasaray fans congregated outside our hotel or to spy a single kamikaze Turk abseiling down the front of the building. After what we had experienced the previous day, I thought anything was possible, fortunately all was calm.

I still needed to confirm with Colin that the previous night's escapades weren't just a dream and we really did experience the Cockney Reds hotel being under siege, we were surrounded by a delirious mob on that bridge and that we saw the Black Maria driving the wrong way down the carriageway waving Galatasaray flags and probably most bizarrely we witnessed a heavily decorated horse with young bare-back riders trotting down a deserted street at three in the morning.

After checking out of the expensive Hilton, we left the reception and went straight down to the restaurant and ordered a slap-up meal. We added five pints to the bill of a random room and asked one of the taxi drivers who was outside the

Hilton to take us somewhere where we could find a cheap hotel.

After driving for almost an hour we arrived in a rundown part of the city that had plenty of low budget hotels and cheap café-restaurants. At first, I was a bit apprehensive about where he had dropped us off, but after checking into a half decent hotel we went for a mooch around and was pleasantly surprised at the warm reception we received from most of the locals. Me being a bit of a history buff, was delighted to discover we weren't too far from the famous Istanbul city walls, which are over 1,500 years old.

As we approached the wall, we were shocked to find small shanty towns set just inside the old walls, all the ram shackled dwellings were constructed from rotten planks of wood and rusty sheets of corrugated iron. They had no amenities / services and most of the kids were shoeless and looked like they were wearing very well-worn hand-me-downs. On the periphery of the shanty towns we stumbled across one of the cities many Artisan Quarters, the winding narrow streets were no wider than five feet, which gave the locals just enough room to push a handcart along, the small hovels that lined the cramped streets and alleyways were used as open workshops where you could stop and watch the old Turkish men making everything from saucepans to Fez's. Talk about a culture shock!

Mainly because of the friendly nature of the locals we had come across, the agro we'd experienced the previous night had been forgotten, Colin and I walked around for hours and hours and in the late evening we found ourselves in small shabby bar that was just around the corner from the prison where they had filmed the seventies cult film Midnight Express. The bar was empty so we hovered in the doorway for a few seconds wondering whether we should go in or not, but when a friendly looking barman beckoned us inside and said in English, "We have good beer and wine at good prices." We thought it would be worth a try. The cordial young barman introduced himself as Ali and he asked us what we were doing in Istanbul, when we told him we were Manchester United supporters and we were at the game the previous night his face lit up and he told us he loved all things English especially the football.

Ali immediately impressed us with his knowledge of the English game and of course he told us United was his favourite English team, with how much history he knew about the Reds, going back as far as the Busby Babes, I think he was probably a true Istanbul Red.

Being the only customers in the bar Ali was more than pleased to sit and chat to us and every beer we ordered he gave us a free shot. We had been in the bar for a couple of hours and the conversation didn't stop, that was until a certain someone walked into the bar. Ali was in mid-sentence when he suddenly stopped and the ever-present smile on his face disappeared, wide eyed he seemed to be staring at someone who had just entered the bar. I was about to turn around to see who he was looking at when a bloke of slight stature appeared at my side. Without saying a word, he calmly opened the bar-flap walked up to the fridge at the back of the bar and helped himself to a bottle of coke, he then returned to our side of the bar. Ali's whole demeanour suddenly changed, he no longer casually lent over the bar, instead Ali stood bolt upright and I could tell he was trying to avoid eye contact with his new customer. As Colin and I started to talk to each other Ali looked at us and slowly shook his head, as he did so the other Turk called him over. They exchanged a few words in Turkish then Ali turned to us and said, "Excuse me this is my friend Radi he wants to buy you a drink". I turned to my left where Radi was standing and was just about to thank him when I noticed what looked like dried blood all over his face and in his hair. I then noticed he also had dried blood all over his tacky silver-grey suit. '*Oh fuck! Here we go again.*' I thought. Radi must have clocked me staring at his blood stained clothes and hands because after another brief conversation with Ali, our barman explained that Radi's best friend had married a Kurdish girl earlier that day, something that Radi had been 100 % against, so to demonstrate his disapproval of the marriage he went along to the mosque where the ceremony was taking place and while the service was underway Radi continually banged his head and hands against one of the internal stone columns. Pretty hard-core stuff! Personally, I would have just sent my mate a telegram stating, 'don't do it – ya cunt'! But each to their own.

I really didn't want to look at Radi again but felt I'd better acknowledge what Ali had just told us. In a timid and half-hearted manner, I gave him a nod of approval, and as I did so I noticed his wild eyes for the first time, and I was immediately filled with dread. He couldn't have been any taller than 5 foot, 4 inches, bordering on skinny and looked as if he was in his mid-twenties. He wasn't really a distinguished looking man, but he certainly had the wildest eyes I had ever seen, he resembled a time bomb waiting to go off. I'm sure even the likes of Ronnie Kray and Mad Frankie Frazer would have thought twice about challenging him. Radi didn't speak any English so a three-way conversation continued to go through Ali. When Radi enquired the reason Colin and I were in Istanbul, Ali nervously asked us, "Is it's okay for me to tell him you're Manchester United supporters?" Radi may not have spoken any English but he certainly understood the words 'Manchester United' as soon as Ali had informed him Radi pointed at us and shouted out, "Manchester United?" Fearing his response, I nervously replied, "Yes" He let out an intimidating laugh then banging one fist on his chest he cried out, "Galatasaray."

Ali, then told us that after the game Radi and his mates drove around Istanbul in an old cattle wagon until it was light and throughout the night, they made thunder many times. When I asked Ali, "by thunder? Does Radi mean fireworks"? He immediately replied, "No, Radi has a gun," "What, like a starting pistol or something like that." I asked. Ali shook his head and said in a low tone, "Radi does not have a starting pistol." No doubt interested to find out what we were talking about, Radi quizzed our barman and Ali told him that we thought he was talking about fireworks. Radi looked a little confused but as Ali was still talking, he put his hand inside his jacket and produced a massive revolver that Dirty Harry would have been proud of. Radi pointed his enormous gun towards the ceiling and shouted out, "BANG – BANG THUNDER!"

He went on to tell Ali that the previous night he had almost shot a policeman who had been beating Galatasaray fans, the policeman was saved when one of Radi's friends persuaded him to get back into their lorry. Straight away I thought, Radi must have been the mad bastard that was pushing the riot police about outside the Cockney Reds hotel. Oh Bollocks!! For a few seconds there was a very uneasy silence, and then seeing that he had frightened Colin and me to death a sadistic smile came across Radi's face and I felt like the proverbial rabbit caught in the headlights. Radi instructed Ali to get us another drink and also added two large glasses of Moonshine Raki which were put on the bar. We both downed the drinks in one, and then telling a little porkie I said to Ali, "We have an early flight in the morning so we will be off now, can we buy you and Radi a drink before we leave?" As Ali told Radi that we wanted to leave the bar Radi gave us a cold hard stare, which seemed to last for an age. But as soon as Ali confirmed Radi's approval we quickly said our thank you's and goodbyes and walked calmly out of the bar. Thinking that crazy Radi could well decide to come after us, as soon as we got outside, we ran like Olympic sprinters and didn't stop running until we found a taxi.

The next few days passed without any major incidents, but I did get an offer of marriage from a gorgeous Romanian Brass, which after due consideration, I politely and courteously declined. I also declined all her other suggestions of carnal bliss even though she was very reasonably priced.

We arrived back in Manchester a few hours before the derby game at Maine Road. Needless to say, the Bitter Blues were overjoyed that Galatasaray had knocked us out of the European Cup and they gleefully sang, **"United is our name – United is our name – two nil up and fucked it up – United is our name."** We were gutted that City were 2 – 0 up at half time and the blue half of The Kippax sang their latest song all the way through half-time.

I'm delighted to remind you all that the second half was a completely different story. Two goals by Eric made it 2 – 2 then with just over 10 minutes to go Keano put United 3 -2 up. From then to the end of the game it was the ecstatic Reds who were delirious chanting **"2 - 0 up and fucked it up – City is our name"**. I don't think I have ever left an away ground where the home supporters were so quiet and dejected.

As we mingled with the Berties in the Moss Side streets you could hear a pin drop. That 3 – 2 win over City certainly helped to ease the disappointment of being knocked out of the European Cup by the Mad Turks.

CANTONA IS SENT OFF TO COMPLETE UNITED MISERY

By Collin Malam in Istanbul
Galatasaray 0, Manchester United 0
3-3 on aggregate, Galatasaray win on away goals

ENGLISH football suffered its second crushing blow in four weeks last night when Manchester United were knocked out of the European Cup by Galatasaray of Turkey. This setback follows the defeat in Holland that virtually ended England's hopes of appearing in the finals of the 1994 World Cup. So now that the English have lost they're highly regarded champions from Europe's most important and lucrative competition, there is nothing for them to look forward to this season and into next summer. And as if that were not bad enough, United's Eric Cantona was sent off here in an undignified scene after the final whistle. The temperamental French international was shown the red card by Swiss referee Kurt Rothlisberger for something the player said to him. Cantona had complained throughout about Galatasaray's time-wasting tactics, and he went straight up to the match official at the end of the game.

After shaking Rothlisberger, a teacher of French, by the hand, the Frenchman pointed to his own eyes and obviously expressed an problem that was not at all flattering. It had Rothlisberger reaching angrily for the red card and flourishing it over the Frenchman as he punched the ball away in frustration. It had not been a happy night for Cantona.

During the second half, his one-man campaign against Galatasaray's tactics had seen him cause an ugly scene on the running track as he went to retrieve the ball from among officials of the Turkish team and their substitutes.

Perhaps Cantona was giving vent to the frustration he had earlier experienced. His tall, strong German marker, Reinhard Stumpf, did not give him an inch of room and, in doing so, put a question mark against the decision of United manager Alex Ferguson to leave out Mark Hughes. Ferguson did not mince his words afterwards. "We were disappointed with the performance," he said. "Our passing wasn't good enough and when it became a matter of desperation, the game turned into a shambles. "Asked if United might protest to UEFA about the incidents in the tunnel at the end of the match. Ferguson added:

"We'll have to examine the evidence, but we aren't out of the cup because of that. We can't use that as an excuse, it's very flimsy."

Ferguson went for speed and mobility in his attempt to get the result United needed to win the second-round tie and reach the money-spinning Champions' League. Instead of playing with two strikers as usual, Ferguson flanked Cantona with the pace of Ryan Giggs and Lee Sharpe.

With Roy Keane, Bryan Robson and Paul Ince forming a solid wedge in midfield, United looked the sharper and brighter team in the early stages. Indeed, Sharpe cannot have been far offside when Robson put him through to slip the ball past Heyrettin in the opening minutes of the game.

Galatasaray began cautiously, their packed mid-field suggesting strongly that they had decided on a safety-first approach to protect their 3-3 draw in the first leg. They got forward only sporadically and threatened United's goal just twice in the first 28 minutes. The first shot flew wide and the second was deflected for a corner by Paul Parker, the injured Gary Pallister's replacement in central defence. It came as something of a surprise then, when United's control of the match dissolved so suddenly, and they might have conceded three goals in two minutes.

Haman's low angled shot through Mike Phelan's legs was parried by Peter Schmeichel, sprawling to his left, but when the Turks closed in again for the kill, Schmeichel made an even better save to block Hakan's shot from point blank range. Then Kubilay flicked the ball wide after beating Schmeichel to Tugay's lovely chipped pass.

United's only response, indeed, their only legitimately dangerous attack of the half, came not long before the interval. Robson put Giggs through to the left of goal, but the young Welshman's centre sailed harmlessly across the face of goal.

United buckled down to their work with a new sense of purpose at the start of the second half but their play became more and more ranged as desperation set in. Ferguson sent ton Dion Dublin for Keane after 72 minutes 72 minutes, but the substitution did little to improve the balance of penetration of United.

Lightning Source UK Ltd.
Milton Keynes UK
UKHW021017140620
364908UK00004B/530

9 781916 346253